THE POLITICAL ECONOMY OF CO-OPERATION AND PARTICIPATION

A Third Sector

EDITED BY
ALASDAIR CLAYRE

OXFORD UNIVERSITY PRESS

1980

Oxford University Press, Walton Street, Oxford OX2 6DP

OXFORD LONDON GLASGOW
NEW YORK TORONTO MELBOURNE WELLINGTON
KUALA LUMPUR SINGAPORE JAKARTA HONG KONG TOKYO
DELHI BOMBAY CALCUTTA MADRAS KARACHI
NAIROBI DAR ES SALAAM CAPE TOWN

*Published in the United States by Oxford
University Press, New York*

British Library Cataloguing in Publication Data
The political economy of the third sector.
   1. Employees' representation in management
   I. Clayre, Alasdair
   658.31'52   HD5650   80-40470

   ISBN 0-19-877137-1
   ISBN 0-19-877138-X Pbk

*Typeset by Anne Joshua Associates, Oxford
and printed in Great Britain by
Billing & Sons Ltd.,
London, Guildford and Worcester*

PREFACE AND ACKNOWLEDGEMENTS

The papers in this volume arose, for the most part, out of a small conference held late in 1978 to discuss the political economy and practical workings of co-operation, participation, and profit-sharing. Three main alternatives were presented: a fully co-operative economy, by Peter Jay; a growing co-operative sector in a mixed economy, by Robert Oakeshott; and value-added sharing in conjunction with participation (but stopping short of full employee ownership or control), by Felix FitzRoy. Criticisms of the whole range of ideas were also made.

Most of the papers in the book were written or amended after the conference, bringing out in more detail points made at the discussion. The main exception is Peter Jay's opening paper, which was taken as the starting point for the first part of the discussion itself. This has already been published by the Manchester Statistical Society, to whom thanks are due for permission to reproduce it here.

The editor is grateful to the editors of the *Economic Journal* for allowing Professor James Meade's paper on 'The Adjustment Processes of Labour Co-operatives' to appear in this volume as well as in the Journal; to the Editor of *The Economist* for permission to reproduce part of a Business Brief on profit-sharing; and to the editors and publisher of *Work and Power* (Tom R. Burns, Lars Erik Karlsson, and Veljko Rus (eds.), Sage, 1979) for permission to reprint parts of a contribution to that volume. For fostering interest in these ideas generally over recent years thanks are due to the Acton Society, to the Anglo-German Foundation for the Study of Industrial Society, and also — though its interest has been severely critical — to The Institute of Economic Affairs. The greatest debt is owed to the Outer Circle Policy Unit and to its Director, James Cornford, for their generous help and hospitality in bringing the conference together.

A.C.

CONTENTS

I. INTRODUCTION

II. THREE ALTERNATIVES

A CO-OPERATIVE ECONOMY

A CO-OPERATIVE SECTOR IN A MIXED ECONOMY

THE COMPARATIVE ADVANTAGES OF PARTICIPATION COMBINED WITH PROFIT-SHARING

III. COMMENTS

IV. NEW CONTRIBUTIONS TO THE ECONOMICS OF CO-OPERATION AND PARTNERSHIP

I. INTRODUCTION

1. The Political Economy of a 'Third Sector'

by Alasdair Clayre

Can a 'third sector' grow in the west between the forces of big business on the one hand and the state on the other, based on co-operation, in which people will have more control over their working lives through hiring their own managers rather than being hired and fired by them? Should this — and could this — ultimately be the main form in which the economy is organized, either through spontaneous growth in a third sector, or through its replacement of the nationalized sector, or, as Mr Peter Jay suggests, through the conversion by law of all enterprises over a certain size to self-management?

Alternatively, can the main benefits hoped for from co-operation be achieved by a spread of participation and value-added sharing even inside more conventionally organized industry in the west today?

Discussion of the question of worker-managed enterprises in the west has for some time been dominated by the example of Yugoslavia. However the social ownership of capital in Yugoslavia and the influence of a single party, visible and invisible, in differing ways throughout the Yugoslav system make it exceptionally hard to draw direct inferences from the Yugoslav example to a western-style economy.

Only one contributor to this volume, critical of the idea of co-operation altogether, suggests that the Yugoslav experience has certain bearings on Peter Jay's theoretical model. In the main body of the book, the reasoning is based exclusively on assumptions applicable to a western-style market economy. No special attention is given here, either, to the type of co-operative that relies on state finance in the mixed economies in the west; all enterprises discussed in this volume are taken to be competing with their own, or with voluntarily subscribed, resources.

These limitations of scope do not in themselves imply judgements of value; they arise from the sense that, whatever the virtues of these other kinds of worker-management and of the literature that describes them, there is a strong need today for examination of co-operation, participation and value-added sharing within the normal framework of western political economy, with no special assumptions about the role of a single party or of the State. That is the object of this volume.

Certain criticisms have recently been made of the viability of fully co-operative third sector enterprises in the west from the point of view of economic theory, and in particular of 'property rights' theory (e.g. Chiplin and Coyne, 1977). The main arguments appear to be these:

(a) If individual workers own their own enterprises:
   (i) the workers bear the risks as well as doing the labour and this is an unfair double burden;
   (ii) their risks are not spread, like those of most shareholders in the west. If their firms go bankrupt their jobs and their savings vanish at the same moment;
   (iii) they are also led to invest their savings in one particular enterprise (their own) rather than having the whole range of savings outlets to choose from freely. It is argued that (unless their firm happens to be the best in the market) they are not getting the best possible return on their savings and, therefore, that worker-owned firms are being subsidized economically at their own workers' expense;

(b) if workers do not own their enterprises, yet have control, it is argued that they will tend, instead of investing adequately, to push up their wages at the expense of whoever does own, or — if 'society' owns — at the public expense;

(c) if workers in all enterprises try to do this simultaneously, or if those in less productive firms, reasoning from arguments of fairness, call for the same wages as those in the most productive, they will tend to push down the value of the currency;

(d) if capital is 'socially allocated' — that is to say, distributed from public funds through political rather than market processes — and if losses are subsequently met out of public funds, short-term political considerations (e.g. propping up unproductive local enterprises) and personal political influence will have strong and arbitrary effects on the allocation of resources, and everyone will be poorer than necessary;

(e) (i) if co-operative enterprises rely wholly on internally raised finance, they will not have enough and will be producing below their most efficient level;

 (ii) if they rely on finance raised from outside, they will have difficulty in preventing outside control, by banks or the State;

 (iii) if all the equity is retained by the co-operative and a fixed rate of interest is offered on all borrowed money the third sector enterprise is likely to suffer in competition with other firms in a western-style market economy, since it will be raising more of its external capital with heavy fixed interest burdens than its competitors, who can spread their finance between loans and equity shares;

(f) All these criticisms apart, it is often argued that the history of third sector enterprises or producer co-operatives in the west is not impressive; that few have been economically successful, or have even rivalled the ordinary achievement of average shareholder-owned firms in what they have done for the consumer and for their employees or members.

For all these reasons (it has been argued) it is misleading people to encourage them to put either their savings or their working lives into such structures.

These objections raise questions about the relationship between 'economic' values and other human values; for some of the advantages that third sector enterprises may offer are hard or impossible to quantify and consist of possible improvements in the 'quality of working life' of those who take part in them. What is easily measurable is of course not for that reason alone more 'real'. However, if the economic objections to third sector enterprises can be discussed in economic terms, this is clearly more satisfactory than a general contention that the non-economic advantages are likely to outweigh any economic disadvantages; even though for some people this may well be true. The present paper can do no more than point to three ways — without following them to their conclusions — in which the economic case against self-management outlined here may perhaps be helpfully investigated.

One way is through further arguments, also from neoclassical principles, which may suggest economic benefits likely to accrue to self-managed enterprises, and to self-managed market economies, capable of outweighing the disadvantages suggested above.

Many of these have been spelled out by Peter Jay (see pp. 9–45) below). Put in its simplest form, the argument may simply be that no alternative kind of economy will work without compulsion and State control; and that inflation will otherwise rise by degrees as voters–workers require governments and trade unions to deliver simultaneous increases in take-home pay and in public spending, and to bid competitively for their votes by uncosted promises to do both. Other arguments have been presented by Jaroslav Vanek, again at the level of the economy as a whole.

Until recently, it has generally been assumed in theoretical discussions that the introduction of self-management to any economy would result in a loss of efficiency. Thus self-management is often assumed to involve a net loss to production from expenditure of time in debating and voting, the avoidance of measures such as wage-restraint, unpopular in the short run though necessary for long-term expansion, and failure to deal severely with offenders against rules. It has not generally been argued until recently that there could be gains that might outweigh such factors in economic terms. However, the argument of Jaroslav Vanek (1970) is that, even in terms of neoclassical economic assumptions, the presupposition of greater inefficiency on the part of a labour-managed system does not have to be made. Firms in a labour-managed economy, according to Vanek's micro-analysis, would have a long-run equilibrium at least as 'Pareto-optimal' as in a privately owned or Russian-style state-centralized system; and while, as in privately owned systems, firms could have reached equilibrium at less than optimal levels of output in the short-run, a labour-managed economy would tend to have more flexible prices and a more competitive market, with less need for advertising and product differentiation; and thus disequilibria would tend to be more readily corrected.

In terms of macro-analysis, Vanek argues that there would be less danger than in privately owned economies of trade cycles, and less danger of long-run unemployment or long-run inflation. More dramatically, the gain from higher incentives, which Vanek believes would follow from the principles of labour-management, are suggested in his model as amounting to 'hundreds of per cent' of the national product.

There are problems in Vanek's theory, some of them mentioned in the well-known review article by James Meade (1972), which is, however, generally sympathetic to the main lines of the argument.

One problem may be mentioned here. Vanek sees capital assets as liable to be 'socially' owned or the property of the state, though his system is compatible with private or public owners and lenders, provided all are prepared to accept the available guarantees for the security of their investments, and fixed rates of interest. Control is exclusively in the hands of those who do the work. Some of the difficulties created by this assumption from the point of view of 'property rights' have been mentioned earlier and will undoubtedly require further examination.

A second way in which the case against self-managed enterprises may be questioned in the future, also at the level of theory, is through an examination of certain aspects of the behavioural foundations of neoclassical economics — particularly those dealing with the 'maximizing' behaviour of the individual — which may affect the weight that should be given to 'property rights' considerations against others. Sen, for example (1977) has argued that there are valid alternatives to the traditional neoclassical assumption of the individual maximizing his personal gain (or it may be his personal utility, or expected life-time utility) which stop short of the assumption of total altruism which (Sen argues) has too often been presented as the one alternative. In particular Sen shows that concepts such as 'commitment' can in principle be built into models as theoretically elegant as the traditional ones of neoclassical economic theory, and that models of man so constructed are not only more like real men in general, but better represent the behaviour required by men in any productive system that actually works. From the point of view of industrial relations, Fox (1974) has stressed the importance of similar factors, especially of trust, in any functioning economic organization. These emphases contrast sharply with those of writers such as Alchian and Demsetz, who in an influential article (1972) stress the unique importance of supervision in the enforcement of contracts. Self-managed systems are likely to be poor at hierarchical supervision, but may well benefit not only through gains resulting from mutual supervision, but also possibly from commitment and trust. The primacy given to individual maximizing behaviour and to supervision (its corollary in organizational terms) has led quite naturally to the assumption that these last two factors can be largely neglected in calculating likely economic returns within organizations. But this has been only an assumption, not a conclusion of empirical observation. Of course it cannot be assumed on the other side that self-managed enterprises will necessarily generate unusual degrees of trust and commitment. Nevertheless these differences of emphasis, some of them at the roots of behavioural theory in economics, are likely to have a considerable impact on the way self-managed enterprises are considered in future theory.

The benefits from such features of self-managed enterprises as participation and profit-sharing (not only for 'job satisfaction' and motivation but also for productivity) have often been considered unquantifiable in economic terms, and this is no doubt one reason for their comparative neglect in economics. A long series of experiments by industrial psychologists up to the late 1960s had yielded the result that no correlation (or a very low correlation, sometimes positive and sometimes negative) could be established between 'satisfaction' and productivity in general (Argyle, 1972). However, the possibility remained that there were changes in the forms of work organization where gains in both these areas could be independently made, and an impressive list of examples was assembled by Blumberg (1968) where greater participation had been accompanied by increases in both. John Cable and Felix R. FitzRoy (see pp. 141–60) have more recently developed a theoretical model for investigating quantitatively the effects on motivation, productivity, and 'job-satisfaction', of workers' profit-sharing and participation in decision-making. The importance of work like this can only be guessed in advance, but an optimistic guess would be that such studies could succeed in bringing these factors into the field of quantitative measurement and therefore of serious economic treatment alongside more readily measurable factors such as output and money income – for long the main concern of serious quantitative economics, yet (as all economists agree) only part of the total 'utility' which even the maximizing individual is supposed in neo-classical theory to be pursuing.

Thirdly one may examine direct empirical evidence of self-managed enterprises that meet in practice some of the most forceful arguments from 'property-rights' theory by combining self-management with individual ownership and well-designed organization: for instance cases where third-sector enterprises enjoy a considerable amount of internal (equity) finance through retained profit but do not rely on it exclusively; where there is a federation of like-minded enterprises supporting a co-operative bank that lends without seeking to control; where the federation has a good reputation locally so that outsiders are willing to lend to the co-operatives through the bank; and, finally, where workers build up deferred private ownership in their enterprises individually through the reinvested sharing of the profits. These conditions can be found in at least one apparently successful group of third sector enterprises – possibly the most successful co-operative system in the western world – Mondragon, which has been described in some detail recently by Campbell and others (1977) and by Oakeshott (1978).

Finally there may be ways of combining participation in decision-making with profit-sharing or value-added sharing in what James Meade calls partnership, which can achieve many of the advantages without some of the difficulties of full co-operatives. Whether partnership is likely to be preferable to co-operation, and the merits of piecemeal over once and for all change, are probably the two most frequently recurring questions debated in this book.

BIBLIOGRAPHY

Alchian, A. and Demsetz, H. (1972), 'Production, Information Costs, and Economic Organization', *American Economic Review*, 62, 27–52.

Argyle, M. (1972), *The Social Psychology of Work*, London, Allen Lane.

Blumberg, P. H. (1968), *Industrial Democracy: The Sociology of Participation*, London, Constable.

Campbell, A., Keen, C., Norman, G., and Oakeshott, R. (1977), *Worker-Owners: the Mondragon Achievement*, London, Anglo-German Foundation for the Study of Industrial Society.

Chiplin, B. and Coyne, J., with Sirc, L. (1977), *Can workers manage?*, London, Institute of Economic Affairs.

Fox, A. (1974), *Beyond Contract: Work, Power and Trust Relations*, London, Faber.

Meade, J. E. (1972), 'The Theory of Labour-Managed Firms and Profit Sharing', *Economic Journal*, Special issue in honour of E. A. G. Robinson, March 1972, 402–28, reprinted in Vanek, J. *Self-Management: Economic Liberation of Man*, Harmondsworth, Penguin, 1975.

Oakeshott, R. (1978), *The Case for Workers' Co-ops*, Routledge and Kegan Paul.

Sen, K. (1977), 'Rational Fools: A Critique of the Behavioural Foundations of Economic Theory', *Philosophy and Public Affairs*, 6, 317–44. Reprinted in F. Hahn and M. Hollis (1979), *Philosophy and Economic Theory*, Oxford University Press.

Vanek, J. (1970), *The General Theory of Labour Managed Economies*, Cornell, Ithaca, N.Y.

A NOTE ON TERMINOLOGY

1. The same term 'self-management' tends to be used of two different types of system:

(a) one where there is State or one-party control of the political apparatus;

(b) one in which self-managed enterprises operate in the private sector of a mixed or free market economy with democratic political institutions.

This volume will generally be concerned with the latter.

2. The term 'self-management' is normally used as a shorthand for a system in which employees' control is inevitably indirect. Typically, an assembly of all members of an enterprise, meeting perhaps three or four times a year, may elect a council which meets, say, monthly, and in turn appoints a director and a small board, which selects middle management. The crucial point is that the director and all who manage, though they may be on a year's notice rather than dismissable instantly, are in the end accountable to the members of the enterprise, and not to the State or to outside owners of capital. If the term 'self-management' is no more misleading than 'self-government' it is probably harmless and the best available term to describe this system.

3. 'Self-management' and 'employee-ownership' are distinct though related concepts. How they can best be combined or separated in practice forms one of the leading topics for discussion.

4. There are also various degrees of participation and/or profit-sharing, without full self-management or worker-ownership. The term 'partnership' is used sometimes to describe this range of alternatives.

5. The terms 'value-added sharing', 'profit-sharing' and 'residual-sharing' are all used by different authors in this book without necessarily implying systematic distinction between them. Different accountants can give different definitions of profit and the term carries an ideological load. Value-added sharing as a more objective concept seems likely to be more widely used in the future.

6. The term 'third sector enterprises' is used here as an intentionally loose term for firms that are either self-managed or worker-owned or both (fully or to a significant degree), or that embody a significant degree of both participation and profit-sharing or value-added sharing together.

II   THREE ALTERNATIVES

A CO-OPERATIVE ECONOMY

2. The Workers' Co-operative Economy

by Peter Jay

1. The purpose of this paper is to raise for discussion certain theoretical and practical questions about a market economy in which the predominant enterprises are workers' co-operatives. By workers' co-operatives I mean business enterprises in which the freehold ownership of the assets of the business is vested in the members collectively, in which the sovereign body is the members each having one vote and in which all employees and only employees are members. The rest is negotiable.

2. By an economy in which workers' co-operatives predominate I mean, for the sake of argument, an economy in which by law all enterprises employing more than say 100 people are workers' co-operatives as defined above. By a market economy in which workers' co-operatives predominate I mean an economy as above in which the relationship between enterprises and between producers and consumers is regulated by free competitive markets, in which monopolistic tendencies are effectively discouraged under law and in which the activities of government are confined broadly to the traditional foreign and domestic functions plus interventions by way of taxes, subsidies, and regulation in the manner developed by Professor James Meade to correct clearly defined and established market imperfections involving public goods and other externalities.

3. My interest in this economy has arisen neither from academic curiosity nor from socialist idealism *per se*. I have no ambition to improve upon, for example, J. Vanek's classic *The General Theory of*

Labor-Managed Market Economies (1970). Nor am I primarily concerned to build directly on the heritage of syndicalism and those sub-
plots in socialist theory which have emphasized workers in their work
place rather than the state as the proper embodiment of the public or
society for the purposes of the public, common, or social ownership
and control of productive activities.

4. My concern is more with policy and practicalities, even though
at this moment the perspective may appear heroically futuristic and, as
today's politicians might see it, unrealistic. In my 1975 Wincott
Memorial Lecture, later published by the Institute of Economic Affairs
under the title *A General Hypothesis of Employment, Inflation and
Politics*, I argued that our present political economy suffered a central
contradiction which portended a catastrophic failure of the system
within a finite number of years.

5. I suggested, but did not develop at all far, the notion that the
contradiction might be resolved and the catastrophe therefore avoided
if and only if labour were in general to replace capital as the entrepreneur of the predominant productive unit, dealing at arm's length
with the saver through free capital markets just as the capitalist
entrepreneur deals at present at arm's length with the workers in the
labour market (with the one important difference that monopolistic
practices would and could be more effectively prevented in the capital
markets under such conditions than they can now be in the labour
market).

6. This is not the place to go again over the same ground. But the
briefest summary of the hypothesis is needed as background to the
present discussion.

Our present political economy was defined as a system with government dependent on renewable consent on the basis of universal man-
hood suffrage and with widespread free collective bargaining in the
labour market. It will be seen that political economies satisfying this
definition are broadly conterminous with the membership of the
OECD, in other words the so-called 'western industrial democracies.'

7. The fact of renewable popular consent to government entails,
it was argued, a political imperative to deliver some approximation to
full employment and a general stability of the inflation rate, if not
actual stability of prices. If this imperative were breached in either or
both respects and if the breach appeared to be indefinite without an
early prospect of rectification, then the basis of consent to government
— to any government based on the representative democracy, not just

to this or that coloured administration — would dissolve and, after such lags as were implied by the political process, some or other sequence of anarchy and authoritarianism would ensue.

8. The fact of collective bargaining in the labour market entails, it was argued, a high equilibrium rate of unemployment, certainly higher than any conventional post-war interpretation of full employment as implied by the political imperative. This arises because collective bargaining is of its nature an exercise in monopolistic supply, the essential character of which is that a higher than market-clearing price is charged and a smaller quantity than under perfect competition is supplied to the market.

9. Under these conditions governments are confronted with a threatened breach of that part of the political imperative which requires full employment. If they move to meet this by stimulative fiscal or monetary policies — and for these purposes it matters not whether you prefer the monetarist or the Keynesian canon — the only effect beyond a temporary rise in economic activity will be a rise in prices while employment remains at its low equilibrium point.

10. If governments keep stimulating by fiscal and monetary means, after a rather longer lag, equilibrium will be found with a higher rate of inflation and the same high level of unemployment. If governments try to beat this, as they will be obliged to do, by constantly increasing the fiscal and monetary dose, they will in theory be able to maintain or at least approach the target employment level at the price of continuously and logarithmically accelerating rates of inflation. But in the end either this breach of the other leg of the political imperative will force abandonment of the policy, or hyper-inflation will be reached. In the latter event money illusion will break down; and the temporary stimulative power of expanding monetary demand faster than people are discounting inflation will evaporate because it becomes literally impossible. Either way, there will then be a catastrophic rise in unemployment, almost certainly far over-shooting the long-run equilibrium point. Either way, government is then seen to be in breach of either or both aspects of the political imperative; and its previously supposed remedies against such evils are exposed as ineffective. Then the basis of political consent to government disintegrates.

11. In support of this hypothesis it was argued that what have come to be known as incomes policies offer no escape from the explosive nature of the model for basic economic reasons as well as for practical political and industrial reasons. You cannot indefinitely abolish

collective bargaining without either establishing a totalitarian state or abolishing trade unions by law, it was argued. The first takes one outside our present political economy as defined, while the second appears inconceivable in a modern democratic state.

12. The historical evidence was said to corroborate the hypothesis. In all the main OECD countries, though most graphically in Britain, a steady logarithmic acceleration in inflation rates (abstracting from the usual four-year cyclical movements) is detectable from the middle or late 1950s.

This has, however, been diluted by a progressive rise in the average level of unemployment through each cycle; and it has been temporarily distorted or alleviated from time to time by exporting the problem to each other and to the third world.

This is not observed in the pre-war period only because the political imperative did not then effectively exclude in all countries (though it clearly did in Germany and perhaps in Italy) a very high level of unemployment. It is not observed pre-1914 because collective bargaining was not then the pervasive norm of the labour market.

13. So it is argued that, if the OECD countries, with Britain in the lead, are not to suffer the fate of Germany between the wars, some way must be found consistent with the constraints of political democracy and free societies of eliminating collective bargaining other than either outright legal prohibition of trade unions or incomes policy. It was suggested that only the conversion by law into workers' co-operatives of all enterprises, other than the technical monopolies, above a certain small size could achieve this and that it would.

14. The questions to be discussed here are not how valid that argument is, but, given that it is broadly valid, how an economy of workers' co-operatives would work. Would it lead to the withering away of collective bargaining and would it have such other grave defects as to outweigh any benefits it might have of the kind advertised above?

15. Among the questions to be asked are:

(i) How would a workers' co-operative raise finance for investment?

(ii) Would there be a general tendency to under-investment by the standards of optimal capitalism?

(iii) Would there be a tendency to under-employment by the standards of optimal capitalism?

(iv) What is the maximum practical size for a workers' co-operative — how would an economy of workers' co-operatives cope with much larger firms of the kind which account now for an increasing proportion of national output?

(v) What arrangement should be made for the present statutory monopolies in the public sector?

(vi) What about the 'technical monopolies'?

(vii) Why should labour behave differently in respect of its monopoly power under such conditions?

(viii) Would governments be any more able than they are now to confine their functions and to abjure discretionary fiscal and monetary policies in the way suggested?

(ix) In what directions could the market economy be extended?

(x) Why is the record of workers' co-operatives so poor?

(xi) Does it work in Yugoslavia?

(xii) Is there an evolutionary route to market socialism? ·

(xiii) Do workers want co-operatives?

Sources of Finance

16. Once the employees of a firm collectively rather than the suppliers of capital are the entrepreneurs of that firm it will no longer be reasonable to expect capital finance to come from the entrepreneurs individually. For one thing, employees individually do not have personal access to savings in the necessary quantities. For another, even if they did, it would be unwise for them to invest their individual savings heavily in the enterprise on which their employment and earned income also depended. For a third thing, they will not have individually differentiated and realizable stakes in the enterprise; and, if they did as a result of putting up money for new investment, the character of the co-operative as a collectively owned enterprise would be modified. Moreover, if there were individually owned stakes in the enterprise, either departing workers would take away their entitlement with them, in which case the spectre of the capital shareholder would rise again from the ashes of conventional capitalism or departing workers would have to be bought out by newly arriving workers or by the co-operative itself.

Either arrangement would impose unacceptable cash burdens on the buyer to the detriment of the vitality and flexibility of the enterprise.

17. Indeed, it would be a misunderstanding of the whole concept of workers' co-operatives, defined as an enterprise in which the supplier of labour is the entrepreneur, to try to reimport the concept of the

limited liability company in which the entrepreneur is supposed to supply the capital. Capital and labour are distinct factors of production; and it would be surprising if it were appropriate for both to be supplied by the same group.

18. Instead investment would be financed, as now, from a free capital market and from retained surplus earnings, with banks continuing to play the role in short- and medium-term finance which they play now. The main novelty will be in the terms on which workers' co-operatives deal with the capital market, since *ex hypothesi* they will not be in a position to offer investors an equity in the enterprise where an equity implies a freehold ownership of the assets and the right to appoint the directors.

19. It is likely that two main forms of investment in co-operatives will be used: fixed interest and 'equity-type'. Fixed interest investments will be modelled on the present form of obligations and present no new problem. 'Equity-type' investment will be new in that it will entitle the investor neither to appoint the board of directors nor to realize the net worth of the enterprise on liquidation.

20. 'Equity-type' investors will be entitled to receive all of the 'profits' of the enterprise; and it may also prove desirable to assign them a mortgage on the relevant assets. The 'profits' will correspond to the distributed earnings of a limited liability company and will amount to whatever the board of directors, appointed by the employees, says they amount to. This is likely to work more similarly to present arrangements than many who believe that distributed profits are the residual earnings of a company suppose.

21. Distributed profits, though in the long run inevitably influenced by the success of the company, are at present whatever the board of directors decides they should be, whether this mean drawing on reserves or adding to reserves. The reserve movement is the true residual on a short-term view. The motive now to make a distribution of suitable size is essentially to maintain a reasonable price for the company's obligations on the capital market, though at present the shareholders can petition to have the company wound up if the directors' distribution policy dissatisfies them.

22. This motive — of maintaining a reasonable price in the secondary market for the co-operative's obligations — will continue to apply. For, on that will depend the co-operative's ability to raise new finance in the future at reasonable cost. It is true that the additional spur of warding off threatened takeovers will not apply; but in the presence of

one adequate motive to reasonable distributions secondary motives are not needed.

23. It would be possible to include in the legislation establishing the co-operative economy a provision giving 'equity-type' investors an entitlement to petition for foreclosure on the assets mortgaged to them in specified circumstances of inadequate distribution. But it is hard to see why this artificiality should be needed to reinforce a natural market equilibrium between those who lend and those who borrow, unless it were to overcome irrational hesitation during the initial stages of transition or because there was some public interest in the encouragement of 'equity-type' investments. There probably is such an interest, since the alternative of either over-gearing the co-operatives or forcing them to excessive dependence on received earnings for financing future investment would tend to damage the financial resilience of the new structure and perhaps to inhibit investment which could show a good social as well as private return. But this is what might be called a 'committee-stage' point on which either view is tenable without being integral to the principle of the scheme itself.

24. Another committee-stage point on which either of the opposing views seems tenable is whether the co-operative economy would need to surround itself with tight exchange control regulations in order to prevent savings which need to be invested in the co-operative economy at home flowing overseas in pursuit of the more familiar form of capitalist investment in which, at least at first, investors may be expected to have greater confidence. The argument for it is obvious and, in effect, as just stated.

25. The argument against it is more subtle. First, in so far as all the free industrial economies are supposed to be suffering the same morbid condition the attractions of capitalist investment overseas must be presumed to be diminishing and, if they exist at all, only to reflect the differing stages of morbidity of the various conventional economies. So at worst the need for exchange controls would probably only be temporary.

26. Secondly — and quite apart from what may be happening in other economies — the existence of alternative investment outlets offering attractive returns abroad may be regarded as a necessary and proper protection of savers at home and as a desirable incentive to workers' co-operatives to earn and make reasonable distributions. Thirdly, it is a technical fallacy to regard home and overseas investment as direct alternatives, however much it may look like that to the investor. The quantum of home investment is constrained by the

quantum of home savings, in the sense of available non-consumed resources. This quantum may or may not be affected by overseas investment whose direct impact is on the balance of payments, short-term capital movements, the reserves, and the exchange rate.

27. On balance it seems desirable to seek to avoid exchange controls as anything more than a transitional measure. But, if it should prove necessary to retain them longer than this, there is nothing in the nature of workers' co-operatives which makes that impossible; and certainly it would involve no loss of freedoms and efficiency now available.

28. In sum then the expectation is that the financing of industries and enterprises would be less different from present arrangements than may at first blush have been supposed. The essential and desirable character of a market relationship between savers and entrepreneurs is conserved. Moreover, all of this is in relation to the free enterprise concept working as it is supposed to work, not working in the warped and sickly manner which the essential contradictions of our political economy have in practice made inevitable, with society earning little or no apparent return on its productive assets, with savers — including pensioners and small insurance beneficiaries — suffering manifest injustice, with new investment disastrously depressed, with employment and international competitiveness increasingly threatened and with a growing dependence on government as the only large source of new investment funds. By that comparison the arrangements for investment and capital markets under the co-operative economy may be expected to work much better. The entrepreneur has legitimacy, which contemporary opinion does not allow to the capitalist entrepreneur. Competition between co-operatives will provide an incentive to new investment, as will the natural desire of each co-operative to maximize its income per head and to protect future employment. Governments will have been extracted from their heavy industrial involvement by the nature of the market socialist settlement here considered. The motive force behind the progressive acceleration of inflation, of a kind which is necessarily destructive of private investment, will have been removed by the withering away of collective bargaining.

29. It is even tempting to speculate that in the new environment the taxation of savings and capital should become less penal. In a world of workers' co-operatives the people will hardly thank the government for raising the cost of capital finance by taxation, more particularly when the conventional capitalist against whose excessive wealth such measures are supposed to be directed has been removed

from the scene, or at least from the mythology of the society.

Moreover, with the government's role severely restricted its revenue requirements will be correspondingly reduced. This too may create a better environment for savings and investment.

Will Co-operatives Under-invest?

30. A workers' co-operative seeks, to the extent that it conforms to the archetype of the economically rational unit, to maximize income per head of its members. This is a different, though substantially overlapping, maximand from the conventional limited liability company's maximand of profit for the shareholders.

31. An investment which would show a good return to capital, by for example building a new factory employing new workers at the same rate of reward as existing workers, but no return per head to labour would appear to be more attractive to a privately owned enterprise than to a worker's co-operative. Conversely an investment which raised rewards per head of the labour force, for example by equipping the workers with more efficient machinery, without necessarily earning any return to capital would seem to be more attractive to the workers' co-operative than to a firm where the decisions are made in the interests of the owners and providers of capital.

32. But this analysis is too simple. The reality is more complex. All returns to new investment are by nature returns to capital; and, if in the event labour partakes of part or even of all the benefits, under capitalism this can only occur either because trade union bargaining is in a position to scoop a large proportion of any new surplus earnings or because more generally throughout the economy investment is raising the demand for and therefore the opportunity cost to each employer of the labour which he needs to operate new investments.

33. Both the capital and the labour entrepreneur has to pay the cost of capital finance, whether it is the actual cost of market borrowings or the opportunity cost of using retained earnings to finance new investments.

If there is a surplus return on the investment, then it belongs naturally to the entrepreneur, whether capital or labour is playing that role.

34. The capital entrepeneur will be interested in any investment which produces such a surplus return. The labour entrepreneur will only be interested in investment which produce a surplus return per head of workers. The second category appears to be more limited than the first. In other words in an economy of workers' co-operatives the

kind of investment which creates new employment at the going rate of pay seems not to be attractive to existing enterprises, though it should be attractive to those who are unemployed if they can organize themselves to go into business.

35. But this leaves out the distribution of the surplus which the new investment has earned. Under a capital entrepreneur this is distributed, or at least attributed, to the shareholders. With a labour entrepreneur it can be distributed amongst the workers; and therefore there will always be a return to labour per head where there is a return to shareholders under the traditional arrangements. It may on occasions be very thinly spread; but then so it also is when there are very large numbers of shareholders, who indeed can often outnumber the employees.

36. This analysis, however, assumes that the cost of capital to a workers' co-operative would be the same as to a capital entrepreneur. Yet this can hardly be so when the different distribution of risks and benefits are considered. If, of course, all investment were to be financed by fixed interest borrowing or retained profits, then what has been said would be true. But that would be a very unsound arrangement. External finance is likely to be needed; and in a healthy market economy an efficient market in funds between savers and investors is important for efficiency in the allocation of capital resources. Total reliance on fixed interest borrowing to finance new investment, which is sometimes called 100 per cent gearing, leaves an enterprise extremely vulnerable to bankruptcy in a trading recession because capital's reward has to be paid whether or not any trading surplus has been earned.

37. Some 'equity-type' finance will certainly be needed by workers' co-operatives if they are to survive such recessions. This means that the risk which the investor accepts in making such an investment — and it is greater where he does not own the freehold of the assets created and does not appoint the directors who will manage the investment — will have to be rewarded by the prospect of at least a share in the surplus earnings from the investment.

38. This indeed was the arrangement already described in the first main section of this paper. Market forces in the capital market, if they work in textbook fashion, will tend to drive this share up towards 100 per cent of the surplus earnings, because it will always pay any workers' co-operative to outbid its competitors for investment funds up to this limit. In practice workers' co-operatives will begin to lose interest in this auction as the share approaches the level which would leave the return to workers per head at what they would see as a negligible level.

39. If investors are left no other outlet, then equilibrium will probably be found with rather a lower level of effective interest rates in the
capital market, a rather lower rate of savings in the economy and a
rather lower rate of investment than under conventional capitalism. Or
so again it would appear. But even this leaves out of account the
interest of unemployed workers. If there are such and if they can overcome the inertial difficulties of forming themselves into a new co-
operative, then it will pay them to enter the capital market and offer
investors up to 100 per cent of the surplus earnings from new capital.

40. If investors are free to invest overseas in conventional capitalist
enterprises, then domestic co-operatives will indeed have to offer close
to 100 per cent of the potential surplus earnings in order to attract the
funds they want for new investment. If they do not, savings will flow
overseas and the exchange rate will eventually move to restore equilibrium by reducing the real value of the monetary rewards which
the co-operatives are awarding themselves.

41. There is still a problem. The investors have no stake in the
capital appreciation of the assets of the enterprise, although they may
have a fall-back mortgage at historic real cost on the assets and they
may well enjoy capital growth in the market value in secondary markets
of their conditional stake in the enterprise. This difference may be
more apparent than real. If the enterprise is a going concern, then what
matters is the value of their 'equity-type' shares in the secondary
market. If it is not a going concern, then the mortgage at historic real
cost on the assets may well be as good a protection as a freehold in a
bankrupt enterprise would be under traditional arrangements.

42. Even so the risk to the equity-type investor is clearly greater to
the extent that he cannot appoint the management and that he cannot,
except perhaps under limiting conditions, petition for liquidation of the
enterprise. If, therefore, his prospective return is only as great as under
existing arrangements, the investment will tend to be less attractive.

43. The difference may be very small once investors have become
accustomed to the new system, although during the period of transition, before workers' co-operatives had demonstrated that they have
the same interest in appointing and the same capacity to recruit professional management which conventional enterprises have, suspicion of
the new enterprises may create a larger temporary confidence gap.

44. But there are two other very important factors to be taken into
account before reaching a definite conclusion about the investment
behaviour of an economy of workers' co-operatives:

(a) The effect of co-operative organization on labour productivity; and

(b) the effect of co-operative organization on collective bargaining.

45. So far we have been comparing the rational investment behaviour of workers' co-operatives with the rational behaviour of idealized capital enterprises working according to textbook optimization. If we actually lived in the latter world, we would hardly be considering the problem discussed in this paper at all.

46. The classical texts on producer co-operatives, mainly written in the late nineteenth and early twentieth centuries, tended to argue that worker co-operatives would suffer lower productivity than their capitalist contemporaries and so would fail to survive in competition with them. The historical evidence in both western Europe and North America tended to confirm this view.

47. The failure was blamed mainly on less efficient management and deficient investment, arising from failure to amortize past investment properly, leading to lack of finance for capital replacement. This view of the history, especially in North America, has recently been challenged by Professor Derek Jones, who puts more of the blame for failure on an artificially hostile legal and political environment.

48. Certainly, I would reject on an elementary point of logic any inferences drawn about the systemic characteristics of an economy of workers' co-operatives from the experience of particular workers' co-operatives operating in the framework of a conventional private enterprise economy. There is no private advantage from behaving in the jungle as if the rule of law applied; but there may yet be advantage for all jungle-dwellers in establishing together the rule of law.

49. It is in fact an open question whether the favourable effects on productivity of better motivation and enhanced credibility of managers under a system of workers' co-operatives would outweigh the unfavourable effects — which are not inherent, but possible — of any disinclination on the part of the co-operative to accept or pay the market price for good professional managers.

Even if the advantages to productivity — and the recent cases of Meriden, Kirby, and the Scottish Daily News have not been in business long enough to substantiate the first favourable impressions — did outweigh the drawbacks, workers' co-operatives still might not prosper in a capitalist economy.

50. Capital markets might still discriminate irrationally against them. Trade unions might well discriminate against them, perceiving

them quite correctly to be in the long run a threat to the existence of trade unions, since the abolition of private enterprise would eventually destroy the *raison d'être* of collective bargaining. In other ways the law and the tax system might discriminate against them; and certainly the existing system of patents, marketing, and sophisticated corporate finance makes it difficult for workers' co-operatives to get off the ground in areas where large conventional enterprises predominate. Moreover, the tendency for workers' co-operatives only to come into existence where a conventional enterprise has collapsed suggests that the seed has been sown on peculiarly recalcitrant soil.

51. Against the visceral feeling that sceptics may have that workers' co-operatives will tend to be less productive per head of their work force is the fact that for a workers' co-operative the direct interest is in maximizing labour productivity, because that determines income per head which is the natural maximand of a workers' co-operative. A conventional firm seeks to maximize capital productivity because maximizing returns to shareholders is its natural maximand.

52. As Professor Jim Ball and others have pointed out, the discrepancy between the over-all economic interest in maximizing labour productivity and the private interest of the enterprises which comprise the conventional economy in maximizing capital productivity can under certain conditions be a source of sub-optimal performance by the economy. An economy of workers' co-operatives would not suffer from this apparent conflict of private and social goals.

53. Another possible reason for predicting lower productivity in workers' co-operatives is their presumed soft-heartedness about laying off redundant workers. The co-operative will prefer, unless faced with literal bankruptcy, to carry surplus workers as a form of disguised social insurance for and between the members of the co-operative.

54. This seems undeniably true; and historical experience seems to confirm it. On the other hand, for the very reasons discussed above in relation to possible reluctance of workers' co-operatives to invest in employment-creating expansions unless this can be shown to produce more income per head for the existing members of the co-operative, they can be expected to be more reluctant than conventional firms to take on new labour. Therefore, where co-operatives are expanding they may well be more inclined and able to stretch the productivity of the existing work force than a conventional firm.

55. The whole question, however, becomes very much less moot when we drop the artificial comparison between the workers'

co-operative and the idealized capitalist firm of free market textbooks and compare the potential performance of the workers' co-operative in the workers' co-operative economy with the performance of the capitalist firm in the capitalist economy as it has in fact developed. For, the moment that the comparison is extended to the macro level from the micro comparison of disembodied enterprise units, one confronts the pervasive fact of trade unions.

56. Trade unions are a natural and probably politically inevitable response of the suppliers of labour in capitalist market economy to the opportunities, if not indeed the exploitative tendencies, of a *laissez-faire* labour market. It is theoretically arguable that combinations should be prohibited by law, as in parts of the nineteenth century they were.

57. Beyond much doubt the common interest would be served by such a prohibition, just as the common interest is also served by the prohibition of other forms of monopoly and cartel. The greater efficiency and dynamism of the economy would make up within a very few years for the once and for all reduction in labour's share of national income; and from there on it would be pure gain, at least in real income terms.

58. But that is hardly consistent practice with the assumption of universal suffrage operating in the wake of the political heritage of the last hundred years. To any individual group of workers a combination will always be a superior option to free individual bargaining so long as blacklegging can be prevented by force, industrial strength, or custom.

59. The perception of a social advantage in general abstention from collective bargaining is too remote from the circumstances of the individual worker for him even to support through the ballot box a general prohibition on trade unions, let alone to abstain privately from their immediate protection in a world where there is no reason to expect other workers to confer a reciprocal advantage on him by similar abstention. Since workers and their families predominate in the electoral process, it would be an extraordinary triumph of abstract macro-economic reasoning over concretely perceived private realities to secure a political mandate for the suppression of collective bargaining in favour of free individual bargaining; and the occasional political support for incomes policies offers no counter-evidence because, while it bespeaks a popular appreciation of certain macro-economic realities, the consent is given strictly on the assumption of some principle of fairness in its application which necessarily implies an administered

control rather than perfect competition in the labour market.

60. So, it is right to regard free and independent trade unions as an inherent feature of real world-market capitalism, even if they are a gross disfigurement of the original ideal of a private enterprise economy. It is therefore also right to compare the workers' co-operative economy with the capitalist economy on the assumption that the latter works not as in the classical textbooks, but as it does in the second half of the twentieth century.

61. We then confront a quite different standard of performance although it is more pronounced in Britain than in most of the other OECD countries and although the very rapid and in some ways geometrically accelerating advance of technology in the post-war era has engendered more rapid growth even in Britain than in almost all previous eras. If the argument in the preamble to this paper is accepted, then we are at the end of the era in which we can expect, on the basis of the characteristic institutions of post-war political economy, sufficient stability in the economy for these impressive growth achievements to continue without an insupportably accelerating rate of inflation.

62. This arises not because of any constraint imposed by the physical environment, as the Friends of the Earth would argue, nor because of any exhaustion of technological novelties or superabundance of savings forcing down the rate of return on capital as contemporary neo-Marxists argue, but quite simply because collective bargaining has advanced to the point where there is no, or virtually no, return on the capital assets employed in industry and commerce. The effects of money illusion disguised this fact from us for some years, until the techniques of inflation accounting were properly applied; but the recent NEDO study leaves us in no doubt, cyclical fluctuations apart, that industry in Britain is now earning virtually no return at all.

63. This does not of course mean that there is no social return, in the sense that we should all be equally well or better off, on a conventional present value calculation, discounting future benefits for society's time preference, if we were to consume our existing stock of capital, although we are now in fact very close to doing just that because of the alarming discrepancy between private and social goals which collective bargaining has caused. It does mean that there is very little incentive under existing arrangements for capital entrepreneurs to undertake even those new investments which would show a return to workers and shareholders added together, because the whole or more

than the whole of the return would be taken by labour under pressure of collective bargaining. The current position over the introduction of new technology into Fleet Street is a classic case in point and may well now lead not merely to the cancellation of the new investment but also to the liquidation of the existing assets and widespread closure of newspapers.

64. It is a symptom of this condition that more and more enterprises find themselves driven to turn to government for investable funds; and it is not surprising that workers' co-operatives born of the collapse of conventional firms under these pressures (as well sometimes as under the pressure of normal market forces) also turn to government when private investors are so demoralized. But this offers no permanent solution to the problem of under-investment because government is prevented from simulating the behaviour of a competitive capital market by the political constraints under which it operates. Even if it could — which would depend not merely on all voters being wholly rational and wholly informed but also on their having entered into an enforceable mutual contract to refrain from seeking to press any sectional advantage through the political process (itself a quite breath-taking exercise in constitution-making) — government would still confront the difficulty of financing its lending without either coercive taxation, which impairs the efficiency of the labour market and final markets, or a formidable burden of fixed interest borrowing.

65. There may be certain formal schemes which could theoretically reproduce through government the operation of a perfect capital market without unacceptable fiscal and monetary side-effects.

But the government would still be faced with the yet further problem of how to recognize investments which would yield a positive return to workers-cum-shareholders in a world where profits as conventionally defined were always nil. The problem might not be unanswerable in principle if there were a limitless supply of virtually costless teams of government cost–benefit accountants and economists to examine and compare investment propositions put up by every enterprise in the country. But the mind and the heart recoil from such an extension of bureaucracy; and any realistic consideration of the fallibility of government congruent with the widely celebrated fallibility of markets puts the matter beyond serious doubt.

66. So, we are back comparing the likely investment performance of the workers' co-operative economy with the investment performance of the private enterprise–trade union economy as we know it. If there is

adequate force in the earlier argument that the workers' co-operative economy, from which *ex hypothesi* collective bargaining is absent, would only perform slightly less well than the idealized free enterprise economy without trade unions, then it follows that it would perform a great deal better than an economy in which, once its internal contradictions have fully matured, no one will invest at all.

67. As an afterthought it may be added that, insofar as investment is regarded as important because of the contribution it makes to growth, any tendency of the workers' co-operative economy to under-invest by the standards of idealized capitalism is less serious to the extent that growth is less highly regarded as the sovereign aim of economic processes or to the extent that growth is seen as a subordinate objective to or predicated on the stability of employment and prices which, as we have seen, our present political economy cannot deliver.

Would the Workers' Co-operative Economy Tend to Under-employ?

68. This is two questions disguised as one. The first is, 'Would the workers' co-operative, at the micro level, tend not to recruit new employees and members where a conventional firm would?'

The second is, 'Supposing that the answer to the first is "yes", would that imply a tendency to higher unemployment at the macro level of the economy as a whole?'

69. The first question has already been discussed at some length in the context of the kind of investment which workers' co-operatives might be expected to reject where a conventional firm would go ahead. The conclusion was that to some degree the workers' co-operative would be less inclined to make the kind of new investment which would increase employment without increasing distributable rewards per head of the pre-investment members of the co-operative.

70. Whether there would as a result be a macro tendency to unemployment as a result – and some observers have claimed to identify such a tendency in Yugoslavia, though we may wonder how they distinguish this element in the observable unemployment from other causes such as structural and frictional unemployment, regional unemployment, voluntary unemployment, unemployability, and so forth – entirely depends on the efficiency of the mechanism for forming new enterprises.

71. If we assume that the combination of a neutral fiscal and monetary policy, in Professor Friedman's sense, with access to technological

improvements and an initial level of incomes sufficient to engender an adequate savings potential will always guarantee the possibility of employment for all those who are not the victims of structural, frictional, regional, or voluntary unemployment or of unemployability or the collective enforcement of a higher than market-clearing price for labour — in other words that there can be no long-run demand deficiency in Keynes's sense — then anyone who is unemployed could be employed provided that a new co-operative could be formed to exploit the market opportunity which, *ex hypothesi*, is there and would have been exploited by lateral expansion of existing enterprises under pure market capitalism.

72. This then is purely a problem of friction in enterprise formation. But it is a real problem.

73. It is for this reason — and in order to preserve the important competitive condition of freedom of entry for new enterprises — that I have suggested in *Employment, Inflation and Politics* (1976) a threshold size of enterprise, measured by number of employees, below which conventional capital entrepreneurship would continue to operate. The assumption behind this is that the creation of new enterprises to fill market gaps and to exploit new technologies is by its nature more easily undertaken (and therefore more likely to be undertaken) by an individual than by a spontaneous workers' co-operative sprung ready-made from the dole queues.

74. As a direct corollary of this, provision has to be made for the conversion of a privately owned enterprise into a workers' co-operative when the threshold size is reached. This is made significantly easier than it might otherwise be by the form of relationship described already between workers' co-operatives and those who supply its capital. The founder-owner would himself be the owner of all the 'equity-like' obligations of the new workers' co-operative; and he might also be entitled to a mortgage on the assets at their historic real value.

75. He might choose to sell his rights in the ordinary secondary market. He might be offered and accept a post as a senior manager in the enterprise by the new workers' co-operative. He might choose to go and found a new venture, if that was his temperament. He might decide to rest on his laurels and his share in the future 'profits' of the co-operative.

76. It may still be argued that a tendency to under-employment in the workers' co-operative economy will persist because the change in the company law whereby the new era would be accomplished

necessarily introduces a friction into the operation of the classical labour market which was not there before.

However nearly this friction can be eliminated by simulating the mechanisms of capitalism for absorbing unused labour into commercially viable activities, the full efficiency of the classical labour market cannot be reproduced.

77. The shortest way with this objection is to accept it. Indeed, the experience of Yugoslavia, for what it is worth, tends to corroborate the conclusion of *a priori* reasoning.

78. But, once again the point must be made that the comparison here is with the capitalist economy working with textbook perfection. Anyone who has accepted the argument on which the case for the cooperative economy is predicated must accept that that is not the choice that actually has to be made. Anyone who has not accepted that premise must be met on that ground anyway.

79. If, as is implied by the diagnosis of instability in our existing political economy, the choice for conventional capitalism, with its inevitable corollary of strongly developed collective bargaining, is between stability of a kind with a permanently very high level of unemployment and a progression towards hyper-inflation and then even higher unemployment, a considerable tendency to underemployment in a stable and workable alternative political economy may still be acceptable.

80. A direct quantitative comparison of the levels of unemployment implied by the alternative systems is not possible, since both magnitudes are unknown and extraordinarily difficult to estimate. But judgement may be assisted by the reflection that, whereas the unemployment implied by capitalism with conventional bargaining is inherent and structural in the sense that it is the direct counterpart to the fact of monopoly in the labour market, unemployment in the workers' co-operative economy is inertial and frictional and will constantly tend to yield to market opportunities for new enterprises.

How Big can Workers' Co-operatives Afford to be?

81. This is a large issue and cannot be adequately treated here. There is no question that experience and *a priori* reasoning both suggest that workers' co-operatives work best when they are small — up to maybe a maximum of 1,000 members — and that their supposed advantages tend to evaporate as size rises much above that level.

82. These impressions need to be assessed rigorously and critically

to establish how far they are universally true, to identify the precise reasons why they are true and to consider how far modifications of the design — including possible federal and confederal arrangements — may be able to raise the acceptable limit on numbers.

83. Of the 18 million people employed in the UK private sector in 1973 just over 7 million were employed in firms employing more than 1,000 people, of whom over 5½ million were in enterprises employing over 5,000 people, and over 3,700,000 were in enterprises employing over 20,000 people. This is the picture given by the Bullock Report (Table 2, page 7).

84. Another 2 million are employed in public corporations, including nationalized industries, which tend to be large employers. A further 5 million are employed in central and local government administration and services. This leaves about 11 million people employed, predominantly in the private sector, in small enterprise units.

85. So, on the face of things about nine million people appear to be employed in enterprises which may well be too large for effective workers' co-operative functioning; and another 5 million government employees are not in the market economy at all, but may require in varying degrees and ways to be brought into it under the general concept of market socialism.

86. The question of the public corporations will be discussed in the next section. The question of marketizing existing public services is briefly discussed under a later section in this paper. So, attention here is focused on the seven million or so private sector employees in enterprises which may at present be too large for easy conversion into workers' co-operatives.

87. The first question which naturally arises is whether or not the present size of existing enterprises (and as Bullock very carefully acknowledges the Committee had to make some pretty heroic definitional stipulations in order to reduce the chaotic heterogeneity of the real world of diverse corporate structures to the neat categories of their statistics) reflects an objective industrial and commercial logic which could only be disturbed at great real cost.

88. This is a subject on which the literature is extensive and by no means unanimous. It is worth bearing in mind that the number of establishments in which more than say 2,000 people are employed on a common enterprise is small and accounts for a small fraction of the seven million private sector employees in large companies.

89. The new study this year by Professor S. J. Prais, *The Evolution*

of Giant Firms in Britain, tends to throw doubt on the industrial objec-
tivity of the reasons for high concentration of employment in large
firms. Instead it emphasizes the role played by artificial financial
factors, to say nothing of the natural temptations to monopoly
wherever government policy and the law do not stand in the way (let
alone where they actively encourage concentration, as in Britain during
the post-1964 craze for restructuring British industry to meet the
alleged competition of foreign-owned super-corporations).

Professor Prais concludes with the view that 'the encouragement of a
progressive and competitive economy now requires a systematic series
of policy measures aimed at tilting the balance throughout the range of
firm-sizes; measures are required to offset the private financial advantages enjoyed by the largest firms, *to encourage individual plants to
be run as independent businesses rather than as subsidiaries of a distant
head-office*, and to foster an increase in the number of smaller independent firms to the level found in other economically advanced countries'
(my italics).

90. Certainly, many conventional managements of large enterprises
regard it as most efficient to run their component enterprises as if they
were independent firms, with head-offices merely monitoring financial
performance and intervening only to supply new capital and to ensure
consistency on certain broad questions of corporate policy and
strategy, labour relations commonly being an important head-office
issue. In a world where the present artificial financial incentives to size
and concentration were removed and where the conventional problem
of labour relations had been replaced by the mechanisms of a workers'
co-operative, the need for firms to be larger than the appropriate size
for individual plants might well appear weaker than it now is.

91. Nor have I involved any of the broader social and social psychological arguments for smaller units in which the individual feels less lost
as a meaningless cog in an unintelligible, even hostile, machine. For
what they are worth, they appear to favour smaller self-directing groups
against giant hierarchical and remote structures.

92. The only general conclusion to be ventured at this stage is that
the present state of knowledge does not warrant the automatic assumption that workers' co-operatives cannot work above a certain size,
which size is too small to accommodate modern industrial realities.
There remain very important questions of fact and analysis to be
investigated, including the degree to which there may be important
economies of scale in marketing, research, and design even where there

are no real economies of scale in production. Even here it will be important to know how far these economies could not be equally well realized on an inter- rather than intra-enterprise basis, and how far the economies are specific only to the environment of a conventionally structured economy.

93. Finally, we have to remember yet again that the standard of comparison being made, when the pure artificialities have been excluded, is with an idealized free enterprise economy, not with the political economy we actually have.

What About the Statutory Monopolies?

94. This question can be quickly answered, so far as issues of principle are involved. Insofar as existing statutory monopolistic public corporations (and indeed public services) are so structured for reasons other than the effective impossibility or absurd diseconomies of competitive enterprise in the activity in question, then they should be split into competitive enterprises. The question whether such component competitive enterprises would be too large for organization as workers' co-operatives is no more than a special case of the general question of size already discussed.

95. Insofar as existing statutory monopolies are so structured because competitive enterprise would be impossible or absurd — say in sewage and some few other public utilities — then they must so remain. The question whether and to what degree they could then be organized as workers' co-operatives can then be put on one side as a genuinely special case, the treatment of which does not have any critical significance for the general viability of the workers' co-operative economy. My personal leaning would be against trying to establish workers' co-operatives in such cases, preferring instead to adopt the model of, say, the police force where employment by such a public monopoly carries with it certain natural and widely accepted restrictions on the scope for collective bargaining.

What About the Technical Monopolies?

96. This question has now been considered as a special case of public monopolies.

Would Trade Union Monopoly Power Really Wither Away?

97. This is a critical question for the whole argument for a workers' co-operative economy as a viable alternative to our present supposedly doomed political economy.

98. The case to answer has been well posed by Mr Samuel Brittan in a volume of essays published in 1977. He writes:

There is . . . no reason to suppose that industry-wide monopolistic behaviour by organised workers would stop. It would, of course, take the form of raising prices rather than wages, but the distinction would be one of form. Indeed, workers coops could more easily combine directly with each other to raise return by limiting output, if they did not have to go through the inconvenience of threatened or actual strike behaviour first. Nor is there any reason to suppose that the tensions produced by an unstable balance of power between different groups of workers, and the resulting threat to employment and temptation to inflationary policies, would be any less than they are today. The most difficult wage issues and confrontations have even under the existing system been in the public sector, where the issue of profits has not even arisen and where the argument is clearly one with the rest of the community over relative shares.

99. If this view were correct, then indeed the thesis presented in the final part of my *Employment, Inflation and Politics* would fall to the ground. But this critique appears not to give sufficient weight to the following points:

(i) Strict competition between co-operatives in final markets is an essential element in the market socialist new political settlement, as I have proposed it;

(ii) effective anti-trust enforcement of this condition by law will be politically possible in a way that anti-combination laws are not enforceable, because, in the face of the threatened collapse of existing political economy, the political settlement itself will be able to command general assent in a way that what would look like a union-bashing capitalist counter-revolution would not, because individual co-operatives will have assets against which legal sanctions can be enforced and because of point (iv) below;

(iii) small government, balanced budgets, and Friedmanite 'neutral' monetary growth are also essential features of the new settlement so that government will not be, and will be seen not to be, available as a universal provider and supporter of commercial enterprises;

(iv) Once working people are organized, willy-nilly, into co-operatives the natural forces which tend eventually to undermine producer cartels of all kinds can begin to work, which is effectively impossible so long as the only perceived group identity of working people is as members of their union. (Rival unions do not commonly produce close substitutes in final markets for each other's particular products and their sense of solidarity against capital in general prevents them from competing to supply cheaper labour to employers — but once the co-operative identity has been established the temptation to break ranks and undercut any collusive cartel price which might be illegally proposed will operate directly on the members of the co-operative wishing to extend its market share. If it did not, the provisions for new entry into the industry already described would put heavy pressure on them to do so and would anyway undermine the cartel price); and

(v) the arrangements already described for transforming public corporations into competitive workers' co-operatives, technical monopolies apart, and the proposed marketization of other public services are other integral elements in the political settlement and so dispose of the danger of special difficulties in the public sector except in the cases of the technical monopolies, where the proposed adoption of the police model of industrial relations would be easier in the context of the general settlement proposed.

100. In short my answer to Mr Brittan is that there are indeed reasons to suppose that industry-wide monopolistic behaviour by organized workers would stop. These are that:

(a) it would be politically possible to make such behaviour illegal (in the sense of collusive price-setting);

(b) it would be politically and operationally easier to enforce such anti-trust legislation;

(c) it would be politically possible drastically to reduce the government's role as direct employer;

(d) workers organized into co-operatives would perceive much less need for trade unions (which are essentially a response of labour to the capitalist entrepreneur); and

(e) whether they perceived this or not, collective bargaining would disintegrate under the pressure, that eventually breaks all cartels, of the free-rider temptation which will operate on co-operatives as on conventional producers — though perhaps to a weaker degree because of the co-operative's interest in maximizing income per head rather than conventional profit and because of its acknowledged hesitancy over increasing its membership — because the imposition of a cartel is bound to mean reduced output and employment which each participating co-operative has an interest in minimizing.

101. I am puzzled by Mr Brittan's reference to 'an unstable balance of power between different groups of workers'. He would be the last person to describe the relation between firms in a competitive market as an unstable balance of power, although of course he would not expect it to be static. The relationship between co-operatives is congruent with that between firms on the conventional competitive market.

102. Lastly, he misconstrues, I am sure through unclarity in my original exposition, my contention that workers 'need somehow to be disalienated enough to become infected with the entrepreneurial realities which confront their employers, so that they will accept a non-inflationary market-determined environment as setting the level of rewards that can be afforded', if he thinks that by that I meant that workers are alienated by the fact of private profit as such.

I meant that as employees of enterprises, often large and remotely managed, the residual effects of whose financial successes and failures fall upon third parties (either shareholders or the government), employees have little perceived direct interest in the commercial performance and viability of those enterprises, except in certain moments of extreme crisis when it is usually too late. They simply want better rewards and have no opinion about how their employers will meet the cost. This point applied at least as much to public sector employees as to private; and therefore Mr Brittan is wrong to infer that the behaviour of public sector employees can only stem from a conscious claim on the rest of the community for a larger share (though that of course can be the only reality in what they are doing, just as it can be the only reality in the private sector except where profits can indeed be squeezed).

103. Mr Brittan also raises the spectre of all the co-operatives in a particular industry banding together to confront the government with a demand for privileged treatment − say, authorization of a cartel − on pain of stopping all output. Why, he asks, would they be less likely to do so under market socialism?

104. This leads one into an important discussion of the differences between the economic realities of trade union behaviour and the purposes of such behaviour as perceived by the people who are instrumental in leading and supporting it.

105. It is certainly true that the only rationally predictable consequence of some forms of trade union behaviour in stateable circumstances would be, if that behaviour were successful in its declared purposes, to divert claims on the real disposable national income from

the rest of the community to the affected members of the trade union in question. It does not follow that this is the purpose of the action as those members see it; and to make this distinction it is not necessary to suppose that the trade unionists in question are any less rational, informed, well-motivated, patriotic, altruistic, or healthy in mind and body than those of us who presume to comment on their behaviour.

106. It is perfectly rational and ethical for any given group of producers or suppliers, who are allowed by law to operate a monopoly or cartel to do so to the limits of their self-interest; and this remains true even if it is not sensible or even morally right for a society to allow people in general to behave in this way. Of course, the monopolist's profits can only be secured at the expense of the rest of the community, since there is nowhere else for it to come from. But the people who exploit such an opportunity are merely seeking to promote their own legitimate advantage without harbouring any particular opinion about what the distributional effects diffused throughout society may or should be.

107. It may be said that every man is morally accountable for the foreseeable consequences of his actions, whether taken individually or collectively. But we do not expect a man in a queue to keep moving to the back because this confers a benefit on the rest of the community in the form of the other people in the queue. We merely expect him not to jump the queue because that is the rule established by society for balancing self-interest against group interest in that situation. If queues as such are evil, then it is up to society to change the rules, not to rely on individual sacrificial gestures.

108. It may be said, taking for example a hypothetical threat by the massed co-operatives in the coal-mining industry to refuse the nation supplies of coal until the rules of market socialism are abridged in their favour, that when the coal-miners defied the Heath government in 1973/74, they showed themselves willing to break explicit rules established by society in the form of an incomes policy law passed by Parliament. Leave aside the technicality that they only asked the executive to exercise a discretion which that law specifically provided to the executive.

109. Leave aside, too, the economic fact that what they sought was certainly no more than their economic value following the quadrupling of the price of oil.

Leave aside thirdly the tempting observation that this was precisely the kind of nonsensical situation which incomes policies breed and which market socialism would stand a better chance of avoiding by promoting a more effective and more probably acceptable form of market criterion for setting rewards to labour. The important point is that the miners maintained throughout and evidently believed that theirs was essentially a conventional dispute about wages with their employers, the state, and not a dispute with Parliament about the general framework of industrial and commercial law.

110. Obviously, there can be no way by law of ensuring that no one will ever break the law. What Mr Brittan imagines could happen. But in the wake of the new political settlement supposed — and that could not occur without general political consent having been secured to the settlement and consequent legislation — the mining co-operatives, if they were to fulfill Mr Brittan's speculation, would have openly and directly to demand a change in the framework law, not merely a modification of government policy, on pain of denial of supplies. It would explicitly be a demand on the rest of the community.

111. They would be seeking legal easement to charge monopoly or cartel prices which would fall directly and immediately on the rest of the community as individual and co-operative consumers of coal, without any muffling mediation through the Exchequer. They would also face the consequence that even coal has imperfect substitutes; and the community could decide, each man and co-operative for him and itself, how far they wished to pay the price of such special cases or how far they preferred to economize or switch to alternative fuels.

112. It may be said that there is nothing to prevent the government under present arrangements from passing on the effects of excessive public sector pay settlements and that private sector employers naturally have to do so and that this does not deter collective bargaining.

But this does not mean that the blame is necessarily attributed as it would be under market socialism. For, in advance of a new political settlement we live in a world which expects the government to extract quarts from pint pots, which is indeed frequently encouraged by actual and aspirant governments to expect such results and which accordingly blames governments for any disappointment of such expectations. The attribution of blame matters because it ultimately affects the enforceability of those laws where, as in this area, enforcement depends heavily on support not merely for the principle of the laws but also for the necessary sanctions against those who break the law.

113. Thus, it is seriously doubtful, at the very least, whether the avowed and conscious purpose of trade unionists as at present organized

is to hold the nation to ransom in the customary headline writer's sense; and so they would more probably balk if forced to make their choice in that form. It is also clear that the enforcement of competition laws in the political context posited here would, again to say the least, have a better chance of success than the enforcement under present conditions either of wage control or anti-combination laws.

Would Governments be Able to be Any Less Inflationary?

114. As already stated the political settlement which would inaugurate the world of market socialism under discussion here would commit governments to orthodox fiscal and monetary policies. There would be no discretionary demand management, no countervailing contracyclical judgements (though certain automatic fiscal stabilization might be permitted, if it could be defined in a watertight way) and no scope for financing government outgoings from the literal or metaphorical monetary printing presses.

115. So the question is whether there would develop insupportable political pressures to break these rules. Strong pressures could certainly develop.

Even if the system of competitive workers' co-operatives was wholly successful in suppressing the evil effects of collective bargaining on real labour costs, and thus on employment, a sharp rise in world commodity prices would certainly cause a transitional domestic recession until other prices were forced down sufficiently to restore the previous average price level. If the rise in such world prices is real and not just a reflection of domestic inflation in supplying countries, then the effect cannot stably be absorbed by adjusting the sterling exchange rate.

116. In those circumstances, so long as what may for brevity here be referred to as the Keynesian illusion (though unfairly to Keynes) lingers in the public mind, pressure for reflation may well develop. But there are certain advantages in the new situation. There will be *ex hypothesi* much less prospect of the effects of the higher import prices leading into a domestic pay–price spiral because there will be no such spiral once pay is effectively market determined rather than determined by collective bargaining. If government does seek to accommodate the higher level of import costs by increasing monetary demand through fiscal or monetary means, the effect will be to drive down the sterling exchange rate in such a way as to achieve a new payments equilibrium at the new terms of trade; and with no pay–price spiral waiting to be aggravated that could be the end of the process.

There will have been a once-and-for-all price increase at home, but no permanent increase in the inflation rate, still less any prospect of accelerating inflation of the kind inherent in trying to maintain full employment by expanding monetary demand while labour monopolies seek to earn a monopolist's return.

117. So, economically as well as politically it should become easier for governments to abjure the horn of accelerating inflation because the other horn of the current dilemma, namely an inherent domestic tendency to high unemployment, has been removed; and occasional disturbances from abroad can be accommodated without embarking again upon the old vicious circle.

118. This leaves out the possibility of a domestically generated recession. Since government policy is *ex hypothesi* neutral, this would originate in an imbalance of domestic savings and investment. A modern monetarist may incline to scepticism about the likelihood of such a development and be willing to rely on automatic monetary stabilizers, in the form of falling interest rates, to correct the recession.

119. There is also the possibility, once the new political settlement is established and working well and collective bargaining has faded away more or less entirely, of permitting a cautious revival of Keynesian ideas.

Once the effects of monopolistic bargaining have been eradicated the notion of demand deficiency becomes much less dangerous. A modern monetarist might at least accept that the natural level of un-employment (i.e. the non-inflationary level) would be much reduced by the elimination of the monopoly effect and that therefore the inflation-generating gap between the natural level and likely governmental employment targets would be reduced.

120. A modern Keynesian, who had none the less accepted that incomes policies could not solve the unemployment-inflation problem, would certainly argue that the way was now clear to resume discretionary demand management, provided only that the available quality of forecasting was sufficient to give a substantial probability that action would in practice tend to be contra- rather than pro-cyclical. The modern monetarist will still worry that official employment targets will be set above the natural or sustainable rate and that therefore accelerating inflation could be reborn, because even in the absence of collective bargaining there are plenty of other structural and frictional reasons why full employment will not be fully attainable.

121. If unemployment does tend to settle down at an uncomfortably

high level, effected in part by any tendency of a workers' co-operative economy to underemployment as already discussed, then this condition will have to be carefully and empirically examined. Monetarists will tend to argue that such a tendency is evidence of a high natural rate of unemployment and therefore of the presence of structural and frictional causes which may or may not have been identified. Keynesians will tend to suspect demand deficiency.

122. A careful and jointly monitored experiment might throw light on the correct interpretation. Let the government take up by fiscal or monetary action all or some part of the demand gap as estimated by the Keynesians. Then wait five years. If the employment position improves markedly without any strong tendency for prices to rise correspondingly and for the level of economic activity to fall back after the first stimulative effects wear off, then demand deficiency will appear to have been the right diagnosis and may be acted upon on subsequent occasions.

Whither to Extend the Market Economy?

123. The short answer is in the direction of what is now government activity, including those areas which, though technically in the private sector, are so heavily regulated or dependent on government aid and custom that market criteria do not in effect determine behaviour.

124. It includes the provision of social services as well as the mainstream industrial and other productive activities such as agriculture. It implies that distributional policies, however egalitarian or inegalitarian, will be seen mainly as an operation affecting cash incomes; and, while in some areas it may be convenient for the government or some statutory agency — or even a state promoted workers' co-operative — to continue to provide some or, in the absence of any other entrants to the field, all of a particular service, the concept implies that the consumer would acquire the service on market terms and that the signals so given of consumer preference would determine the scale and direction of future service. The co-operativization of nationalized industries has already been discussed; and the main thrust under this heading will be in areas not traditionally regarded as primarily economic, such as education, housing, health, personal services, and broadcasting.

125. This is not the place to be more specific, although in the case of broadcasting I would draw attention to my evidence to the Annan Committee (*Encounter*, April 1977) which seeks to explain how the principles of the present print publishing market could and should be applied to electronic publishing when the next generation of spectrum

technology becomes available towards the end of the century. Much work done by the Institute of Economic Affairs has opened up a number of interesting avenues for investigation of the possible application of market principles to education, social, health, and personal services in ways which need not conflict with the original compassionate and social purposes of those services. In the context of a market socialist political settlement these would become germane, just as many of the ideas developed over many years by Professor James Meade for correcting specific and ascertained market failures in areas involving public goods and external diseconomies would be even more obviously necessary than they already are, as well as being more easily distinguishable from extensions of state intervention which have quite other rationales.

Why is the Record of Workers' Co-operatives so Poor?

126. There is a popular knock-down argument against almost all claims on behalf of the workers' co-operative economy, namely that if co-operatives had the advantages attributed to them they would, as Samuel Brittan and Peter Lilley imply in their book this year *The Delusion of Incomes Policy*, spread 'like wildfire' through the economy without benefit of statutory imposition. And they have not. Therefore, either they cannot have the advantages claimed or there must be other, more than offsetting, unconsidered disadvantages.

127. This is a little too fast. For one thing there have been and are a number of impediments to such a spontaneous combustion. More importantly the argument for the workers' co-operative economy is an argument for a change of system because of systematic defects in the present political economy; and it is often the case that the switch to a better system is not self-propagating, as for example with the adoption of a 'Keep Left' or 'Keep Right' rule of the road.

128. This is not the occasion to review the evidence of producer co-operative successes and failures in North America and Europe. Experience is concentrated in the two hundred years from the middle of the seventeenth century to the middle of the present century; and in very broad terms it leaves an impression that producer co-operatives have tended to be small, to be short-lived and to have difficulty surviving in the prevailing environment, although there are some important exceptions.

129. But this evidence has to be interpreted with great care, if morals are to be drawn about the viability of market socialism. The

American evidence and literature have been usefully examined by Derek C. Jones (of Hamilton College, Clinton, New York) in a privately circulated paper, *The Economics and Industrial Relations of Producer Cooperatives in the United States 1791–1939*. He throws considerable doubt on the conventional view that American producer co-operatives failed through inherent internal weaknesses.

130. He draws attention to the extent to which many American co-operatives were not truly workers' co-operatives in the sense in which self-management is defined by J. Vanek (the chief modern theorist of labour managed market economies; see his *The General Theory of Labor-Managed Market Economies*, Cornell University Press, 1970), namely enterprises where all control, management, and income remains in the hands of those who actually work in the given enterprise on the basis of equality of vote.

131. The European experience has some similar features, although there are also many differences of which the most important is that the record is by no means so seemingly dismal as in North America. There is little doubt that in Britain the extreme hostility from the end of the nineteenth century of trade unions and socialist intellectuals to workers' co-operatives discouraged their development.

The Webbs were peculiarly fierce against them on the dubious grounds that workers' co-operatives were necessarily an element in a world of producer sovereignity to which they quite rightly preferred consumer sovereignity as the only coherent basis of legitimacy for any economic activity (see their *Cooperative Production and Profit-Sharing*, New Statesman Special Supplement, 1914, and *A Constitution for the Socialist Commonwealth of Great Britain*, Longmans, 1921).

132. But the stronger point is the purely logical one that nothing necessarily follows about the rival merits of labour- and capital-managed economies from the experience of individual co-operatives operating in the context of a capital-managed economy. Insofar as the crucial advantage urged for the labour-managed economy is that it would cause collective bargaining (in which incidentally the Webbs and the classical American consumer supremacists strongly believed) to wither away, so dissolving the catastrophic dilemma of high unemployment or accelerating inflation, that cannot be tested by examining the experience of individual co-operatives in a capital-managed economy where the general need for trade union organization and collective bargaining is bound to be strongly felt.

133. We have already discussed whether and why collective

bargaining would wither away in a labour-managed economy. Manifestly it would not do so just for the benefit of an odd co-operative here and there. Trade unions with a powerful base in the conventional sectors of the economy will take good care to see that it does not, unless they regard the individual case as too small to matter, as has occurred with some small or commercially doomed co-operatives. One only has to reflect on the attitude of the TUC and key national trade union leaders to the forms of industrial democracy urged upon and accepted by the Bullock Committee to appreciate what would be and indeed has always been their natural and inevitable attitude to the creation of a genuinely independent expression of workers' power.

134. Obviously so long as the main power-base of collective bargaining remains, as it is bound to do in a free society with a capital-managed economy, ways would be sought and probably found of preventing any serious tendency for workers' co-operatives to undercut union labour prices. What is more, the entrepreneurs of potential workers' co-operatives, themselves workers, are virtually reluctant to embark upon ventures which could and would be represented as anti-union and therefore, under our present political economy, anti-labour and anti-working class.

135. In these circumstances it will seldom pay any individual enterprise to become a workers' co-operative, overcoming all the substantial inertial and transitional problems at the same time. It follows that the lack of evidence of a general tendency for workers' co-operatives to propagate themselves except in circumstances of total commercial failure of the conventional enterprise proves nothing about the potentialities of a workers' co-operative economy. As every social thinker knows, in a theatre on fire it does not pay the individual to behave unilaterally as it would pay him to behave if he had good reason to think that everyone else would so behave on condition of his so behaving. For the benefit to him, in the form of a better chance of escaping the theatre unharmed, flows, not from his own orderly restraint, but from the orderly restraint of everyone else; and orderly restraint on his part would be irrational, albeit heroic, if it were not the price of the orderly restraint of others from which he can expect to benefit more than he expects to benefit from disorderly self-assertion in the absence of a mutual restraint agreement. In other words conduct which in the context of a changed system of rules would benefit the whole community and all or most individuals in that community is not self-propagating merely by the individual's pursuit of private advantage

as perceived in an unchanged context. This phenomenon is a cliché and should not need to be laboured.

Yugoslavia

136. The description 'market socialism' has commonly been applied to the economic system which has prevailed under Marshal Tito in Yugoslavia.

It is natural to inquire, when market socialism is proposed for other economies, how it has fared in the one place where it is supposed to have been tried.

137. I am not able here to answer that question. Impressions of tendencies to under-employment, inflation, and under-investment have certainly been reported by some observers. Others have detected some successes. Any final evaluation must allow fully for the differences in the circumstances and system of Yugoslavia from any other economy to which the model of market socialism might be applied.

138. Yugoslavia is far from having a fully developed industrial economy. It is poor. It is under authoritarian Communist rule, though it is not part of the Moscow-dominated Communist bloc in eastern Europe. It relies heavily on state planning as the predominant mode of resource allocation; and the outside capital for investment by co-operatives comes mainly from the state, not from private savers through a free capital market. It is most doubtful whether free trade unions would be possible in the western sense, whether or not co-operative forms of enterprise management made them otiose.

139. In these circumstances it is uncertain how much could be definitively learned about the potentialities of a workers' co-operative economy in western Europe and North America from the experience of Yugoslavia, but clearly it should be examined more thoroughly than it yet appears to have been by English-language economists.

Can We Go Step by Step towards Market Socialism?

140. The argument already presented for regarding the change to market socialism as unlikely to be self-propagating because the private and social advantages will only be enjoyed after the system has been changed must tend by parity of reasoning to weaken the idea of a step-by-step approach. If it is an all-or-nothing choice, then it cannot be had bit by bit.

141. This is a real difficulty, because any practical politician who sees merit in the general thrust of the argument will want to find ways

of moving gradually towards the goal, that being the nature of non-revolutionary politics. Moroever, others who see prima facie merits in the argument, but who would like more evidence from hard experience before trying to turn a whole modern economy inisde out, will naturally and properly look for some limited experiment.

142. Alasdair Clayre, writing (in *The Economist* for 5–11 March 1977) sympathetically to the idea of self-managed enterprises, explains his own preference for 'self-management as one sector of a mixed economy'. Any sensible man would prefer at least to start out by this route, provided that the general systemic advantages of a workers' co-operative economy would be expected to be given a fair trial in a mere sector of a conventional capital-managed or mixed economy.

143. It may be that experiments could be conducted in some fairly self-contained sector, where the existing trade union organization and collective bargaining procedures are specific to that industry or sector alone. Coal-mining is a tempting example. Schools, postal services, newspapers, professional and technical services, railways, fisheries, and parts of the entertainment industry may be others. But the heart of the matter is manufacturing industry, where general and craft unions predominate over industrial unions and where, even if they did not, it is hard to see how one could bite on a mere part of the bullet without forfeiting the prospects of a transformation of the patterns of pay determination.

144. There is also a real danger that in the next few years the creation of a co-operative will become the standard response of workers to the bankruptcy of their conventional employers and that, as a result, the idea will be put on test in hopeless circumstances in which neither the systemic nor even the internal benefits of co-operatives will have a fair chance. The Scottish Daily News and the Meriden Co-operative are a warning. The Plessey plants at present under threat of closure may be other cases in point.

145. The central argument is for a workers' co-operative economy and should continue to be pressed as such. If ways can be found to conduct genuine and fair experiments, so much the better. But the advocate of a market socialist solution to our macro problems will have to be vigilant against the real danger of unfavourable conclusions being drawn from partial and biased contexts which do not and cannot test the main thesis.

Do Workers Want Co-operatives?

146. They may or they may not, according to the prospects as they see them for job security, living standards and influence over those aspects of their working lives which most concern them under conventional and alternative management. They cannot reasonably be expected to appraise the macro-economic arguments for a workers' co-operative economy on the basis of the information at present given them by their employers and trade union leaders; and, even if they could so appraise the arguments and did appraise them favourably, that would be very far from giving them sufficient reasons of private advantage in each or any of the particular employments for preferring a co-operative form of management. Anyone who is in a position to rip off the taxpayer, negligent shareholder, indulgent proprietor, or exploitable consumer is clearly well-advised to continue doing so as long as people are foolish or kind enough to let him get away with it.

147. But the argument here, unlike that in the Bullock report, in no way depends on what the currently expressed or even eventual preference of workers may be. It is not to be done because workers want or demand it. It is to be done whether they prefer it or not, although of course subject to the basic democratic sanction of the ballot box and the Parliamentary majority, because this is the only or best way of preventing a calamity for the whole community.

148. An unintelligently hostile expression of the underlying thought would be, 'O.K., you've fought capitalism to a standstill and it won't work anymore; the government's cupboard is bare and it can't play sugar-daddy so now you run it, but without coercing consumers, taxpayers, or savers.' That would be unintelligent because it confuses in the word 'you' working people as organized in trade unions with working people as such and because it imputes either folly or malignity to them, where the fault lies not in the intentions of any man, but in the institutional framework for expressing his intentions.

149. The problem would not be essentially different in character from what it is if every single participant in the economy had a Ph.D. in economics, was a devout supporter of the traditional principles of the United States Republican Party and was as fully concerned for the welfare of his neighbour as is commonly thought to be desirable. It would of course be different if every participant were a saint and an ascetic because in that case there would be little call for any economic activity at all.

150. In the circumstances of a community of wise, understanding,

well-motivated, and normally materialistic individuals, they will and must behave broadly as they now do, so long as they are organized into pressure groups and sectional lobbies, because in a world of what Samuel Brittan has called 'collective extortion' the loner is a sucker and his dependants suffer.

151. But in such a community the individuals would also jointly decide, if they perceived the option, to abstain by collective agreement from mutually stultifying and eventually destructive modes of pursuing sectional advantage. That would be a political and not an economic or industrial decision; and in that decision the voices that count are the voices of every individual as a total human being, not just the voices of one economic category, however large, expressing only one aspect of themselves.

152. It would pay every motorist to get free petrol; and the overwhelming majority of the adult population are motorists. Yet, we are very far from providing free petrol. No more can the opinion of workers *qua* workers, still less trade unionists *qua* trade unionists, supposing it were sceptical about co-operative organization, be decisive if it conflicts with the general interest of the community, although as has been said no political action can be taken until the democratic conditions are fulfilled. To fulfil them is the political task for market socialists.

A CO-OPERATIVE SECTOR IN A MIXED ECONOMY

3. Piecemeal

by Robert Oakeshott

I have two main objectives in what follows. The first is to argue that, provided the correct conditions are satisfied, there is a strong case for encouraging the piecemeal, though at the same time interlinked, promotion of worker-owned co-ops: we are not confronted here with an all-or-nothing choice between a wholesale swapping over to a worker-owned co-operative economy on the one hand and leaving things as they are on the other. Secondly I want to argue that the optimum financial arrangements for such workers' co-ops are likely to resemble those which have evolved in the co-operative grouping centred on Mondragon in the Basque provinces of Spain — and apparently in Poland — rather than, say, those which have developed in Yugoslavia. On both issues my theoretical position is sharply at odds with Peter Jay's. So, for that matter, is my practical position. For in working for the recently established Job Ownership Ltd. (JOL) I am engaged with others in the piecemeal encouragement of worker-owned co-operatives on Mondragon lines.

The Piecemeal Approach

Essentially Jay sees the choice as one between a wholesale switch-over to a workers' co-operative economy, brought about by legislative fiat, and leaving things as they are. Only by a wholesale switch-over, he argues, will a political economy of workers' co-ops be able to deliver the benefits which it has to offer. The analogy suggested is with the rule of the road. Piecemeal decisions by individuals to adopt a rule of the road are unlikely to produce any great benefits either to themselves or to the community. It is only when everyone drives on the left (or the right) that real advantages start to accrue. And so it is, Jay argues, with workers' co-ops.

The grounds for this belief of Jay's are straightforward enough. Only in this way, he argues, can the monopoly power of the trade unions in the labour market be broken and only thus, therefore, can the UK

economy break out from its secular path of progressively higher unemployment and progressively higher inflation. Moreover, in Jay's
view, it is not only unrealistic to imagine that a piecemeal elimination
of trade union monopoly power would be associated with the
piecemeal promotion of durable workers' co-operatives. It is also most
unlikely that a successful enclave or enclaves of workers' co-ops could
be created in an economic environment still dominated by trade unions.
It may even, Jay argues, be dangerous and counter-productive to
attempt any such piecemeal promotion on the grounds that failure, the
most likely outcome, will make the task of persuading the electorate to
believe in a workers' co-op solution that much harder. As against this
position of Jay's I propose to contend:

(a) that those workers' co-ops or similar enterprises which survive successfully in today's world have largely eliminated, within
their own organizations, the most negative aspects of trade union
monopoly power;

(b) that the key requirement, if we are to persuade the electorate of the virtues of a workers' co-op solution to the problems of
inflation and unemployment, is that we should be able to point to a
significantly larger class of actual, and robustly prospering, workers'
co-ops. Moreover I shall also contend that this may not be as difficult a goal as a superficial reading of the evidence suggests: histori-
cally most workers' co-ops have suffered from various specific but
theoretically avoidable handicaps. If these can be overcome then we
can be cautiously optimistic about successful co-op promotion;

(c) that a gradual process of transformation, brought about very
largely from the bottom upwards, is much more likely than any
legislative fiat to bring about those changes of attitude which are at
the heart of the matter.

Even leaving aside for the moment the astonishing Mondragon
experience, there is now a solid body of evidence that, as compared
with what happens in a conventional company, the shop-floor in a
successful workers' co-op may well be prepared to strike a new balance
between its own short-term 'wage packet interest' and the longer-term
interest of the enterprise as a whole. I have tried to present some of
that evidence in my recent book. And though I would be the first to
acknowledge that a systematic job on this issue remains to be done, the
particular cases with which I was able to deal do seem to me to tell
a modestly encouraging tale. For there is evidence that whether we are
talking about glass workers in Albi, or ex-Miners in South Wales, or a

chemical work-force outside Wellingborough, or a group of part-time young mothers in Sunderland — or, yes, the Meriden motorcycle shop-floor outside Coventry — or, for that matter, waitresses in Dublin, we find a readiness where necessary to forgo some part of the wage packet for the sake of preserving employment. To make just one of these examples more concrete, the achievement at Meriden in this respect seems to me to have attracted much less attention and favourable comment than it deserves. For well over four years now the shop-floor in that motorcycle enterprise has accepted significantly less — currently some £10 per week — than the going rate for the job in their neighbourhood. That may not be an example of *breaking* trade union monopoly power in the labour market. But it is surely an example of transcending it.

But, of course, if working people are going to be convinced that co-op structures are worth trying, we need upside examples as well as, indeed much more so than, examples of a readiness to make short-term sacrifices. Though in some respects it is not a workers' co-op (and certainly not a worker-*owned* co-op) the case of John Lewis Partnership is worth mentioning here. The partnership's policy on wage and salary rates is to pay at or marginally above the going market level. In addition the work-force receives each year a share in profits, originally paid in fixed interest shares, but since the early 1970s in cash. The cash bonus which an individual receives has never, since it was introduced, fallen below 11% of his or her annual wage or salary. It is hard to dispute the contention that, as compared with a conventional enterprise, the workers at John Lewis are thus receiving a significantly larger percentage of net value-added. It would be perverse to deny that they are better off as a result.

As a second upside example I can introduce a small cluster of workers' co-ops which operate in the plywood industry in the Pacific North West of the US. The American Federal Income tax officially acknowledged some years ago that because worker productivity in these enterprises was significantly higher — by an average of some 25% — than in their conventional counterparts so also were their members' incomes. There is evidence too that over the years the members have enjoyed a significantly greater measure of job security than workers in the outside world. It is true that these particular workers' co-ops are to .some degree flawed, in that there is not a total identity between the membership and the work-force, and some non-members have been employed. On the other hand non-member workers have always been in a minority in these plywood co-ops. What is clear in any case is that they point the way to precisely those benefits — greater job security, higher incomes — which could convince working people that it was worth attempting a co-operative solution.

It is with precisely those benefits to the shop-floor — greater job security and higher incomes — that the group of largely industrial co-operatives centred on Mondragon has come to be associated. Over the period of now nearly 25 years since the first of these enterprises was started there has not been one single case of involuntary redundancy. Since we are talking here about a work-force total, distributed between 60 to 70 co-ops, of now about 13,000, this looks like a considerable achievement. As for Mondragon incomes, a number of points are worth recalling. In the first place the policy combines a quite narrow pre-tax set of differentials — they must not be more than 4.5:1.0 — with an insistence that the lowest rates must be the same as, or slightly above those prevailing in the neighbourhood. Secondly, under a rather complex formula (the details of which need not concern us) up to 70%* of the profits of these enterprises are distributed to their worker-members in the form of credits to their personal accounts. These profit shares have frequently amounted to the equivalent of three months' pay, or exceptionally even more, on top of normal annual income. Thus as in the case of John Lewis, and in fact substantially more so, the Mondragon workers are receiving a much larger percentage of net value-added than their counterparts in conventional industry. The beneficial demonstration effects of these arrangements can hardly be exaggerated. And if there are any lingering doubts on that score it should be enough to point to two key facts. First, ever since the late 1950s there have been more applicants to join the co-ops than available places. Second, after the recent legalization of trade unions in Spain, co-op members voted overwhelmingly that there should be no union organizing within their enterprises. There could scarcely be more convincing evidence that in the eyes of those working in them the Mondragon arrangements are highly valued.

Of course it will be rejoined that as against this evidence of success there is much *more* evidence of failure. If that rejoinder means that only a minority of all those workers' co-ops which have been launched over the last 150 years are still alive and well, then it is unquestionably

*The bulk of the balance is assigned to indivisible, collectively owned co-operative reserves. We can thus think of Mondragon ownership as partly or mainly — but not exclusively — individual.

true. It is also almost certainly true that there have been more failures than successes in this area of endeavour and it is fair to conclude that their successful promotion is a difficult business. But once the reasons for the widespread failure of the past have been properly understood I believe that a policy of cautious promotion in the future can be supported by hard heads as well as soft hearts.

I have tried elsewhere to analyse the causes of failure and there is not the space to repeat that exercise here. In rough and ready terms on the other hand I would argue that we can boil down the main causes of failure to four:

 (i) workers' co-ops have generally failed to attract good managers;
 (ii) the finance available to workers' co-ops has normally been much less than that available to their conventional counterparts;
(iii) the enterprise structures adopted by the vast majority of workers' co-ops have been faulty in that they have not ensured that there should be an identity between those who work in the co-operative on the one hand and those who own and ultimately control it on the other;
(iv) most workers' co-ops for most of the last 150 years have been operating on their own in a largely hostile environment. To survive they need to be linked together in mutually supporting groups.

I would go on to argue that by a mixture of good luck, imagination, and plain business horse-sense the leaders of the Mondragon co-operatives have overcome these traditional workers' co-op difficulties. They have attracted good managers; they have developed their own highly successful bank; they have evolved structures in which all, or virtually all, the workers are at once owners and voting members of their co-operatives. And they have formed themselves into a mutually self-supporting group of enterprises. Of course it is true that they have had the great advantage of local feelings of loyalty and solidarity, in the shape of Basque nationalism, to build upon. All the same there is clearly more than an outside chance that a new set of workers' co-ops, if it could overcome the traditional difficulties in the way that Mondragon has shown to be possible, could be successfully promoted on a piecemeal basis.

Such a piecemeal approach also looks more convincing than Peter Jay's wholesale and government-precipitated switch-over if we reflect for a moment about attitudes. The first point is that the negative aspects of present UK union behaviour, whether within the enterprise or in the labour market, is not simply or perhaps even mainly a matter of monopoly power. It derives at least as much from a widespread shop-floor feeling (particularly in the Midlands and North) that our present arrangements are not the beneficent, even-handed, and pluralistic ones which they are presented as being by liberal apologists. On the contrary they are widely seen as being loaded against the interests of working people and they generate hostile attitudes as a result. A Government-precipitated wholesale switch-over to workers' co-ops would stand a poor chance of changing these attitudes. By contrast a piecemeal approach, if it resulted in the establishment of successful co-ops, could perhaps begin to change attitudes as well as economic structures. The reason is that workers would then normally be involved in co-ops only if they chose to be. Moreover the extension of the new co-op sector would largely depend on shop-floor preferences to work in this way. The Mondragon experience is, I think, again relevant. It is one of the rules of the men of Mondragon that new initiatives (which may or may not eventually result in new co-op launches) must originate from the bottom and must not be imposed from the top.

The danger with Jay's strategy is that it will change structures but not attitudes. Sometimes, to be fair, he seems to write as if that would not matter; because the change of structures, even if everything else in the new workers' co-ops remain the same, would do the trick. If that is what he believes then that is perhaps where I disagree with him most fundamentally. For in my experience the structural change will not by itself be enough. The realities inside the new workers' co-ops have got to be different and to feel different from those in a conventional enterprise: otherwise the old conflicts between shop-floor and management and the familiarly negative shop-floor attitudes to productivity improvements and change are all too likely to soldier on.

Optimum Financial Arrangements for Workers' Co-ops

Among those who believe that workers' co-ops are worth trying at all, there is as yet no consensus about the most promising financial arrangements they should adopt. The chief point of controversy is about whether the assets of the enterprise should be in the undivided collective ownership of the co-op (or of some outside agency, perhaps the state) on the one hand, or at least partially* owned by the individual worker–members on the other. Put in another way the question is — should the individual worker–members be able to participate in the

---

*There is obviously a case for having an element of indivisible, collectively owned reserves.

capital growth of the co-op (with a corresponding exposure to the risk of loss if its results are negative); alternatively should they be protected from any direct involvement in balance sheet changes, with the co-op as a collective (or some outside institution) picking up the final responsibility and taking the long-term downside — and upside — risks.

There is a secondary point of conflict among those who support the collective ownership variant of the two main alternatives. If its assets are collectively (or externally) owned should the workers' co-op enjoy access to capital on only fixed interest terms? Or should it be permitted (or encouraged) to sell on the money markets some kind of non-voting shares in its distributed profits? Among those who favour collective (or external) ownership Peter Jay advocates the second of these positions.

I can deal only briefly with this secondary issue. Essentially I see no case for restricting the right of workers' co-ops to raise money by selling non-voting shares, if they are in fact able to do so. The crucial point is, of course, that such shares should be non-voting and thus there could be no risk that outside capital would simply acquire control and so defeat the object of the workers' co-ops' very existence. On the other hand both on general grounds and because financial markets have normally been unenthusiastic about non-voting shares, I would not expect that very much money would be raised in this way.

Turning back to the main area of controversy between the advocates of collective (or external) and those of partially individual ownership in workers' co-ops, the first argument to consider is whether *any* individual ownership arrnagements carry with them an unacceptable degree of risk. The collective ownership advocates argue, of course, that they do. Under any such arrangements in their view both the employment security and the personal savings of the individual co-op workers are committed to the fortunes of a single enterprise. The individual is thus effectively forced to have all his or her eggs in one precarious basket. Common prudence tells us, or so it is argued, that such a degree of risk is unacceptable.

In relation to the particular and mainly individual ownership arrangements — and other relevant practices — which have been pioneered by the Mondragon co-ops this argument has never seemed to me to be very convincing. In the first place we need to be clear *what* is at risk, as between genuine personal savings and accumulated profit-shares, for the individual Mondragon worker. By far the larger part will normally be accounted for by accumulated profit-shares and thus be something 'extra' compared with the position of a worker in a normal company. As we have seen and at least at the shop-floor level Mondragon wage-rates are as high as, or higher than those in conventional business. So any profit-share which the co-op member receives, like those profit-shares of the workers in the John Lewis Partnership, represents a net increase in his or her share of co-op income. Of course such profit shares cannot be guaranteed and are to that extent at risk. But it would be perverse not to prefer the risky prospect of a larger share in enterprise income when the alternative is no prospect of any such share at all.

What about any downside risk? To begin with, by the logic which we have just been through, the risk of losing their accumulated profit shares cannot properly count as a downside risk for the Mondragon workers. They are thus exposed to downside risk and their personal savings are threatened only to the extent of the initial capital contribution which they are all required to put up as a condition of co-op entry. With perhaps a tiny minority of exceptions, the level of these entry contributions at Mondragon has never exceeded six months of the lowest rate of shopfloor earnings. Thus in relation to average expectations of life-time earnings, the downside risk to which Mondragon workers are exposed is modest enough. Given the permanent waiting list of applicants anxious to join, we know, in any case, that this degree of downside risk is acceptable to the people concerned. One additional reason why they see it in this way is perhaps that their pension money is invested outside the co-ops. Another is that the individual Mondragon co-ops should not mainly be seen as isolated enterprises on their own. They can rely on support from other enterprises of the co-operative grouping and in particular on the resources of the bank which is at the nerve centre of this whole co-operative effort.

The other main argument against individual ownership arrangements in workers' co-ops is that they will result in inefficient investment decisions. This is the central argument on which Vanek rests his case in favour of removing ownership from the actual operating co-ops and assigning it to some outside institution. Only thus, he believes, can an efficient capital market operation be achieved. He would presumably concede that his case is weakened when co-ops are grouped together and when investment decisions can therefore, as at Mondragon, be taken at least partly in terms of the group as a whole. He might also concede that if only because of the immense distance which often separates capital markets from actual physical investments on the ground the efficiency of those we normally work with may leave a good deal to be desired.

Certainly in relation to the Mondragon co-ops which have an astonishing and almost bankruptcy-free record of investment success, I do not find this capital market efficiency argument all that persuasive. What I do find persuasive on the other hand are the psychological arguments which the Mondragon leaders adduce in favour of their mainly individual ownership arrangements and of the capital contributions which they require on entry. There is all the difference in the world, they argue, between the attitudes and feelings of a man who has put some of his own money into a business and the man who simply enjoys the benefit of working for an enterprise financed by outside loans. Both common sense and personal experience confirm the force of this contention. The workers' commitment to the long-term success of the enterprise will surely be immensely stronger if it is underpinned by the responsibility which a measure of actual ownership brings.

Looked at the other way round the temptation to behave with insufficient responsibility will surely be far stronger if commitment is not underpinned by a measure of ownership. This is not the place to review the evidence from elsewhere, nor am I familiar with it in any detail or at first hand. But Dr Ljubo Sirc is not, I think, alone in arguing that the worker-managed enterprises in Yugoslavia suffer from precisely this drawback. Figures quoted by Dr Sirc imply that in the last financial year worker-managed enterprises in that country voted to pay themselves out in wages and salaries 6% more on average than the total net value added of their operations. Opponents of worker-management are, of course, fond of arguing that such arrangements are almost bound to result in irresponsible decisions of this kind. But the point to emphasize here is that the individual ownership system which has been evolved at Mondragon gives a real measure of protection against irresponsible excesses of that kind.

THE COMPARATIVE ADVANTAGES OF
PARTICIPATION COMBINED WITH PROFIT-SHARING

4. Notes on the Political Economy of a
Co-operative Enterprise Sector[*]

by Felix R. FitzRoy

1. Introduction

Much has been written on the advantages to be expected from replacing
capitalist by co-operative enterprise, ranging from increased productivity through reduced 'alienation' to the preservation of liberal democracy itself. (For a sample of such views, see Jay, above; Oakeshott,
1978; Vanek, 1975.) Critics have focussed on the incentive problems
leading to inefficient allocation and even expropriation of capitalists by
impatient and opportunistic workers. (See for example Meade, 1972;
Furuborn, 1976; Pejovich, 1978.) Neither side has seriously attempted
to come to terms with the other's arguments, nor often shown much
awareness of them. In these notes an attempt will be made to discuss
the evidence available in an open-minded manner, and draw conclusions
on balance for industrial policy and legislation. Our approach thus
continues in the tradition of eclectic inquiry in this area developed
particulaly by Meade (1972), Fox (1974), and Oakeshott (1978) from
quite different standpoints.

The incentives stabilizing traditional capitalist organization are
analysed, and a contractarian co-operative model is proposed as a
natural outgrowth of a 'human capital' market. Existing experiments in
participative management, their benefits and problems, are discussed.
Removal of institutional barriers and support of organizational innovation are suggested as components of an evolutionary political strategy
which emphasizes efficiency rather than redistribution, but offers
advantages on both counts.

*For comment and discussion I thank John Cable, Alasdair Clayre, Edward
Goodman, Paul Kleindorfer, Dennis Mueller, Hans Nutzinger, Robert Oakeshott,
Joe Stiglitz, and Christian von Weizsäcker, none of whom, however, are to be
held responsible for any opinions expressed here.

2. *Finance and Risk*

Early proposals for co-operative-design suggested pure debt financing with workers as residual claimants. A major criticism of this model is that workers with a limited time horizon and no transferable claims to future income may lack incentives to maintain capital or to maximize present values. Thus, if workers are mobile in the sense that they can easily find comparable alternative employment, it may be difficult to avoid bankruptcy during a temporary downturn. If higher interest rates are demanded by creditors the incentive to default increases, and credit may be limited or unavailable as a result.

Another apparently obvious disadvantage of debt finance is that there is no risk sharing with external holders of diversified portfolios. Peter Jay and others have thus proposed financing by non-voting equity or residual shares. This can be defended on the same lines as the arguments for the efficiency of managerial corporations where small stock-holders are effectively 'voiceless': as long as the firm depends on the capital market for further net investment, 'exit' by stockholders or sale of their shares will adequately discipline managers or co-operative workers through the market. However, the argument breaks down in the case of a mature firm which is no longer dependent on the capital market; then workers or managers can — and, on the evidence, do — transfer resources from stockholders to themselves. The original members of a successful co-operative may well find this course more profitable than further expansion and 'dilution' of their shares.

The only solution to the problem seems to be that either workers must share managerial or control rights with suppliers of capital, or they must themselves supply sufficient capital or otherwise immobilize themselves and hence remove the incentives for default. This would be feasible if workers could borrow on the security of their future earning-power or human capital. Traditionally banks have refused to lend without tangible collateral because the cost of enforcing repayment, say by garnishment of wages, is considered too high. Suppose, however, that liability for interest and principal repayment of such a loan were assigned to all the debtor's future employers, who would then deduct the bank's claim from wage or residual payments to the debtor, while change of employment automatically switched liability to the new employer. Alternatively, interest payments to private creditors would be made through the tax system; either way, transaction costs should be tolerable.

If workers could thus 'liquidize' some of their human capital they could buy majority holdings in their employer's firm in the stock market, and then control management as in a co-operative, as well as possibly expropriating remaining outside stockholders. In a co-operative with debt finance, new workers could be required to put up an 'entrance fee' or loan to the co-operative, repayable at a contractual rate only after some period of years. The fee and the time for repayment could be calculated so that workers' capital plus liquidation value of assets covered outside creditors' claims. Young workers would then bear the risk of losses from bankruptcy, and hence be willing to take temporary income-cuts in difficult times to avoid bankruptcy.

Since the co-operative residual with capital rental has much less variance than the traditional profit measure with fixed-wage costs, the lack of portfolio diversification is ameliorated. Indeed, the foregoing considerations suggest that complete diversification suffers from 'moral hazard' incentive-problems neglected in the usual theory of risky allocation. The use of debt rather than equity capital also has informational advantages, which are discussed below.

Equity capital requires outside investors to estimate the probability distribution of future returns, a costly procedure which explains why small and new firms make little use of equity finance since the costs of estimation may still be as large for small firms, and so deter investors unless expected returns exceed the informational set-up cost. Hence, also the prevalence of internal capital markets and the rationale for much growth by merger with attendant problems of size, hierarchy, and impersonal bureaucracy. Since the presence of adequate guarantees or collateral for debt capital is relatively easy to monitor, the transactional costs of an efficient capital market could be considerably reduced if workers became residual claimants. Inflexible wages and fixed costs on the other hand, increase the variance of residual shares, and hence necessitate a cushion of owner's equity capital to absorb temporary shocks without excessive monitoring costs for external creditors trying to distinguish temporary ill-fortune from managerial or entrepreneurial incompetence.

Even with this cushion, the 'fixed' costs of inflexible wages may exceed revenues in a recession and hence cause bankruptcy which would be avoidable under residual sharing; co-operatives are sometimes born out of bankruptcy. We shall have more to say about flexibility later, but it does seem that the risk-allocating properties of debt-financed co-operatives could be better than suspected — with the help of entrance fees or similar financial commitments by workers. Meade's (1972) suggestion to restrict 'exit' rights of key skilled workers with irreplaceable, firm-specific skills will not be effective unless these workers bear financial liability for losses they impose on other workers or creditors through striking, working-to-rule, or just shirking on the job. In the traditional firm the tables are turned; it is immobile or older workers who are vulnerable to opportunistic or unscrupulous management — and hence the emergence of seniority rights discussed in the next section. We turn now to the other main stumbling block for co-operation-collective decision processes and their problems.

3. *Industrial Democracy*

Allowing workers to elect their management has appealed to reformers since Mill. Yet experience in Yugoslavia and elsewhere generally shows managers appropriating effective power from workers, just as they do from stockholders. Information costs explain this tendency quite well. Majority voting, despite certain desirable properties like simplicity and familiarity, can easily lead to polarization and exploitation of a minority group. As an example, consider the seniority system. Older workers without special skills are generally immobile; whatever abilities they have are firm-specific, so job-change would imply loss of income as well as psychic costs. The seniority system, which has been a priority goal for organized labour, protects immobile older workers, and helps to retain skilled mobile workers by maintaining their income during recession, while younger workers are laid-off as demand declines. This accords with greater mobility and preference for leisure of the young, but in a prolonged recession the utility of leisure is likely to decline drastically, and the downwardly-sticky wages and prices which are necessary to maintain senior workers' incomes also impede recovery and reduction of inflation. During the Great Depression real wages of those employed actually rose due to the collapse of food prices, but there was little work-sharing or shorter weeks for all. Such measures would have spread the burden and reduced the decline in demand as older workers could have drawn on savings to maintain consumption.

Against the polarization thesis it could be claimed that if 'voice' rather than 'exit' became the institutionalized response to individual discontent, so the scope for solidarity should grow, at least among those with similar commitments to their organization or costs of mobility. Mondragon is a rare example of this, in a co-operative setting (Oakeshott, 1978).

The lack of democracy or 'voice' in the miniature polity called the enterprise has been traditionally justified by the fiction that exit is costless. Recognition of mobility costs could justify a contractarian solution, to be discussed below, but at present the tendency is rather to suggest centralized, legislative constraints on the freedom of association of individuals in productive organization. This has disadvantages. Thus a requirement of union representation in − or worker 'control' of − management above a certain size of firm would divert much entre-preneurial effort into evading the laws by restricting firm size, and into internal political activity in larger firms. More fundamentally, different organizations suit different people and situations; size is but one of many dimensions, and variety rather than uniformity of structure best serves the needs of an individualistic, liberal society.

There is a thesis that experimentation is stifled by social conditioning and market forces in a competitive capitalist environment, and that co-operative successes could loosen these restrictions, threatening managerial and union−bureaucracy prerogatives. There is some truth in this, as will be enlarged upon slightly below, but then public support of experiments with public-good properties in the form of new information on organizational behavior is called for, rather than blanket legislation of an uncertain ideal.

Much of the motivation behind labour-movements in the past and discussion of industrial democracy today, is redistributive. Economists know how to transfer wealth or income with much less distortion of effort than by industrial democracy, but more subtle qualities of working-life depend directly on the organization of production, and it is to these questions that we now turn.

4. *Alienation and Job Satisfaction*

The most significant critique of capitalist and industrial society, based on division of labour, appears already in Adam Smith: the psychic costs of material productivity in the form of 'alienated', repetitive, non-fulfilling tasks for a large proportion of the working population.* Economists who have noticed the phenomena subsequently have usually postulated an optimal competitive trade-off between job satis-faction and pecuniary reward for each worker's level of ability, without

*See Alasdair Clayre (1977) for an anthology on these matters, and FitzRoy (1978/79) for a review of the literature. Clayre provides a detailed discussion in his book *Work and Play* (revised edition, Oxford University Press, forthcoming).

inquiring very closely into the causes and consequences of non-market work organization. On the other hand, more critical observers from Marx to modern radicals have relied upon the capitalist's 'power' to control and exploit in the work-place without explaining the failure of competition to throw up a (Pareto-) efficient, if not an equitable, distribution of goods and bads both inside and outside of the market-place.

Capitalism grew out of the dissolution of feudal ties, and in the employment relationship at least, freedom of contract was dominated by freedom to recontract. Binding long-term commitments were associated with indentured servitude, and mobility in a free labour market was supposed to optimize welfare. But since most productive skills are the result of on-the-job training and experience, mobility meant that skilled workers could only be kept after training by paying them premium market wages, and competition ensured that employers would minimize the amount of costly training given and expensive skills employed to produce a given output. This in turn meant minimizing the tasks performed by any one person and utilizing informational economies of scale to concentrate skills and decision-making functions in upper layers of a pyramidal hierarchy, or just maximal division of labour (FitzRoy and Mueller, 1977).

Workers without property and forbidden by their new-found freedom to alienate future wage income could only offer lower current wages for better training, but were limited therein by consumption needs and uncertainties over future prospects. Employer's investment in training free workers would in any case be less than socially optimal because workers who change jobs are not obliged to share the continuing quasi-rents on their initial training with the original employer who provided it. Attempts by the employer to increase returns by lowering wages are self-defeating because the incentive to search for alternatives is thereby increased. Only by paying higher wages than competitors can employers reduce turnover and lure skilled workers away from other firms. If all employers follow this logic, wages will settle at an equilibrium level which is high enough for the resulting unemployment to reduce turnover and demand to levels which induce no further bidding up of wages. To return to our starting point, it seems that the unrestricted mobility of 'free' labour leads to capitalism's main problems of 'alienation' and unemployment!

Notice also the consistency of the resulting state: 'too high' wages depend on excessive division of labour (with resulting alienation), while the scarcity of skills due to the divergence between social and private (employer's) returns to training investment increase wages for skilled work so that firms have to minimize skilled employment. Thus additional workers who would prefer more skilled work at less than the going (market-) rate cannot get the training because employers know that as soon as they are qualified they can demand the full market premium. The extension of formal schooling has not changed the supply of jobs to match raised aspirations; instead applicants are screened by their credentials and dissatisfaction with poor jobs is increased by exposure to more education.

Ever increasing investment in schooling and other 'positional' goods thus appears individually desirable in order to gain a competitive edge over one's rivals in the 'rat-race' for desirable jobs and promotion. Socially, however, such investment may be increasingly wasteful and even divisive (Hirsch, 1976).

5. *A Contractarian Alternative*

We concluded that a co-operative in a capitalist environment which reduced division of labour and offered above-average training for less alienated jobs may face serious survival problems. Workers will probably leave unless they get competitive wages, but competitive markets require minimizing average labour costs and skill levels. Co-operative experiments in many countries have had considerable success (Oakeshott, 1978), but they do not seem to be leaders in job-redesign and humanization-of-work programmes. On the other hand, it would be possible for workers to choose lower wages in exchange for more satisfying work if they agreed to pay back to the supplier of training some fraction of all extra wages earned after changing employment. The original employer or co-operative which provided the training could then obtain a return on its investment over the worker's whole lifetime, irrespective of job-changes, and hence the socially optimal investment would be provided. Putting liability for repayment on future employers would again minimize enforcement costs.

This scheme has interesting potentialities for improving the quality of working life. Workers could bid for jobs and training opportunities by offering higher repayment rates in case they quit. Such bids have valuable signalling properties, revealing workers' determination to persevere and succeed at the job and firm in question, and could thus replace some costly screening procedures such as educational credentials. The way would be opened for major reorganization of production, with team-work and high average levels of training and skill replacing fragmented, machine-placed tasks. Some such changes, and in particular the replacement of destructive intra-worker rivalry and worker-management conflict by improved co-operation and communication may also increase material productivity, but in any case, different firms could offer a greater range of combinations of job-satisfaction and pecuniary reward.

Flexible wages would be an essential complement to the scheme, so workers would not be dismissed or laid-off when demand declined temporarily, but shorter weeks for all and more flexible pricing would spread and soften the impact of recession without fear of losing 'immobilized' key skilled workers.* With more widespread skills there would be fewer bottlenecks and less need to hire specialists away from other firms in boom times, while repayment commitments would raise the cost of change to workers. Firms would not have to try and pay above-average rates, when labour-markets tighten, because turnover imposes no loss when repayments or entrance fees are sufficiently high.

Instead of maintaining a pool of applicants for jobs by excess wage offers in order to reduce screening costs, firms would encourage workers' bids by competing to provide improved training opportunities. Related to this proposal, the entrance fees discussed earlier could alternatively be used to pay for training, with a somewhat different risk structure for the worker and firms resulting. While further details cannot be treated here, it is worth emphasizing that the benefits of residual sharing and extended on-the-job training can be realized only under a system of individual bargaining. These proposals thus face major political opposition from powerful union–government coalitions which have thrived on the combination of collective bargaining and increased government involvement in demand-management. The limitations and dangers of the latter are being increasingly recognized by economists (Pringle, 1977).

6. On the Distribution of Power and Wealth

In effect we have argued that the problem of alienated work could be overcome to a considerable extent by individual contracting if human

---

*It is shown in FitzRoy (1979) that flexible wage *rates* indexed to firm's value-added would reduce the variance of both workers' and capitalist's *incomes*, as well as increasing allocative efficiency. This surprising result contradicts the widely held Knightian notion that fixed wage rates transfer risk from employees to employers.

capital was not artificially handicapped by institutionally imposed illiquidity. Worker's control seems to be neither necessary nor sufficient to provide fulfilling work opportunities on a large scale. There is, however, a political argument that vested interests in the collective bargaining system can only be overcome in exchange for an explicit shift of power inside the individual enterprise.

Difficulties with legislating industrial democracy have been mentioned above, but residual sharing and some degree of voluntary immobility on the part of workers do carry implications for the distribution of power and worker-participation in management in the long run. As the expected duration of the employment relationship increases, the necessity for close supervision declines, and 'high-trust-relations'* are more likely to develop. A major precondition for meaningful worker involvement in decision-making is possession of requisite knowledge, and precisely this is provided by the 'market' for training outlined above.

Individual contracting is based on mutual benefits, and of course, entrepreneurs are unlikely to relinquish 'ultimate' power even in exchange for better labour relations or increased efficiency in the broadest sense. However the results may not differ much in practice from the situation with well-established managers of a co-operative who are periodically re-elected by their workers. Employees who immobilize themselves by investing in firm-specific skills will demand explicit contractual protection of the training and job-rights they have 'purchased'. These rights are in themselves infringements of the employer's traditional right to re-contract at any time. The contractarian model espoused here tends to subvert authoritarian structures, and holds promise of growth by example and imitation rather than by fiat.

If the arguments in favour of residual sharing made above hold up, the original entrepreneur might be left with a small fraction of the residual if his firm became large. This capital gain would be shared with original employees, whose effective status as partners rather than purely as 'workers' would be reinforced by their wealth in this case. The entrepreneur's power as a minority holder would be circumscribed even if he retained the rights to fire and hire within contractual limits. Workers' long-term claims on their jobs would reduce mergers by

*See Fox (1974) and Oakeshott (1978) for the role of trust in labour–management relations, and FitzRoy and Cable (1979) for economic theory and empirical implications thereof; also Nutzinger (1977).

empire-building entrepreneurs, thus effecting a sort of decentralized anti-trust policy.

It seems plausible that in the long run a society of contractarian firms would generate a more equal distribution of income and wealth because the rationing of access to good jobs and valuable information which characterizes the internal organization of traditional capitalist firms would be eroded by market forces. As 'human capital' multiplied, the returns to given skills would decline, thus narrowing differentials. Inflationary pressures in boom-periods would subside, and with work-sharing instead of lay-offs unemployment would become unambiguously voluntary. While capital gains would be shared, capitalist fortunes would not be abolished, and neither would poverty. Indeed, workers would tend to share the fortunes of their firm, and income dispersion for the 'same' job in different situations, entered under different expectations, would increase.

In these notes the efficiency properties of extended property rights have been the main focus, in line with the tradition in economics of separating allocative and distributive issues. This does not of course imply that the latter are unimportant, but it is worth remembering that any redistribution through the coercive power of the state which violated existing property rights has considerable social costs in the form of conflict, uncertainty, and diversion of resources into evasive or predatory activity.

7. *Political Conclusion: A Tale of Two Strategies*

The details of the optimal route to what might equally be called 'human capitalism' or workers' partnership remain to be worked out. But there is a major and politically attractive if not easy initial step which is worth considering as a policy package in its own right.

Nationalized industries without public-good or natural monopoly properties, which survive only with massive state subsidies, should be turned into co-operatives by giving their workers the choice between residual sharing with election of their own management on the one hand, and cessation of state subsidies on the other. The second alternative would lead to bankruptcy and massive unemployment, while the first could be coupled with credit availability for investment purposes if workers accepted reduced incomes in the short- to medium-run. Decentralization by plants would help the democratic process, and undermine union bureaucracy, whose opposition would surely be vehement. Since generous unemployment benefits have taken some of the sting out of bankruptcy for redundant employees, additional pressures might be needed to make the first choice palatable. A natural role for government here would be to facilitate the credit necessary for ongoing investment without immediately demanding the long-term repayment commitments discussed above from workers as yet unused to the rigours of a competitive market.

Among small firms at least here is some precedence, with a number of successful co-operatives in Europe having grown out of threatened bankruptcy. The switch to residual sharing can actually be regarded as a device to overcome the downward inflexibility of wages which frequently triggered bankruptcy and crisis under declining demand in the first place. The combination of co-operative sharing with an overt shift of power to give workers the rights of electing their management does have a powerful rationale in these crisis situations, a rationale which is not contradicted by the arguments against legislating abrupt redistributive changes in general which were made above.

It can be argued that inflexible wages represent rational contracts under uncertainty in low-trust situations. Flexibility at the discretion of employers would involve costly bargaining and conflict since all parties would be uncertain about how much wage reduction would really be necessary, while employers would have incentives to exaggerate the need for cuts. With contractually specified shares in residual income or indexed wages and elective power over management, employees or 'members' of a co-operative would have the kind of assurance against managerial opportunism which is required to overcome the long history of conflict and mistrust that characterizes much of traditionalist capitalist enterprise. The dramatic change from state-guaranteed wages or unemployment benefits to entrepreneurial risk-bearing most probably requires for political realization an equally dramatic and visible guarantee that ultimate entrepreneurial power has alao devolved upon the new risk bearers.

Co-operatives would thus seem to be an attractive alternative to costly bankruptcy and equally costly subsidization of inefficient concerns. Implicit in this faith is the belief that in the long run three things will happen:

(i) the most mobile or the most sceptical workers will drift away as they find better alternatives;

(ii) this gradual attrition will solve some of the problems which destroyed viability initially;

(iii) the combination of residual sharing and 'participation' in management will generate 'horizontal monitoring' by peer groups and co-operative interactions instead of conflict and diversive inter-worker competition, with significant efficiency gains (even in the short run);

Participative management has been introduced in various forms and degrees in a large number of usually entrepreneurial firms, with no question of workers' control. Particularly when combined with profit-sharing these pragmatic experiments have had considerable success in terms of productivity gains (see Cable and FitzRoy, 1979), and the support of such organizational innovation should be the other main prong of current policy in the co-operative area.

There are strong theoretical grounds for expecting participation and profit-sharing to increase both efficiency and job-related satisfactions, developed in detail in our other cited papers. Briefly, workers who mistrust management and are only rewarded with individual incentives and promotion opportunities may rationally collude to restrict effort. Such collusion can be enforced by peer-group pressure, and is rational because unrestricted competition among workers for a fixed number of promotion slots reduces average expected welfare: everybody works harder and only the winners are promoted faster. Piece rates may also be lowered if all work too hard, hence sanctions against 'rate-busters'.

On the other hand, group reward structures (of which profit-sharing is one), and participation in decisions affecting rewards and tasks (which ultimately include all managerial decisions), can together mobilize enhanced co-operation. Thus if extra effort by one worker benefits his co-workers there will be social pressures to increase effort, and sanctions against shirking. In cohesive groups such horizontal monitoring can be much more effective than sole reliance on traditional vertical monitoring. Communication, and particularly active participation, tend to break down barriers of low trust and deception, improving the reliability of information flows to management. Finally, co-operation amongst employees can be improved if the gains are shared and the incentives to hinder rivals are reduced by group incentives.

These efficiency gains do provide scope for increasing both earnings and skill levels, as well as encouraging further moves towards contractarian partnership. Decentralization of decision-making inside the firm does, however, represent a shift of functions away from the administrative hierarchy, which will naturally resist such moves. It is no accident that typically entrepreneurs with democratic ideals rather than managers have instituted such changes. Existing tax laws too provide major hurdles in the way of replacing wage income with residual sharing.

The evidence suggests that most entrepreneurs believe their own (authoritarian) management style to be optimal, though their knowledge of alternatives may be non-existent. It is possible that many would prefer to retain that style rather than introduce participation and some sharing of a larger profit-pie. Profit-sharing without participation merely adds a random variable to worker's perceived incomes, while the combination of tax and other legal barriers, idiosyncratic entrepreneurial preferences, and simple managerial self-interest can explain the slow spread of pragmatic experiments.

It is not clear how rapidly reform of tax and other company-law would succeed in overcoming the internal barriers to organizational innovation. Competition from more successful participative firms is a slow process; substantial profit differences can persist over long periods (Mueller, 1977). More concrete assistance in the form of advisory services, dissemination of information, and even financial support of promising organizational models in their early stages can be justified by the public-good properties and informational economies of scale involved.

Government support in various ways of participative and (voluntary) co-operative experiments does hold promise of overcoming traditional animosities in an evolutionary manner, with minimum creation of new divisions and bureaucracies. The greater the variety of successful models observed in practice, the weaker the attractions of collective bargaining with its inevitable rigidities and dysfunctional uniformity. Nevertheless there is a constructive role for unions to play in the context of individual or plant-level bargaining. Efficient internal organization, we have argued, depends on effective transmission of information in a co-operative, high-trust setting. An efficient labour-market depends equally on the dissemination of information between firms, and individualistic bargaining imposes greatly increased informational requirements on individual workers. The public-good properties of information strongly suggest some form of public intervention, and unions would seem to be natural candidates for the job of doing for workers what consumer associations do for consumers. Indeed, there is strong evidence that unionization increases productivity in traditional capitalist firms in the US by improving communication, and thus reducing dependence on costly 'exit' or mobility to match workers and employer's requirements. (See Brown and Medoff, 1978; and Freeman and Medoff, 1979.) This, and other evidence cited above, clearly refutes the old-fashioned property-rights approach, which relies on perfect mobility under complete information to attain efficiency, and sees any modification of traditional capitalist organization without worker-participation as steps on 'the road to serfdom'. (For glaring examples of this still-popular approach, see Pejovich, 1978.)

Finally, there should be broad political support for the two main measures proposed here. Ending costly subsidies to ailing concerns, and supporting promising experiments in participation and partnership instead, looks like a popular exchange. The long-term benefits from removing tax and other institutional barriers to co-operation and finally moving a long-polarized society toward industrial partnership may indeed amount to the preservation of a liberal social order.

BIBLIOGRAPHY

Brown, C. and Medoff, J. (1978), 'Trade Unions in the Production Process', *Journal of Political Economy*, 46, 3 (June).

Cable, J. R. and FitzRoy, F. R. (1980), 'Productive Efficiency, Incentives and Employee Participation: Some Preliminary Results for West Germany', *Kyklos*, 33, 1.

Clayre, A. (ed.) (1977), *Nature and Industrialization*, Oxford University Press.

—— *Work and Play*, revised edition, Oxford University Press, forthcoming.

FitzRoy, F. R. (1978-9), 'Alienation, Freedom and Economic Organization', Acton Society Trust, London, Occasional Paper.

—— (1979), 'Wage Contracts and Risk Sharing by Implicit- and Firm-Indexing', presented at Constanz Seminar on Monetary Theory and Monetary Policy (June).

—— and Cable, J. R. (1979), 'Economic Incentives and Social Interaction in the Firm', paper presented to the Arne Ryde Symposium on Theories of Economic Institutions, Lund, Sweden (September).

—— and Mueller, D. C. (1977), 'Contract and the Economics of Organization', IIM, Berlin, forthcoming.

Freeman, R. B. and Medoff, J. (1979), 'The Two Faces of Unionism', *The Public Interest* (Fall).

Fox, A. (1974), *Beyond Contract: Work, Power and Trust Relations*, Faber.

Furubotn, E. G. (1976), 'The Long Run Analysis of the Labour-Managed Firm', *American Economic Review*, 66 (March).

Hirsch, F. (1976), *Social Limits to Growth*, Harvard University Press.

Mueller, D. C. (1977), 'The Persistence of Profits Above the Norm', *Economica*, 44, 176 (November).

Nutzinger, H. G. (1977), 'The Firm as a Social Institution: the Failure of a Contraction Approach', *Economic Analysis and Workers' Management*, 11, 3–4.

Oakeshott, R. (1978), *The Case for Worker's Co-ops*, Routledge and Kegan Paul.

Pejovich, S. (ed.) (1978), *The Codetermination Movement in the West*, Heath Levington.

Pringle, R. (1977), *The Growth Merchants*, Centre for Policy Studies, London.

Vanek, J. (ed.) (1975), *Self-Management: Economic Liberation of Man*, Penguin.

III. COMMENTS

5. Discussion of the Alternatives

1. *Gradualism, or once-for-all change to a workers' co-operative economy*

JAMES MEADE: I would associate myself in general with Peter Jay's analysis of the dangers facing the economy, and of the catastrophe that they could lead to. But I differ from him about the cure.

I am attracted to the idea of workers' co-operatives. But I would make two modifying points.

First, Peter Jay says trade unions must either remain as they are or be 'bashed' through Combination Acts. But if people become aware of the problems he has described, it is not impossible that trade unions' actions might change and pressure on money wages might be reduced.

Secondly, I am not sure the rule of the road analogy is right. On the one hand the setting up of successful co-operatives may gradually change the present position. On the other hand, there may be advantages for 'the first driver' — the first firms to change to labour-management.

I would suggest that we look at some of the things that are already happening — at the 'lump' in building, at moonlighting, at the way lorry drivers have been organizing their incomes — as ways already in existence of seeking to dodge not only the taxman, but also the trade unions.

PETER JAY: I agree with James Meade that trade unions might learn from warnings about the present situation, and change. But I still have doubts whether this would result in changes in enforceable behaviour at the place of work.

I would not see my solution as merely restrictive. It offers working people a benefit (although it may not be perceived as a benefit); it is not a mere outlawing of 'free collective bargaining', but a replacement of free collective bargaining with something which better achieves the aims that free collective bargaining is intended to achieve.

I also agree that some degree of gradualism is possible and desirable. I merely want to protect my proposals against two arguments: one is the argument that if there were benefits from worker-management it would have come about already under the present system. If the benefits arise only or mainly from a change of system, this argument is invalid. I also want to protect it from the argument that any general conclusions about the working of a labour-managed economy can be drawn from single experiments under the present system. If those two arguments are ruled out, I would be willing to agree that gradualism could be effective.

2. *Residual sharing as an alternative to worker-ownership and possibly to worker-management*

FELIX FITZROY: Downward rigidity of wages is a block to the working of the economy. One of the arguments in favour of the workers' co-operative is that it replaces fixed wages with residual sharing, and residual sharing is necessarily variable, particularly if workers pay themselves a fixed *share* of the residual.

However, residual sharing is a distinct concept, not necessarily connected with either labour-management or worker-ownership. There are examples of wage contracts being replaced by residual sharing, without either worker-management or worker-ownership, but with the advantages that have been attributed to both. And this solution avoids the conflict-ridden redistribution of property rights that Peter Jay's proposals entail. It is a gradualist solution, and encourages the learning processes necessary for its working. It is a solution which might be acceptable in Britain, as it has been in other countries (see below, p. 141) as an alternative to either bankruptcy or state subsidy: individual workers, unions, and taxpayers might all prefer it. Control by workers might or might not follow. By contrast the massive change in property rights advocated by Peter Jay would divert energy into avoidance, evasion, and irrational restrictions on size; while it might lead to ineffective control over managers, by workers as owners, with misallocation of resources, as in the limited company today.

3. *Inflationary pressures through government support for prices, and producer cartels; and the question of their persistence in a worker's co-operative economy*

BRIAN CHIPLIN: If inflation is to be attributed to the actions of both governments and trade unions, in so far as governments underwrite the prices of final products, why should that change under labour-management? Why should governments be expected to cease underwriting prices in a labour-managed economy?

Secondly, why should powerful groupings between workers be

expected to vanish under a labour-managed system? Why should we expect no cartelization, for instance among worker-managers controlling both labour and management in key industries? These might be more powerful than the monopoly groupings among unions of workers in key industries today.

4. *Would workers want the risks entailed in residual-sharing, and how great would its incentive effects be?*

CHIPLIN: Thirdly, why should it be supposed that workers would want 'the residual', rather than a fixed wage? Most of the best-fitting wage-equations fit the maintenance by workers of real wages. Why should this change? Surely only those workers who are risk-preferrers will want the change? The risk to the worker is greater in residual sharing than to the capitalist in lending money through the stockmarket — even if workers do not put up a capital stake on entry to co-operatives, or build up capital holdings by individual deferred stakes from their residual shares. The capitalist can spread his risk across a portfolio: the worker can choose — in general — once only, when choosing a job (cf. Meade, 1972).

Furthermore too great emphasis should not be laid on the incentive effects of residual sharing. They might be considerable in, say, a small mining enterprise with 3 to 25 workers; but negligible in something as big as British Leyland.

JAY: My proposals are part of a package which necessarily includes changes in the behaviour of government, and its withdrawal from intervention in the market in supporting prices and in other ways.

On the second point, widespread anti-trust legislation would also be needed in the labour-managed system: my proposals form part of a political solution with several features besides labour-management, anti-cartel laws being prominent among them.

Thirdly, Mr Chiplin has brought out the point that incentives work less well across larger numbers. I agree, but that is a separate point from the question whether a co-operative solution is the best for the political economy as a whole.

The optimum size for a co-operative is probably not much more than 1,000. On the other hand there are very few organizations in Britain or America where more than 2,000 people are doing the same thing in the same place, and I believe that there are very few companies which could not be helpfully broken down into units of between

1,000 and 2,000; a 'unit' being a body that deals with other bodies on a market basis.

But that is a separate question from the optimum size of the working group with separate incentives, which might well be as small as 4 or 5 people. British Leyland could no doubt benefit from being broken down into units of 1,000 and 2,000 and into working groups of 4 or 5. Of course there would be legal problems to be solved.

5. Inflationary pressure from the presence of two arguments for higher wages: profitability and fairness

LJUBO SIRC: The idea of residual-sharing conflicts with a fundamental feeling among workers that the shares or wages of workers should be equal. This is a main source of inflationary pressure, and the two systems of value together are inflationary in a spiralling way: workers in more profitable industries or enterprises enjoy a higher residual than others, through market forces, and workers in less profitable industries or enterprises then call for equally high wages on grounds of fairness. (Cf. Chiplin and Coyne/Sirc, 1977.)

6. Conflicts between workers as consumers and workers as producers

SIRC: There is a conception of 'producer sovereignty' which needs to be clarified. Workers have interests as producers and as consumers. In Italy in 1968 the trade unionists said they had broken out of the labour market, and that workers as producers had complete sovereignty over workers as consumers. Is this desirable? And would this be an implication of labour management?

JAY: One of the advantages of a labour-managed system would be that it made clearer the nature of economic conflict. Conflicts would be visibly between workers as producers and workers as consumers because the third party would be removed.

7. The importance of ease of entry both for the individual to a firm and for new businesses to the market

MEADE: Consider the example of a firm raising capital in two ways: either with fixed interest on the debt raised; or — Peter Jay's case — with a variable return on share capital. First consider the case where it hires debt capital. Under capitalism, if there is an expansion in the demand for that firm's product, there is an incentive for it to expand its employment. Under labour-management, there is no such incentive.

(Cf. Meade, pp. 89–118 below; cf. Chiplin and Coyne, pp. 119–40 below.) The same arguments would apply in reverse if there were a fall in the demand for a firm's products.

With an expansion in the demand for a firm's product, there is an incentive for the entrepreneur under capitalism to hire more workers — since the value of their marginal product will be higher.

There is no incentive however for the co-operative group to expand its membership, unless they can take on people somehow at a lower rate than the share they are getting, or would be getting with the extra people.

That is the first big difference between capitalism and labour-management. In so far as there is no cost of entry of new co-operatives the problem disappears. But it means there is much heavier reliance on ease of entry of new businesses than under capitalism. And Peter Jay relies very much on ease of entry of new co-operatives.

FITZROY: I think there are solutions to the problems of the firm with expanded demand and with debt capital, where the workers share the residual. There seems no reason at all in the case of a sudden expansion in demand why workers who took the risk of going in when demand was low should not take the gains and extend membership of the co-operative to new workers at the market rate; in other words when demand has gone up, just offer smaller income shares to new workers and take them on.

MEADE: Then you have two people at the same work bench getting a different rate?

FITZROY: Yes. They would have different shares of residual income, not necessarily capital shares. The workers who went in earlier are earning an above-market return on their entrepreneurial decision. You would have workers with the same skills but earning different sums of money.

MEADE: I agree; this is one of the solutions I suggested in my article [*Economic Journal*, 1972].

JAY: You would have to have that so firmly entrenched in the constitution of the firm that there would be no practical incentive for the majority of the employees, who in my constitution would have one man one vote in the control of the enterprise, to band together to redistribute that benefit back to themselves.

FITZROY: That is just one of the many problems with 'one man, one vote' as a decision rule.

8. Would there be willing lenders under labour-management?

MEADE: Now the second problem is whether there would be any possibility of having outside ordinary share capital — capital with a variable return; because if the enterprise has no incentive to expand it has no incentive to give distributions which will enable it to raise new equity capital. If you have only debt capital that problem does not exist; you will have the same incentive as under the capitalist system for expanding your investment through debt capital.

9. Who bears the cost when the enterprise collapses; do departing workers take away responsibility for losses; do those who retire take away equity shares? How do new recruits enter?

Thirdly, what do you do (assuming that the enterprise is run on debt capital not equity capital) when the thing collapses? Do you give the right of free exit to all the members who are in it, when they can find new jobs, without requiring them to take with them their pro rata share of the debt liability? Because if you don't do something of that kind, the assets against which you are raising the debts are rather unattractive to the capital.

Again, what do you do when people retire: do they take some of the equity? And (as I already said) what do you do when new people come in: do they come in on the same terms or have to buy their way in? I think these are some of the really basic issues. This is an economic theorist, I know, talking in textbook terms, but they are very real issues.

SIRC: This is not economic theory; it is economic practice. In Yugoslavia they have come up against all these problems. In Yugoslavia they discuss them under the term 'past labour'. They have terrible difficulties in establishing any kind of accountability or responsibility at all for capital and for debt. Anybody who leaves has been participating in decision making and yet does not bear the consequences.

10. *Would there be willing lenders under labour-management? Reply to James Meade's question*

JAY: So far as the fixed interest money is concerned, the enterprise behaves in more or less exactly the same way as an existing corporation does.

So far as the flexible money is concerned there is clearly an extremely important difference from the present system, and this brings me to James Meade's points. A contract is entered into between the enterprise and the saver, a free market relationship which is unconstrained by government or the law other than the general law of contract, and the enterprise offers in return for the saver's money what is to be called 'the distribution' in proportion to the units he holds.

Now what is 'the distribution'? The distribution is whatever the enterprise decides that it is, in exactly the same way as at present the distribution a company makes is whatever the board of directors decides that it is.

What incentive does the enterprise have to make an adequate distribution or a distribution adequate enough to induce the saver to part with his money in the first place? The answer to that is exactly as at present: if it does not do so its obligations in the secondary capital market will stand at a very low price which will make it impossible for it to borrow in the future. Provided that the saver thinks he is going to want to borrow in the future – and this is a very important point which James Meade has raised – he will expect a distribution in the future in the same way as with present enterprises.

The distribution is not the residual because we have now inverted things. The residual belongs to the entrepreneur. If capital is the entrepreneur then labour is a paid charge. But if labour is the entrepreneur the return to capital is itself a prior charge on the earnings of the company before the residual is distributed to the entrepreneurs. Partly this will be a straight fixed interest charge, partly it will be 'the distribution' – the variable return to equity capital – which is also a line in the accounts before the final residual is struck.

11. *Would there be an incentive for the firm to expand under labour-management? Reply*

Now on the very important question which James Meade has raised about incentive to expand: it is true that there is less incentive for the enterprise to expand under a labour-managed system; though not necessarily true that there is no incentive. It may be Felix FitzRoy's solution of differential returns would alleviate this problem. My answer as James Meade rightly says depends very heavily on ease of entry, which is another very important subject to discuss. Men standing in hundreds in dole queues do not suddenly spring into new co-operatives.

Even if there is less expansion and less growth than in theory under pure capitalism without trade unions, to bump along with less than the theoretical optimum is still better than catastrophe. But I don't want to make too much use of that argument: in a sense it proves too much.

12. *Would firms want to borrow under labour-management? Reply*

Now we come to James Meade's more subtle point, that if there isn't an incentive for the individual firm to expand, or not to the same degree, and even if the problem in terms of macro-economic growth is solved by ease of entry, or partly solved by ease of entry, there is still the problem that the firm which does not have an incentive to expand does not have an incentive to borrow new money; it doesn't have an incentive to make a reasonable distribution, and, if so, the people in the savings market have no incentive to part with their money to it — or to put it into new firms.

Now that could be true if the only or normal reason to borrow money was to expand in the sense of to increase your productive capacity. But in almost all enterprises you have to keep investing in order to stay in business, coping with changes in tastes, technology, and new methods; and all that requires significant capital expenditure on a quite sufficient scale to give enterprises an incentive to be in reasonably good standing with investors so that they can borrow in the future, and to be seen to be in that position.

Now there is the possibility (raised by some critics) that they will meet all that need from their internal resources. That is hard to reconcile with some other things commonly said about workers' co-operatives: that the workers will over-reward themselves and under-invest. There will only be internal resources if workers reward themselves less than they could. It seems improbable that they will save in this way more than existing enterprises. Thus it seems to me more probable that these enterprises will be more dependent on outside capital.

But I welcome these suggestions about how the thing would best work against a background that time is short and that the alternative is not something that works pretty well but against a background that it is urgently necessary to find something that will work at all: I'm talking about not the next year or so but the next decade.

13. *Should workers have individual stakes in their enterprises, either buying their way in with a capital share or accumulating deferred shareholding within own enterprise? And should they take away equity shares when they leave or retire, and take away individual burdens of debt if they leave an enterprise that has made losses or one that has gone bankrupt?*

ROBERT OAKESHOTT: At Mondragon workers have deferred individual shares in the enterprises they work for. They do not have to borrow outside money with variable returns: they, as it were, lend it themselves from their savings out of previous earnings. These are not just the firms' retained earnings; they are individual stakes; but they are kept invested in the enterprise and they enjoy a return if it does well. Outside finance is basically fixed-interest debt, mainly through the co-operative bank.

JAY: If you do this it seems to me that you get a maldistribution of the workers' investment portfolio. It seems to me inherently undesirable for a man who may have only small savings and his work, to have both of those risks concentrated in the same enterprise. Any system which led to the conclusion that this was a sensible arrangement would seem to me to be inherently defective, which is why I am extremely anxious to avoid workers having a capital stake.

As to debt with both fixed and variable return, I see considerable scope for using a mortgage on the physical assets as a proper way of dealing with that problem. I am not attracted by the idea of members of the firm taking away debt obligations, for instance if the firm closes. The members of a golf club are not (as far as I know) liable for its debt if it closes; this is a characteristic only of Lloyds' underwriters (as far as I know), and I suppose any unlimited partnership. To roll back the basic concept of the limited liability company would be to introduce a major impediment to economic vitality. But I would be perfectly happy to play with the mortgage concept to back up the general charge on the earnings of the enterprise.

I still think that given that the members of it, provided it is not too large, have a strong incentive for it to remain in business, and in order to stay in business to keep investing, there are enough incentives in the system to keep up a proper return to capital and induce a proper financial discipline; and if it works, it is better for the saver to have a stake — albeit legally speaking more limited than now — in something that is working than absolute freehold in something that has become absolutely worthless.

SIRC: You have stressed twice that you are against workers investing in their own enterprises. But does it make any difference? If they are the entrepreneurs and they bear the responsibility for losses they would have to pay for losses either out of their capital or out of their wages, it comes to exactly the same.

JAY: That is true. But it still does not follow that it would be wise for an individual worker to invest a large proportion of his savings through the capital market in the obligations of the firm for which he works. That is not normally something one would advise a man to do now. And so not only would it not be wise for the worker to do so but it would not in my view be right for the law or the system to compel him to. Precisely because he is already exposed to the risk which you describe, and the greater risk to his employment and his future livelihood, it is wrong for him to concentrate in the same basket such further resources as he may have accumulated by saving in the past to protect him and his family against a rainy day. It is a very simple and elementary point.

CHIPLIN: If you have a system of finance through retained earnings ascribed to individual workers' shareholdings the worker has very high transaction costs in changing his portfolio. The individual outside saver by contrast simply has to sell a share, with low transaction costs, if he does not like the distribution; but the worker-shareholder has to change his job if he does not like the distribution and the costs of his moving are much higher.

SIRC: And he will only get the market rate if he lends to his own enterprise.

JAY: He will be on exactly the same terms as any other lender we have been discussing, whether or not that will be adequate to induce lenders to part with their money. I think that the rates will start high and get lower. After all savers have a need to invest their money as well as borrowers to borrow it. A market rate of return will no doubt settle down in real terms quite close to what we have now.

I see a further danger which is an intellectual and theoretical one rather than a practical one. If one does allow the notion of individual stakes in the workers' enterprise one allows a confusion between trying to persuade the worker or the citizen to become to some degree a capitalist — which is a programme that many people have dear at heart and many people regard as anathema — with the argument about whether things might not work better than they now do if labour were the entrepreneur in the sense of the person who puts together the factors of production.

If I can, as it were, seal down all the possible misconceptions that might arise from not making all that absolutely clear then I would be willing to say, 'Conceivably, in some cases, for rather marginal psychological or other reasons, it might be good to allow people — perhaps even in some enterprises to require them — to have some degree of stake.' I still find it hard to see why this should be necessary and I see many dangers in allowing it to seem at all part of the scheme. I don't want to say absolutely dogmatically there are no conceivable circumstances where as a very minor feature of the arrangements, this might happen.

PETER MCGREGOR: I am on common ground with Peter Jay because I had a job with the Liberal Party in the 1960s talking them out of the idea that the solution to Britain's industrial problems was only to go for worker–share–ownership.

Anyone who over the past 30 years had advised an employee to put money into shares rather than into buying his own house would have been very foolish, not to say something stronger than that.

14. *The question of fall-back wages and residuals*

JOHN CABLE: I am confused in Peter Jay's scheme over what the rewards are: whether there is simply a residual share, or whether there is a fixed wage or a fixed fall-back wage in some sense. We are discussing two things: one is the creation of capital — the question of raising the initial capital for the enterprise, and possibly also its continuing need for capital if it has one; and the other is creating an interest on the part of workers in the future of the company — a matter of incentives.

Now if the incentive question can be handled solely by the residual share — and after all that should be sufficient — I can't see any reason why you should want to impinge on workers' freedom to invest their capital, to manage their portfolio, as it were, in any way they choose.

It's only if you don't have a residual-sharing arrangement within the enterprise that then you would want to introduce some kind of enforced shareholding.

ROGER SAWTELL: Residual-sharing is basic in Mondragon, but in this country it is very rare. Nearly all capital contributions in this country are entry fees.

CABLE: Reducing the downward rigidity of wages might be difficult under Peter Jay's scheme.

JAY: Everybody employed by the firm will be paid: there are rewards for skill, rewards for management responsibility, and I imagine any sensible co-operative in manufacturing, say, will pay a good salary for a good export director and good salesmen; otherwise it will go out of business. And these are prior claims. The distribution of the residual — though this will depend on the constitution of each individual enterprise — could be done on a percentage of income, so those paid more would get more.

So there is a basic fall-back wage. If you set it at a too high level, so that your residual is negative, you are in serious trouble; and the whole purpose of the thing is that that kind of commercial reality gets fed back rapidly directly into the system so that you don't set it at that level. It is the job of the manager you hire to make sure you don't set it at that level, and if he does you get a better manager.

JOHN COYNE: Peter Jay says labour is to be the entrepreneur. But an entrepreneur does not normally have a fall-back wage or a fall-back profit.

Labour is wearing two hats: as labour it is enjoying a wage; as entrepreneur it's enjoying the residual. I agree that the owner of capital has previously worn two hats, enjoying a return on capital as a lender, and a residual as entrepreneur. But it seems that in the case where labour is the entrepreneur one of the two hats is a crash helmet.

CHIPLIN: Peter Jay said, 'It's a competitive economy'. If all the employees are being paid their market wage, and if the suppliers of capital are being paid the market rate for their capital, then I can't see, in a fully competitive economy, that there is any more residual.

JAY: Yes, there can be a residual. It can be discounted when the other bargains are struck.

FITZROY: You can have a continuum between fall-back wage and residual; but the higher the paid wage the less the long-term incentive and the more likely the workers are to behave as they do at present.

JAY: There's no theoretical reason not to go the whole hog and let workers draw just a residual. It's partly a matter of what people are used to or what they are used to calling it.

15. *Would the government not continue to subsidize bankrupt firms under a labour-managed system in order to maintain the level of employment?*

COYNE: Would the government not finance the enterprises when they went bankrupt? If governments have a target rate of unemployment, would this change?

JAY: I go back to the point about the all-importance of the political settlement of which this is part; and part of that settlement is that the government doesn't do that kind of thing. There is competition between enterprises. What you are adopting is market socialism. One of the characteristics of market socialism is that the distribution of resources is determined by market forces without government interference except to the degree of those identifiable public goods and externalities which are dealt with by a limited number of mechanisms which Professor Meade in particular over many decades has developed.*

That is the essential guarantee against that kind of government intervention. Of course if that breaks down then the system breaks down.

And in so far as a workers' co-operative economy succeeds in reducing the level of unemployment it reduces the incentive for government to behave in these ways.

16. *Is Peter Jay's plan optimistic about the market?*

HENK THOMAS: I come from a country (Holland) where industries are being wiped out completely because of new technologies.

I am concerned at the apparent optimism that labour management could solve the problems we face. For example entry is a major problem. For many unemployed people it is easier said than done. Changes in the international money market, for instance those that follow the change in the value of the dollar, are far greater than the

---

*See especially *The Intelligent Radical's Guide to Economic Policy*, particularly Chapters I and VI.

kind of changes you have been speaking of in wages. I am uneasy about the market: planning is needed; national incomes policies, regional incomes policies.

SIRC: Planning means again saddling workers with responsibilities for what somebody else has planned.

JAY: There is a real intellectual parting of the ways between the point of view that Henk Thomas represents and the point of view that I represent. He — I would say 'still' — believes that as new problems emerge they merely extend the agenda that the national and regional governments have to deal with. It is precisely because I no longer have any belief in the useful possibility of tackling problems like that through national concerted action, whether of governments, parliaments, national representatives of trade unions, or whatever, alone or separately, that I feel that we have to look for a new political economy which enables the society to accomplish its over-all objectives of prosperity and harmony and freedom of choice, and its other economic objectives, under a system of rules as a result of which free individuals, acting privately in the pursuit of their private interests, will find in an imperfect world that these are conducive to the over-all fulfilment of the society's goals as a whole.

THOMAS: I am speaking of decentralized planning institutions. Furthermore I can see very little promise of market organization coping with the problems of the labour market. I made an issue of incomes policy because I think it is a precondition almost of the stability you are looking for.

We can hardly wait a decade. Even in a co-operative economy, incomes policy will be needed.

17. *A critical assessment of the significance of the co-operative concept*

MCGREGOR: I'm in favour of the co-operative idea. It is necessary to balance expertise against popular control of the objectives and final performance of management. Mondragon is particularly interesting in this respect; though I have to ask myself to what extent it is dependent on the circumstances of that country, that part of that country and the historical point at which it has occurred, and I have some doubts, for instance, about the degree to which it is exportable to Britain.

I think there are some quite clear fundamental factors which underlie what we are trying to get at here, one of which is that there is the need for institutional development at the level of the enterprise to represent a change in the perceived balance within the enterprise compared with what it was a hundred years ago; I don't think we've had any real institutional development of that kind and I think we're going to have to have some.

I think the concept on which the enterprise has to be founded still has to be based on the risk of the entrepreneur: and on, as I see it, the managerial entrepreneur, in cases where the entrepreneur who is also the owner has disappeared from the scene. I think this is an important factor, and is not more difficult in the context of co-operatives than in that of capitalism.

I think the idea that the co-operative concept deals with the general macro-economic problem is quite a different question which I don't go into in detail now.

In my opinion it's much too simplistic to suggest that there is a solution to the macro-economic problem in terms of employment by means of workers' co-operatives; but there could be a solution to the problem of efficiency at the micro level, with its consequences for the macro level, provided the essential fundamentals are not destroyed in the process.

Peter Jay wants to see a change in the balance of power within the company without any change in ownership. How would this differ from assigning more limited rights to employees, though greater rights than now?

Peter Jay says we must change collective bargaining so that it is no longer restricted in content and carved out on a national basis: so that it is unrestricted in content but confined to the firm. And that is a plausible approach.

But I think the idea cannot be sustained that collective bargaining should be about everything. I am always struck by the fact that in Britain we use the term 'industrial democracy' for whatever it is we are talking about, and most people don't seem to know what this is; whereas in Germany, for example, the trade unions made the point that they were not interested in 'industrial democracy', that they were talking about 'co-determination', which means greater rights over a restricted area of the agenda. I suspect that if the agenda were unrestricted the debate could not be confined within the enterprise; and if it were more restricted it would not be necessary to paint such a dramatic picture of change in society as Peter Jay has put forward.

18. *An alternative to a full transition to workers' co-operatives: value-added sharing combined with participation*

FITZROY: I don't believe that what Peter Jay calls market socialism is a realistic concept, because it does not take up the property rights and the incentives issues. It is essentially a transfer of resources from the outside suppliers of capital to those with the decision-making power inside the firm. On the other hand the various very real benefits of the co-operative system can be realized by a combination of modifications of existing property rights, which protect the interests of suppliers of capital.

There is a continuum of control rights between suppliers of labour and suppliers of capital, with the worker-owned or the worker-controlled firm at one extreme and, say, the nineteenth-century capitalist firm at the other. Instead of concentrating on the either/or question between these two extremes, we can show from our empirical work in Germany that there are considerable benefits to be made by exploiting some of the incentive and motivating effects of participation by workers in managerial decision making, plus the replacement to some extent of the fixed-wage payment to labour by a share in a residual, which is enlarged by reducing the fixed-wage-cost element.

I think there are various arguments which suggest that the performance of enterprises of this kind — of which Mondragon is one — will be improved by requiring a capital stake from workers.

Now the traditional argument against this is that workers usually don't have capital. The answer is what you might call 'human capitalism'. What the economist calls 'human capital' is first the discounted present value of workers' future labour earnings, and in a modern economy human capital in that sense dominates material capital — physical capital — by several orders of magnitude. But what Frank Knight — who is generally described as an apologist for capitalism — in a very prescient phrase half a century ago [in *Risk, Uncertainty and Profit*, 1921] called the major failing of capitalism is the inability of people who possess only 'human capital' to liquidize it, in other words to borrow financial capital on the security of their future earnings. The reasons for the institutional lack of this facility are partly historical, partly based on transactions costs; but I think we could make a very good case that given modern communications and modern technology these costs could be very small, and that it would be possible for a young workers to borrow from a bank, committing him to repayment out of his future earnings power. At a very high level of abstraction one could say that all the problems disappear. Automatically the workers can borrow enough to take a majority stake or minority stake in their own enterprises if they wish.

One major advantage would be that it would enable workers to invest in their own training. Another major problem in the modern economy is that generally the people who need training — young workers — do not have the capital to pay for it and the state has to pay for it, and this leads to competitive credentialism — piling up non-productive credentials to get a foothold in good jobs — whereas if workers could invest directly in on-the-job training in the enterprises where they put up a capital stake — roughly as at Mondragan — then there would be a guarantee that the training would be directly relevant, and at the same time the people enjoying the training would have a say in the allocation of funds, in the structure of job design and in the quality of working life, commensurate with their investment in this training; so I think there is a tremendous potential here which is completely ignored in the traditional discussion of industrial democracy and workers' control.

This would solve the incentive problems because workers who have put up a stake themselves in some sense are guaranteeing the outside suppliers of capital that they are not going to run the enterprise down at the cost of the future or at the cost of these outside suppliers of capital.

And the beautiful flexibility of this scheme is that the thing is variable: workers have put up a small capital stake, they have a small mortgage on their own earning power, and a small degree of credibility *vis-à-vis* the outside suppliers of capital, and so they must put up with possibly higher interest rates or credit restrictions; on the other hand the workers who are willing to mortgage their own future earnings to a higher degree will get better credit conditions and so they can invest; so they can increase their own productivity in their own enterprises. So the kind of variations of leverage, financial structure, capital intensity, and so on which are permitted by this system are restricted only by the imaginations, and within very wide limits by the budget constraints, of the people concerned.

19. Re-employment

ALASDAIR CLAYRE: The problem of unemployment might still be left unsolved by Peter Jay's proposals, or left to be solved, as he says,

only through the creation of new firms by old-fashioned entrepreneurial methods. This difficulty may perhaps be met by building in
an idea derived from Mondragon.

Because 'ease of entry' is likely to be so important in any
co-operative economy or sector, one of the most important of all ideas
to be derived from the Basque experience at Mondragon may be the
arrangement whereby an employee agrees to work at any job in the
federation in which he is needed, and, in return, if his firm suffers a
decline in the demand for its product and he becomes redundant, is
guaranteed adequate training and new work and in the meantime generous unemployment support, the guarantee being made by the federation (not by the State, since co-operators are 'self-employed'). The role
of the central management body of the local federation in researching
new ideas, having new projects ready to begin and helping new enterprises to get started — which is a necessary corollary to any such open-
ended commitment on the part of the federation — may be equally
valuable as an idea.

IV. NEW CONTRIBUTIONS TO THE ECONOMICS OF CO-OPERATION AND PARTNERSHIP

6. Labour Co-operatives, Participation, and Value-Added Sharing

by James Meade

I

Much thought is given nowadays to possibilities of improving human relations in industry and also the performance of the economy through participation by workers in the decision-making of the enterprise in which they work and/or in sharing in the profitability of the enterprise. The purpose of this note is to enumerate some of the main analytical issues which are raised by these proposals. The method adopted is (1) to examine the extreme form of labour participation (i.e. the complete, simple Labour Co-operative), (2) to discuss the problems which may be expected to arise in this case, and (3) to consider how they might be met by various modifications of the arrangements for a simple Labour Co-operative.

II

In a simple, unadulterated Labour Co-operative the workers in the enterprise themselves own and manage the business. They borrow at fixed interest the capital funds needed to finance the purchase of the capital goods and land employed by them in the production process (or alternatively they hire at fixed rents the instruments of production and the land which they use). They purchase the current inputs (i.e. of raw materials, energy, transport, etc.) needed for production. They sell their output on the market. The year's Total Net Labour Earnings (TNLE) = Value of sales *plus* value of increase in stocks *less* tax on sales *less* any tax related to the business but not related to the personal incomes of the workers *less* purchase of raw materials and other current inputs (but *not* less purchase of fixed capital goods) *less* depreciation on fixed capital goods *less* payments of fixed interest and rents. Average Labour Earnings (ALE) = TNLE ÷ the number of workers (N). Each worker is paid an amount equal to ALE; or in other words the whole of the net income of the concern is divided equally among the workers, no part of the income being ploughed back into the business.

The basic advantage of this type of institution is the improvement in motivation. No individual worker can lose and indeed every individual worker will gain by acting in such a way as to increase TNLE (e.g. by giving up some demarcation rule or other restrictive practice, by reducing waste of materials, etc.). The gain may take the form of reduced cost of inputs and a greater output for sale, or, if greater sales would spoil the market, an all-round reduction in hours of work.

The individual worker will himself receive 1/Nth part of any increase in the TNLE which is due to his own action. The direct material incentive to increase the TNLE of the concern will, therefore, be small in those cases in which the Labour Co-operative is big and N is a large number. For this reason the small Labour Co-operative will show a greater improvement in motivation than will the larger Labour Co-operative.

But this does not mean that the improvement where N is large will be negligible. Human beings undoubtedly have important 'altruistic' motives in favour of the group to which they belong. A simple and striking example of this is the fact that people bother to vote in democratic elections with large voting constituencies. In a constituency with N voters, where N is large, the probability that Mr Smith's personal vote will decide the choice between two candidates is negligible; and yet we find Mr Smith taking the trouble to vote, his feeling being that the welfare of the group system as a whole requires him to do so since, if every individual refrained from voting, the system would break down. Similarly, in a Labour Co-operative even with N large, Mr Smith may do all he can to avoid waste of materials; although his share of the advantage to the group may be negligible he may be moved by the fact that the welfare of the group to which he belongs depends upon each individual member of the group acting in this way. In short Labour Co-operatives, even if they are on a large scale, may improve motivation by removing the sense of conflict of interest between 'them' (the bosses) and 'us' (the workers).

I turn to a catalogue of Problems to which such an organization of business concerns is likely to give rise. This catalogue makes no attempt in itself to resolve the problems, but only to describe them. Possible solutions will be discussed in a later section of the paper.

Problem I. Would it not be desirable for the Labour Co-operative to be able to refrain from distributing to its members the whole of its TNLE and to plough back some part of it to finance the purchase of additional capital equipment?

The purchase of a new machine by the co-operative should be to the advantage of all the members if the Discounted Cash Flow from the machine (using the rate of interest at which it could borrow funds) were greater than the cost of the machine. The funds for the purchase of the machine could come from the issue of new debt or the use of the accumulation of past depreciation funds. But might it not be wise, indeed perhaps necessary, to enable the concern to finance capital development by ploughing back part of its own TNLE in those cases in which it might have difficulty in borrowing additional funds on the market, even though its own members were convinced of the profitability of the new investment at a rate of return which was attractive to them?

This possibility would raise no great problems if the membership of co-operatives were unchanging not only in size but also in individual persons who made up the membership. But consider a case in which elderly Mr Smith is about to reach retiring age, while young Mr Brown has just joined the co-operative. If part of this year's TNLE is ploughed back into the concern, Mr Brown will gain from the future yield of the machine at the expense of Mr Smith who will lose part of his share of this year's TNLE.

For this reason, if some part of the TNLE were ploughed back into the business, new debt should be issued at some acceptable rate of interest to all the existing members to represent that part of each member's TNLE which had been retained in the co-operative. If this solution were adopted, the question would arise whether the debt of the co-operative (i) to its own existing members, (ii) to its past retired members, and (iii) to non-members should all be treated in the same way. Should existing and/or retired members be free to sell their holdings of the co-operative's debt on the market to outsiders or should their rights of realizing the capital sum of the debt be restricted, e.g., until they retired? Should the co-operative be under an obligation to pay out in cash any debt owed to a retiring member?

Problem II. Should the co-operative's Capital Gains be added to (and Capital Losses be subtracted from) the computation of the TNLE?

The TNLE was defined so that, if any TNLE which was ploughed back into the business was offset by the issue of new debt to the members of the co-operative, then the total debt would remain equal to the total accumulated investment in fixed capital. The repayment of debt to outsiders would come out of the TNLE and would thus be offset by the issue of new debt to the insiders. But how should an unexpected capital gain or loss on the co-operative's assets be treated?*

If the capital gain were included in the year's income, i.e. were included in the TNLE, then it would have to be offset by an equivalent increase in the issue of new debt to the members of the partnership unless it were realized and distributed to them. Conversely a capital loss would either have to be offset by a reduced payment of ALE to each partner or offset by a cancellation of debt due by the co-operative to its members or an actual incurring of debt by the members to the co-operative. In this latter case members might on retirement find not that the co-operative owed money to them but that they owed money to the co-operative.

The alternative would be not to include Capital Gains and Losses in the computation of the TNLE. In this case there would once again be some degree of unfairness between old and young members or between present and future members. Capital Gains made as a result of this year's enterprise would be to the advantage not of this year's members but of the members in future years. Or Capital Losses made this year would have to be made good eventually out of the productive efforts and the TNLE of future years.

Problem III. Would it not be necessary at least in the case of Capital-intensive technologies to raise some form of outside equity capital? People can spread their risks insofar as their capital is concerned by investing small fractions of their property in a large number of different concerns. People cannot split up their occupations at work in the same way and must put all their work-eggs into one (or at least very few) occupational baskets. In the entrepreneurial–capitalist regime workers run the risk of losing their jobs and having to face, if not unemployment, then the cost of movement to other and perhaps less attractive jobs; but the profits of the owners of capital are also continually at risk, including the risk of total loss. In the Labour Co-operative the risk

---

*The estimation of capital gains and losses as well as of the depreciation allowances for the calculation of the TNLE raises the familiar problems of inflation accounting, since it is the co-operative's income and capital in real terms with which the members should be concerned. I do not discuss these issues in this paper.

is much more highly concentrated on the workers. It is true that if the concern goes bankrupt those who have lent their capital to the Co-operative may lose it; but apart from such extreme disaster the whole of the risk of upward or downward fluctuation falls on the workers.

Let us call the TNLE plus the amount paid in interest and rent to those who have supplied the capital the Net Value Added (NVA), since it is the value added in the concern net both of taxes and of depreciation allowances on fixed capital. In a labour-intensive concern in which the TNLE was 90% and the fixed interest and rent only 10% of the NVA, a 9% fall in the NVA would cause a 10% reduction in the TNLE available for distribution to the workers. In a capital-intensive concern in which the TNLE were 10% and the fixed interest and rent 90% of the NVA, a 9% fall in the NVA would cause a 90% reduction in the available TNLE. The risks to labour which was tied down in a capital-intensive Labour Co-operative would be intolerable, unless some arrangement could be made for part of the risk to be borne by the capitalists. (See the Appended Mathematical Note, below, pp. 116–17.)

Problem IV. Should the management of the co-operative be able to dismiss from the co-operative workers who wish to remain members of it?

Problem V. Should members of the co-operative be free to leave the co-operative even if that would be against the interest of the remaining members?

The determination of the number of partners in any Labour Co-operative raises some difficult issues. It may be assumed that the basic objective of the existing partners will be to raise ALE (their income per head) to the highest possible level. With any given capital structure an increase in the number of working members will raise ALE (1) insofar as it will enable the fixed cost of interest and rent to be spread over a larger number of persons and (2) insofar as there are any increasing returns to scale which cause output per head to grow with the growth in size of the output; but on the contrary it will lower ALE (1) insofar as there are decreasing returns to labour applied to the same stock of capital and land and (2) insofar as the other inputs are bought in a monopsonistic market or the product sold in a monopolistic market so that the price of inputs is raised or of the outputs is lowered as more is produced and sold. It is probable that in view of the need to spread the fixed capital cost over a larger numbers of heads, ALE will at first rise but that owing to diminishing returns to a single factor it will reach a maximum and then decline.

The existing members will gain from an increase in the size of the membership if ALE is less than the marginal revenue × marginal product of a worker (MRMP). ALE is what will be paid to the new member; MRMP is what he adds to the TNLE; if MRMP > ALE, there is a bonus to be distributed over the whole membership. Conversely if ALE > MRMP the remaining members would gain if one of their members were to leave the co-operative; the remaining members would save in distribution (ALE) more than the loss in the net revenue (MRMP).

But an individual worker would wish to join or to remain in the co-operative if the ALE were greater than what he could earn outside the co-operative (OE). Conversely he would be unwilling to join and, if a member, would want to quit if ALE < OE.

The partnership is thus confronted with the six following possible situations —

(1) MRMP > ALE > OE
(2) OE > ALE > MRMP
(3) ALE > OE > MRMP
(4) ALE > MRMP > OE
(5) MRMP > OE > ALE
(6) OE > MRMP > ALE.

Situations (1) and (2) do not give rise to any serious conflicts of interest. In situation (1) it is to the advantage both of the existing members (MRMP > ALE) and of any new recruits (ALE > OE) that the membership should be expanded. In situation (2) it is to the advantage both of the remaining members (MRMP < ALE) and of any members who leave (ALE < OE) that the membership should contract.

But in the remaining four situations there is a clear conflict of interest.

In situations (3) and (4) there is an advantage to individual members to remain in the co-operative and indeed for individual outsiders to join the co-operative (ALE > OE) but there is an advantage to any remaining members that individuals far from joining should in fact leave the co-operative (ALE > MRMP).

This situation could arise as a result of the well-known backward-sloping-supply-curve paradox of the Labour Co-operative. (See Section V of the Appended Mathematical Note, below.) If the price received for the sale of a Labour Co-operative's product rose by 10%, this — given no change in the degree of imperfection in the product market —

would raise the MRMP by 10%. But because of the fixed interest and rent to be spread over the membership it would raise the TNLE and ALE by more than 10%. It could, therefore, cause ALE to exceed MRMP.

This situation raises the question whether the management of the Labour Co-operative should be able to dismiss working members against the wishes of those members in the interests of the remaining members. In an unadulterated Labour Co-operative it would seem anomalous that the management should have the power of dismissing members who were unwilling to leave. To have this power means that all the workers are not treated equally. Some (e.g. the latest recruits) would not have the same security of tenure as the others.

But a distinction should be drawn between situation (3) and situation (4). What the members of a co-operative stand to gain by a reduction or to lose by an increase, in the size of the membership is ALE — MRMP. What the individual stands to gain by being allowed to join the Co-operative or to lose by being dismissed from the co-operative is ALE — OE. Thus in situation (3) with OE > MRMP the existing members ought to be able to bribe an individual existing member to leave by an annual payment B_3 where

$$ALE - OE < B_3 < ALE - MRMP.$$

Conversely in situation (4) with OE < MRMP an outsider should be able to buy his way in to the co-operative by an annual payment B_4 where

$$ALE - OE > B_4 > ALE - MRMP.$$

But this solution really offends against the principle that all members should be treated equally. In fact the newly recruited member would be being paid a reward equal to ALE — B_4 while the previously recruited members would be being paid ALE. We will return later to solutions which permit unequal payments.

In situations (5) and (6) the conflict is of the opposite kind where individuals would be unwilling to join and desirous of leaving the co-operative (OE > ALE), whereas the remaining members of the co-operative would gain by an expansion and lose by a contraction of the membership (MRMP > ALE). This is the sort of situation which could arise from a deterioration in the market price at which the co-operative's product could be sold. Because of the fixed cost of interest and rent the

TNLE might well fall in much greater proportion than the MRMP so that ALE fell below MRMP.

It would seem clear that the co-operative could not force unwilling outsiders to join the co-operative. But whether or not individual members should be free to leave the co-operative at the cost of leaving the reduced number of remaining members with the liability of meeting the whole of the burden of fixed interest and rent is a very real and difficult question. If it were possible, the position of a co-operative which was not doing well could be very unstable. Some members would be able to move out to other occupations more easily than others. As they moved out the fixed interest burden would be more concentrated and ALE would fall still further below OE for the remaining members. Others might then move out. The process could go on until the fixed interest absorbed the whole of the NVA so that ALE was reduced to zero.

The alternative rule would be that a member could leave the co-operative only with the permission of the remaining members. What the individual stands to gain by leaving the co-operative or to lose by having to join it is $OE - ALE$. What the remaining members of the co-operative stand to gain by recruiting a member or to lose by losing a member is $MRMP - ALE$. Thus in situation (5) it should be possible to arrange for a payment B_5 from the existing members to a new recruit which would induce the new recruit to join the co-operative or to an existing member to persuade him to stay, where

$$OE - ALE < B_5 < MRMP - ALE.$$

And in situation (6) it should be possible to arrange a payment B_6 to the co-operative by any individual member who wished to leave sufficient to induce the existing members to release him, where

$$OE - ALE > B_6 > MRMP - ALE.$$

But once again rules of this kind imply that members are not always treated equally (and they also encourage the expression — sincere or otherwise — of wishes to leave). Thus the solution in situation (5) would imply that one member was paid $ALE + B_5$ while others received only ALE. Moreover any such arrangements might well undermine morale by encouraging individual members to threaten to leave, simply in order to bargain for specially favourable treatment.

Problem VI. How would differentials be set between payments to different grades of workers in a Labour Co-operative?
We have so far assumed that in an unadulterated Labour Co-operative all the members would receive an equal share of TNLE. There are two possible forms of modification of this rule. One modification would be of the kind to which reference was made in discussing Problems IV and V, namely that workers of the same grade and ability might be paid different amounts in order to permit entry of new members without loss to old members or in order to recruit new members to the advantage of old members. We will return to this case later in discussion of Problem VII.

There remains a less controversial problem of differentiation, namely the setting of differentials in pay as between different grades of labour, e.g. between the skilled and the unskilled. It will probably be recognized that such differentials should exist. If so, two questions arise. First, how should the members of the co-operative decide what the differentials should be? Second, given a set of differentials, how will that affect the operation of the co-operative?

We will first consider the second of these questions and then, in the light of the effect of a given set of differentials, consider on what principles the differentials should be set.

Consider then a case in which there are three different grades of labour, 1, 2, and 3, with N_1, N_2, and N_3 representing the number of members of the co-operative in each grade. The easiest way to think of the effect on the distribution of the TNLE of a differential in payment in which a member in grade 2 is paid twice as much as a member in grade 1 is to imagine the same payment being made for each unit of 'effective work' done and to assume that an hour's work by a grade 2 workers is twice as 'effective' as an hour's work by a grade 1 worker. We can then allot to each grade a multiplier, $\alpha_1 \alpha_2 \alpha_3$, such that $\alpha_1 N_1$, $\alpha_2 N_2$, and $\alpha_3 N_3$, represent the number of units of 'effective work' produced by grades 1, 2 and 3 respectively. The absolute values of the αs are immaterial; all that matters is the relationship between them; thus if $\alpha_3/\alpha_2 = 1.5$, an individual in grade 3 is treated as producing 50% more 'effective work' than a worker in grade 2 and will accordingly be paid 50% more. We can then calculate an average earning per unit of 'effective work' done, namely $\overline{ALE}$ where

$$\overline{ALE} = TNLE \div (\alpha_1 N_1 + \alpha_2 N_2 + \alpha_3 N_3).$$

The payment to a worker in grade 1, 2, or 3 will then be $ALE_1 =$

$\alpha_1\overline{ALE}$, $ALE_2 = \alpha_2\overline{ALE}$, and $ALE_3 = \alpha_3\overline{ALE}$ respectively.

In considering the question whether it would pay the other members of the co-operative to take on more or to dismiss existing workers in any one grade, we can apply an analysis similar to that used for a single body of homogeneous workers in discussing Problems IV and V. Each grade of labour will be making its own marginal contribution to the co-operative i.e. will have its own MRMP. It will pay all the members in the co-operative to increase or to decrease by one individual the members in grade 1 according as $ALE_1 \lessgtr MRMP_1$. The individual in question will want to be a member or not to be a member according as $OE_1 \lessgtr ALE_1$. And similarly for the other grades.

We turn then to the question on what principles the differentials represented by the αs should be set. The easiest way to think of the problems involved in this decision is to imagine a Labour Co-operative with a set of differentials which is fully satisfactory to everybody, and then to imagine a change in circumstances which will introduce a conflict of interest among the members of the co-operative. Suppose then that we start with the happy state of affairs in which $OE_1 = ALE_1 = MRMP_1$ for grade 1 workers; and similarly for workers in all other grades. In each grade no individual wishes to leave or to join the co-operative and in the case of each grade there is no advantage to the other members that there should be any change of numbers in that grade. Suppose then that there is a change in technology which causes $MRMP_1$ to rise and $MRMP_2$ to fall (e.g. typists could do much of the work of skilled compositors). It will be to the advantage of the membership of the co-operative as a whole to reduce numbers in grade 2 and to increase numbers in grade 1; it will be to the advantage of out-side grade 1 workers to join if the differential α_1 is raised; it will not be to the advantage of workers in grade 2 to leave; but the disadvantage to the membership as a whole of maintaining the numbers in grade 2 would be reduced if the differential α_2 were reduced.

This example serves to illustrate the fact that the setting in a Labour Co-operative of differentials between grades of labour raises the same fundamental questions as those discussed in connection with Problems IV and V. Do the other members have the right to dismiss redundant workers in grade 2? Or do they have the right to reduce the differential paid to workers in grade 2 below the level which was previously agreed between all the members to be appropriate? Or do existing members in grade 2 have an inalienable right until age of retirement to work in the Co-operative at the originally agreed rates of differential in the distribution of the TNLE?

One possible set of solutions to these problems raises just the same issue as was discussed in connection with Problems IV and V, namely whether or not the co-operative is prepared to contemplate situations in which workers of the same grade are employed simultaneously at different rates of earnings. If, for example, in the case examined above it were the rule that the unwanted members in grade 2 could not be dismissed, it might be possible to bribe them to leave for outside employment. Or, failing that, it would be possible to let the members in grade 2 run down by retirement. But as this happened would it be legitimate to replace some of the retired members in grade 2 with new recruits in grade 2 but at a lower differential, α_2, than had previously been applied to the workers in grade 2? If the technological change affected grade 2 workers throughout industry, it might well be that the OE_2 of grade 2 workers had fallen and that new grade 2 workers would gladly join the co-operative at a lower differential than previously. But if the pre-existing members in grade 2 had the right to continue in employment at the old and higher differential, this would mean old and new grade 2 members working side by side at different rates of earnings.

In fact the change requires the substitution of grade 1 for grade 2 workers. This calls for a fall in the price of grade 2 relatively to the price of grade 1 workers. Can the substitution take place in a Labour Co-operative by applying it to new members but not to old members? Is it legitimate to argue that the existing members in grades 1 and 2 had agreed to share on old differentials α_1 and α_2 and should continue to do so, although new recruits in grade 1 will be offered a better α_1 and in grade 2 a lower α_2? Will it be ruled that, except on terms agreeable to the other members of the co-operative, existing members in grade 1 are not free to leave the co-operative, simply because they no longer like the old terms and that the old members in grade 2 cannot be dismissed or have their earnings cut simply because their fellow members now find that they are overpaid? If not, what is the solution?

Problem VII. Should all members of the same grade necessarily have the same share in the TNLE?
So far we have discussed problems concerning the rules appropriate for the running of a single Labour Co-operative without consideration of the form of business organization in the rest of the community; we have simply assumed that for each grade of labour there was some

alternative outside earning (OE) (which might presumably simply be unemployment benefit) with which a worker of that grade would compare his earnings (ALE) in the co-operative. But a number of the problems which we have discussed increase greatly in importance if the background in the rest of the economy is one in which all business units take the form of Labour Co-operatives. In particular the question whether all members of the same grade in any one co-operative should necessarily receive the same share of TNLE is of crucial importance in a world composed solely of Labour Co-operatives.

This can be best appreciated by considering the following simple illustration. Suppose that in every co-operative for every grade of labour ALE = MRMP, i.e. that no co-operative had any incentive to take on more members or to get rid of members of any grade. Suppose however that there is a large body of outside unemployed workers whose unemployment benefit is much lower than the earnings of those who are lucky enough to be members of a co-operative (OE < ALE). They would much like to join the existing co-operatives.

There are only two mechanisms whereby the unemployed might be absorbed.

First, the existing members of the existing co-operatives would be willing to expand their numbers if they could take on new members in any grade on less advantageous terms than themselves. The old members would be paid ALE and the new recruit ALE' where OE < ALE' < ALE = MRMP. But this would offend against any rule that all workers in a given grade must receive the same share of the co-operative's TNLE.

Second, employment could be expanded if the unemployed could set up new co-operatives to compete with the existing co-operatives. The new co-operatives should be able to compete with the old co-operatives if they could raise their capital funds on equally favourable terms, since their members would be prepared to accept a lower ALE than the ALE enjoyed in the existing co-operatives. But the snag is, of course, the uncertainty whether a group of unemployed workers could give the security and confidence needed to raise the necessary capital funds, particularly in those cases in which the technology was at all capital-intensive or there were any important economies of scale or any important market imperfections which made it difficult for newcomers to invade the territories of established concerns.

The position is essentially different in a world of capitalist–entre-preneurial concerns. The analogous situation would be one in which the wage rate was equal to MRMP for every grade of labour in every firm, while there existed a large body of unemployed workers. In this case if the competition of the unemployed caused the wage rate to be reduced the existing firms would have an incentive to increase the numbers employed, all of whom would receive the same but lower wage rate.*

It is absolutely crucial for the successful working of a world of Labour Co-operatives that either there should be arrangements for the easy setting up of new co-operatives with full freedom to compete with existing co-operatives *or* it should be the rule that new members can operate in existing co-operatives on less favourable terms than the existing members — or, of course, that both conditions should be fulfilled.

Either of these two conditions also provides answers to the questions already raised in the above discussion of Problems IV, V, and VI.

Thus consider the case of a co-operative in which $OE < MRMP < ALE$. The outside individual would be better off in the co-operative ($OE < ALE$); the existing members will not want to accept him ($ALE > MRMP$). The outsider can hope to improve on his low OE *either* by being accepted into the existing co-operative at a reward ALE' such that $OE < ALE' < MRMP < ALE$ *or* alternatively by finding a number of similar disadvantaged individuals and setting up a new competing co-operative to take advantage of the conditions which allow the existing co-operative to afford so high an ALE.

Or consider the case of a change of technology which in any given co-operative has raised the $MRMP_1$ of grade 1 workers and lowered that of grade 2 workers, so that $ALE_1 < MRMP_1$ and $ALE_2 > MRMP_2$. The situation can be put right *either* (i) by the existing co-operative, while maintaining the ALE_1 and ALE_2 for existing workers, taking on new grade 1 workers at a reward higher than ALE_1 and taking on any new recruits in grade 2 at a reward lower than ALE_2 *or* (ii) by grade 2 workers who can no longer find employment at ALE_2 and grade 1 workers who want to earn more than ALE_1 getting together and setting up a new competing co-operative.

There is one further set of circumstances which underline the importance of these two conditions — of easy entry of new co-operatives or of arrangements to admit new members on terms different from those

*I assume, of course, that there is a macro-financial policy which maintains the total level of money demand for the products of industry when the money wage rate is reduced.

enjoyed by existing members. A Labour Co-operative which requires that all workers should receive the same share in a given monopolistic market will be more restrictive in its policy than would a similarly placed capitalist–entrepreneurial concern. The latter's objective is to maximize total profit; but the former's objective is to maximize total profit per head which can be raised by reducing the number of heads as well as by increasing the total profit. In this case too the extra degree of restriction would disappear if *either* the monopolistic co-operative could take on more members so long as the terms offered to and accepted by the new recruits, though less favourable than those enjoyed by the existing members, were less than the worker's MRMP *or* it was easier in the Labour Co-operative case than in the capitalist–entrepreneurial case for new concerns to enter the market and so to reduce the monopolistic power of the existing concerns.*

III

There are two basic sets of conditions which give rise to the difficulties encountered by Labour Co-operatives which we have discussed under Problems I to VII: first, those which are due to the fact that the payments to capital and land are fixed and bear no part of the risks; and, second, those which arise if it is not permissible for existing members of co-operatives to admit new members on any terms different from the terms set for the existing members. In this section we will outline a possible structure of a Capital–Labour Partnership which avoids both these sets of difficulty.

In a Capital–Labour Partnership there would be no fixed payments of interest or rent. Both those who had provided the capital funds and those who were providing the labour in the enterprise would own shares. What would be shared pro rata among the shareholders would be the annual TNLE without any deduction of interest or rent, i.e. what in the discussion of Problem III above we termed the Net Value Added or NVA. Each share would give to its holder, whether a capitalist or a worker, the same pro rata claim on the NVA and the same pro rata voting power in the direction of the enterprise, e.g. in the appointment of a board of directors and managers at a shareholders' meeting.

But the shares would be of two kinds.

---

*The main result of the analysis in the Appended Mathematical Note is to demonstrate the much greater importance for Labour Co-operatives than for capitalist–entrepreneurial firms of the easy establishment of new competitive concerns.

Capital-Shares would be lasting shares once the funds had been put into the enterprise; the funds themselves could not be withdrawn; but the shares could be bought and sold, e.g. on the Stock Exchange.

Work-Shares would give voting rights and a pro rata claim on the NVA only so long as the worker made himself available for work in the enterprise. No worker could be dismissed against his will once he was admitted to membership, but so long as he was a member he would in principle be under an obligation to do any job in the Partnership which the management might require him to do.

The Partnership would be free to issue a new Capital-Share provided it could do so for a price which, in its opinion, would finance an addition to the partnership's real assets sufficient to produce an addition to the NVA which was greater than the existing ratio of NVA/S, where S is the total number of shares outstanding whether in the form of Capital-Shares or of Work-Shares. In other words new capital would be raised only if the terms were both attractive to the new subscribers and held out the prospect of increasing the income of every existing partner, whether Capitalist or Worker.

Similarly, the Partnership would be free to employ a new worker in any grade provided that the worker would be willing to join the partnership in return for an issue of additional Work-Shares such that the addition to the NVA due to the additional work done was greater than the current NVA/S times the number of new Work-Shares issued to the new recruit. Conversely, any worker who retired would not be replaced on the old terms if the loss of NVA was less than the current NVA/S times the Work-Shares cancelled as a result of the worker's retirement. In other words decisions to increase or decrease the size of the work force would be taken only if they held out the prospect of advantage to all shareholders, whether Capitalist or Worker.

It may be helpful to review the effect of these arrangements on the seven Problems of a Labour Co-operative which were discussed in Section II.

Problem I. Any part of the annual NVA which was not distributed to shareholders should be credited as newly issued Capital-Shares at the current market price of shares pro rata to all existing owners of shares, whether of Capital-Shares or Work-Shares. *All* shareholders would thus receive marketable Capital-Shares equal in value to the amount of their share of the NVA which had been saved and invested on their behalf.

Problem II. The problem of the best treatment of the Partnership's capital gains and losses would be greatly eased though it could still remain an awkward one. In principal, capital gains and losses should be added to, or subtracted from, the NVA. But if at any time there were heavy capital losses combined with some excess distribution of income to shareholders, this could still involve workers ending up with negative holdings of Capital-Shares, i.e. indebted to the Partnership. The problem would, however, be very much less acute than in the case of a Labour Co-operative, since any capital loss would fall on all shareholders, capitalists as well as workers, instead of being concentrated on the workers alone.

Problem III. The problem of risk is met in so far as capital as well as labour now bears the risk of the concern.

Problem IV. No existing partner could be unwillingly dismissed, though it would be permissible for terms to be agreed between him and the management under which he willingly retired early and gave up his existing Work-Shares.

Problem V. Any worker would be free to leave but would have to give up his Work-Shares if he did so. The problem would not arise of workers leaving and thereby causing a fixed sum of interest payment to be concentrated on a smaller number of remaining partners. There would be no fixed interest; and any net loss to the Partnership due to the withdrawal of a valuable partner would be spread over all remaining shareholders, i.e. over all the capitalists as well as over the remaining workers.

Problem VI and VII. On their recruitment individual workers would receive issues of shares which were advantageous in each case to the new recruit and to all existing shareholders. But as circumstances changed these recruitment terms might vary. Thus differentials would come to exist both as between various grades of labour and also as between individuals in the same grade. Early Capital-Shareholders in a venture which was well run and successful would, as in existing companies, make capital gains which would not be available to those who invested funds at a later date. Early workers in such an enterprise would come to enjoy on their Work-Shares an income which it would not be necessary to offer to later recruits to the workforce.

Is it wrong that those who pioneered and were responsible for a successful venture should so gain, whether they were Capitalists or

Workers? This differentiation of incomes is, however, an essential feature of the Capital–Labour Partnership as outlined in this Section. In the light of the discussion of Problem VII in Section II of this paper it can be seen that this may well be a necessary feature of a successful world of co-operatives which absorbs the unemployed and does not lead to excessive monopolist restrictions. The only alternative would be to rely on the setting up of new competing co-operatives, which may be a difficult if not impossible procedure particularly in cases where economies of large-scale production or important imperfections of market competition may exist.

The full Capital–Labour Partnership thus has much to recommend it. But it is not without problems and difficulties.

(1) One problem which would arise with a Capital–Labour Partnership as with a Labour Co-operative is concerned with the qualification for unemployment benefit. Members of such a co-operative or partnership are self-employed. If they leave their work, in what circumstances will they qualify for unemployment benefit? Consider a case in which the market turns against a co-operative or partnership to such an extent that some of the workers are receiving an income which has fallen very low. Will they be free to leave their work (having in effect lost their livelihood in their present occupation) and to claim unemployment benefit? It would seem right and proper that when a worker's income fell below a certain figure he should be free to leave and to take unemployment benefit. But could all persons who left a co-operative or partnership take unemployment benefit? In short could unemployment benefit (UB) be counted as an alternative outside earning (OE), available to any worker?

It is helpful to consider the position in a capitalist–entrepreneurial regime. Suppose that in such a concern MRMP < UB so that the worker would be dismissed if any wage equal to or greater than UB were demanded. It would appear very reasonable to treat it as a case of loss of job which qualified for UB.

Consider then the implications of adopting in a regime of labour co-operatives or partnerships the criterion that UB should be available for any worker who could not find or be placed in a job in which MRMP > UB. If the regime was not based on the egalitarian principle and if the unemployed were always anxious to take any job in which their earnings (ALE) would be greater than the unemployment benefit (UB), it would then be possible to treat UB simply as a fallback OE which any worker could choose if he so desired. For if UB < MRMP the employment of the worker in the co-operative will lead to an excess of income of MRMP − UB which can be divided between the new member and the existing members. It will be to the advantage of all concerned to employ the new member.

The limited problem would remain of the work-shy. It is possible that a situation would arise in which UB < MRMP but UB > MRMP − D where D is the excess of reward in work over income out of work which the workshy would require to induce him to work. This limited problem is similar to that encountered in a capitalist–entrepreneurial regime. Would those administering the system of unemployment benefit have sufficient evidence to ensure that UB was not paid to any-one to whom the offer of an equivalent or higher ALE in an existing co-operative or partnership was available?

The problem would, however, not be quite so straightforward if the egalitarian principle was adopted in the regime of labour co-operatives. A situation can well arise in which ALE < UB < MRMP (cf. situation 5 on page 94 above). Such a situation might be one in which a labour co-operative was being built up. The existing membership is small relative to the capital that, for reasons of economies of scale, has to be installed. The ALE is thus low because of the heavy debt per member. An expansion of the membership may bring success. It would not be feasible for the administrators of unemployment benefit directly to measure the MRMPs of different concerns; and even if they could, it would not be reasonable to insist on a worker giving up his UB for a lower ALE.

There are only two possible solutions. The first is to rely on the possibility of new members being attracted to give up their UB for the low ALE on the expectation of a much higher future ALE as the co-operative developed. The second, more probable and perhaps more sensible, solution is the abandonment of the egalitarian principle and the employment of more workers either as wage hands at a fixed wage (W) or as members with an earnings share equivalent to W, such that ALE < UB < W < MRMP.

(2) The full Capital–Labour Partnership would unquestionably remove many of the conflicts of interests between Capital and Labour in any Partnership since, as we have shown, the main decisions would be taken only if they were to the advantage of all holders of shares, whether Capital-Shares or Work-Shares. But this would not be true of all decisions. A number of things which will cost the Partnership money (e.g. canteen facilities and many other fringe benefits) will be to the

advantage of workers holding Work-Shares but not to the advantage of those holding Capital-Shares, though the cost will fall on both groups. Possibly an even more important case of a conflict of interest of this kind would arise in any decision to reduce hours of work or to increase the length of annual holidays for the workers, thereby taking an increase in real income out in the form of leisure. Holders of Capital-Shares would also sacrifice the return on their shares without enjoying any increase of leisure. It is conceivable that this occasion of conflict might be removed by issuing Work-Shares on condition that the worker performed a certain number of hours of work each year, so that a worker's ownership of shares would be reduced pro rata to any cut in his annual quota of hours of work.

(3) It is to be expected that in a full Capital–Labour Partnership many of the demarcation rules and other restrictive labour practices would be dissolved; if any existing working partner was in any case entitled to retain his existing holding of shares he, like everyone else, would only gain by being willing himself, and by allowing every other partner, to work freely and without restriction at any task in the Partnership which offered the highest MRMP. But, as we have argued, this would have to be combined with arrangements which allowed new recruits to be taken on on terms which were not necessarily as favourable as those which applied to existing members, the value of whose special skills had, for example, been eroded by technical progress. This means that conflict would arise if any group of workers felt that the special restrictive demarcation rules attaching to their work should be maintained in the interests of the future members of their 'guild' – if, for example, existing compositors felt that their skilled tasks must be protected from inroads by other types of worker not in their own interests (since their own shareholdings would not be at risk) but in the interest of the future earnings of their sons on whose entrance to their 'guild' they had been relying.

(4) It is questionable whether the appointments to all posts in the Partnership should necessarily be associated with an initial issue of Work-Shares which would thereafter remain unaltered until the worker concerned left the Partnership. Could an existing worker on promotion to a new post be rewarded with an issue of an additional holding of work-shares? Could a manager be appointed for a limited period, subject perhaps to renewal if he were successful? And, if so, would he receive an issue of Work-Shares which would last only so long as he retained his post as manager? Problems of promotion could give rise to

a direct conflict of interest between the capitalist and the worker-partners. Promotions which involved the issue of additional Work-Shares would automatically reduce the amount of any given NVA which was available for payment on Capital-Shares. Thus a policy of easy and widespread upgrading of the workforce could be a means of redistributing the income of the Partnership from the capitalists to the workers. Should a worker be promoted only when it could be shown that the increase in his ALE was covered by his MRMP and was needed to retain his services as a member of the Partnership?

(5) Finally would there be an objection to the Partnership taking on some workers on a simple fixed-wage-rate basis without any participation in the holding of shares? May there not well be some cases (e.g. short-term temporary needs of labour) and some persons (e.g. those who are specially averse to taking risks) for which employment at a fixed wage is more important than participation? There is much to be said in favour of freedom to arrange fixed-wage contracts or borrowing of capital at fixed interest where this appears advantageous to all the parties concerned. But at what point would the whole nature of a Partnership Economy be undermined by the regrowth of conflict between wage-hands, on the one side, and owners of capital on the other?

IV

It would seem that forms of Partnership in which both Capital and Labour shared in the risks of success and failure hold out more promise than Labour Co-operatives in which labour bears the whole of the risk. There are in fact many forms of profit-sharing or of partial sharing between Capital and Labour of what I have called the Net Value Added (NVA) which are partial steps towards full Capital–Labour Partnerships in that they share the risk of success and failure between Capital and Labour and give both parties a direct interest in the success of the enterprise. Perhaps the way to progress is to develop and build on such schemes. But, if the argument of this paper is correct, many of the improvements in incentives and performance which one may hope to achieve from schemes for the participation of Labour in industrial enterprise rest on the possibility that those who were responsible for the success of a concern should be paid more than those who join later to enjoy the concern's success. But this involves the possibility of two persons working together on the same process but receiving different rates of income. Is this principle acceptable?

7. Appended Mathematical Note: The Adjustment Processes of Labour Co-operatives with Constant Returns to Scale and Perfect Competition*

by James Meade

I

Assume a large number of competing Labour Co-operatives in a perfect market. Each co-operative is producing an output (X) under constant returns to scale with only two factors, labour (L) and capital equipment (K).

For each co-operative we have the production function

$$X = X(L, K) \tag{1.1}$$

which by differentiation gives

$$dX = l\,dL + k\,dK \tag{1.2}$$

where $l = \partial X/\partial L$ and $k = \partial X/\partial K$, the marginal products of L and K respectively.

Since there are constant returns to scale we have also

$$X = lL + kK. \tag{1.3}$$

II

Consider any one of these competing co-operatives facing a market with a selling price P for the product X and a price R for renting a unit of capital equipment K. (It can be assumed either that the co-operative rents each machine for a payment of R per annum or that R measures the interest payable on any sum borrowed for the purchase of a machine.) P and R may vary in the market from time to time but each co-operative acts on the assumption that it cannot affect the level of P or R through its own individual decisions.

Income per head in the co-operative (which we will call W) is given by

*From *Economic Journal*, December 1979. Reprinted by permission of Cambridge University Press.

$$W = \frac{PX - RK}{L} \qquad (2.1)$$

Given P and R, the co-operative can affect W by varying K and L, and so X.

Differentiating (2.1) with P and R constant and using (1.2) and (1.3) we obtain

$$dW = \frac{(Pk - R)(L dK - K dL)}{L^2} \qquad (2.2)$$

From (2.2) it can be seen that if $Pk > R$ (i.e. the value of the marginal product of capital equipment $>$ than its rental cost) W can be raised either by increasing K or by decreasing L. With constant returns to scale and with P and R given it is only the ratio of labour to capital which is relevant for the level of income per head.

Clearly the existing members of the co-operative can gain by taking on more capital so long as the marginal product of capital is greater than its rental ($Pk > R$). It is also true that income per head can be raised in the co-operative by taking on less labour so long as the value of the marginal product of labour (i.e. what will be lost to output by losing one member) is less than the existing income per head (i.e. what is saved to the remaining members of the co-operative by the departure of one member). But with constant returns to scale, if one factor is paid the value of its marginal product then what is left over is just sufficient to pay the other factor a reward equal to its marginal product. If in (2.1) we substitute Pk for R and use (1.3), we obtain $W = Pl$. In other words there is only a single criterion for the maximization of income per head in a constant-returns-to-scale competitive co-operative, namely: 'Adjust the capital–labour ratio until the value of the marginal product of capital is equal to its market cost'. The average income of each member of the co-operative will then be at a maximum equal to the value of each member's marginal product.

III

We consider next the equilibrium conditions for an industry producing an output NX by means of a large number N of perfectly competing identical constant-returns-to-scale co-operatives of the kind described in Sections I and II above, each of which produces X. We assume that the number of co-operatives remains constant at N; there is no entry of new or exit of old co-operatives. We assume further that each co-operative adjusts itself to any change in the industry's market condition (i.e. to any change in P or R) so as to maximize its income per head W by keeping $Pk = R$. By differentiation we obtain

$$\frac{\mathrm{d}R}{R} = \frac{\mathrm{d}P}{P} + \frac{\mathrm{d}k}{k} \ldots \tag{3.1}$$

Assume a demand curve for the output of the industry of the form $P = m\bar{P}(NX)$ where m is a shift parameter, the underlying demand function $\bar{P}$ remaining unchanged. By differentiation we have

$$\frac{\mathrm{d}P}{P} = \frac{\mathrm{d}m}{m} + \frac{NX}{\bar{P}} \frac{\mathrm{d}\bar{P}}{\mathrm{d}(NX)} \frac{N\mathrm{d}X}{NX}$$

or

$$\frac{\mathrm{d}P}{P} = \frac{\mathrm{d}m}{m} - \frac{1}{\epsilon} \frac{\mathrm{d}X}{X} \ldots \tag{3.2}$$

where ϵ is the arithmetical value of the elasticity of demand for the industry's product.

From (1.2) we obtain

$$\frac{\mathrm{d}X}{X} = \lambda \frac{\mathrm{d}L}{L} + (1 - \lambda) \frac{\mathrm{d}K}{K} \ldots \tag{3.3}$$

where $\lambda = lL/X$, i.e. the proportion of the product which will go to labour when, in equilibrium, labour is paid a reward equal to its marginal product; and similarly $(1 - \lambda) = kK/X$.

By differentiation of (1.3) and use of (1.2) we obtain

$$\frac{\mathrm{d}l}{l} = -\frac{1 - \lambda}{\lambda} \frac{\mathrm{d}k}{k} \ldots \tag{3.4}$$

We define σ (the arithmetic value of elasticity of substitution between L and K) as the ratio of the proportionate increase in L/K to the proportionate decrease in l/k with which the change in L/K is associated, so that

$$\sigma = -\frac{(\mathrm{d}L/L - \mathrm{d}K/K)}{(\mathrm{d}l/l - \mathrm{d}k/k)} \ldots \tag{3.5}$$

It was shown in Section II that a single co-operative could adjust to a change in market conditions (i.e. a change in P or R) by adjusting K or adjusting L, since it is the ratio of L/K which matters for the maximization of income per head. Suppose that $Pk > R$. If it is easy to increase K quickly and it is undesired to expel existing members from the co-operative, L/K will be reduced by increasing K. But if it were less easy to increase K rapidly and if at the same time L were being reduced automatically by death and retirement, L/K might rather be reduced by a decrease in L. We will consider the two extreme cases in which

Either
$$\frac{\mathrm{d}L}{L} = 0$$

$$\left.\begin{matrix} \\ \\ \\ \end{matrix}\right\} \cdots \qquad (3.6)$$

or
$$\frac{\mathrm{d}K}{K} = 0$$

Finally from (2.1) by differentiation, with $\lambda = (PX - RK)/PX$ and $(1 - \lambda) = PkK/PX$, we obtain

$$\frac{\mathrm{d}W}{W} = \frac{1}{\lambda}\left(\frac{\mathrm{d}X}{X} + \frac{\mathrm{d}P}{P}\right) - \frac{1-\lambda}{\lambda}\left(\frac{\mathrm{d}K}{K} + \frac{\mathrm{d}R}{R}\right) - \frac{\mathrm{d}L}{L} \cdots \qquad (3.7)$$

We can then use equations (3.1) to (3.7) to solve for $\mathrm{d}K/K$, $\mathrm{d}L/L$, $\mathrm{d}k/k$, $\mathrm{d}l/l$, $\mathrm{d}P/P$, $\mathrm{d}X/X$, and $\mathrm{d}W/W$ in terms of $\mathrm{d}m/m$ and $\mathrm{d}R/R$.

IV

With adjustment wholly through changes in K we obtain the following solutions:

$$\frac{\mathrm{d}K}{K} = \left(\frac{\mathrm{d}m}{m} - \frac{\mathrm{d}R}{R}\right)\frac{\epsilon\sigma}{\epsilon\lambda + \sigma(1-\lambda)} \cdots \qquad (4.1)$$

$$\frac{\mathrm{d}L}{L} = 0 \cdots \qquad (4.2)$$

$$\frac{\mathrm{d}k}{k} = -\left(\frac{\mathrm{d}m}{m} - \frac{\mathrm{d}R}{R}\right)\frac{\epsilon\lambda}{\epsilon\lambda + \sigma(1-\lambda)} \cdots \qquad (4.3)$$

$$\frac{\mathrm{d}l}{l} = \left(\frac{\mathrm{d}m}{m} - \frac{\mathrm{d}R}{R}\right)\frac{\epsilon(1-\lambda)}{\epsilon\lambda + \sigma(1-\lambda)} \cdots \qquad (4.4)$$

$$\frac{\mathrm{d}P}{P} = \frac{\mathrm{d}m}{m}\frac{\epsilon\lambda}{\epsilon\lambda + \sigma(1-\lambda)} + \frac{\mathrm{d}R}{R}\frac{\sigma(1-\lambda)}{\epsilon\lambda + \sigma(1-\lambda)} \cdots \qquad (4.5)$$

$$\frac{\mathrm{d}X}{X} = \left(\frac{\mathrm{d}m}{m} - \frac{\mathrm{d}R}{R}\right) \frac{\epsilon/\sigma(1-\lambda)}{\epsilon\lambda + \sigma(1-\lambda)} \dots \quad (4.6)$$

$$\frac{\mathrm{d}\overline{W}}{W} = \frac{\mathrm{d}m}{m} \frac{\epsilon}{\epsilon\lambda + \sigma(1-\lambda)} - \frac{\mathrm{d}R}{R} \frac{(\epsilon-\sigma)(1-\lambda)}{\epsilon\lambda + \sigma(1-\lambda)} \dots \quad (4.7)$$

All the signs in these equations are what common sense would suggest with the possible exception of the sign of $\mathrm{d}R/R$ in (4.7).

Thus a rise in the demand curve relatively to the cost of capital (i.e. an initial rise in P and/or fall in R) will upset the existing equilibrium by making $Pk > R$. Each co-operative will have an inducement to increase K which will cause an increase in output X, a fall in the marginal product of capital k, and a rise in the marginal product of labour l; and the increase in output will exert a downward influence on demand price P. Pk will fall back until equality with R is restored. There will finally be a net rise in P insofar as it was an upward shift in the demand curve which caused Pk initially to exceed R, but a net fall in P insofar as it was a reduction in R which caused the initial change.

In a perfectly competitive capitalist economy with constant returns to scale and given market prices for the factors, an upward shift in the demand curve would induce an equal proportionate increase in both K and L until output at a constant cost per unit was so increased that the demand price had fallen back to its initial level. With a Labour-Co-operative economy an upward shift of the demand curve may also give an inducement to expand output, but by taking on more K without taking on more L. In this case the expansion of output will not be on a sufficient scale to bring the price down to its old level, since if the old price were so restored the whole of the inducement to employ more K with the given amount of L would have disappeared. The price would remain at a higher level than before the change, and income per head in each co-operative would be raised above its present level. Only if new entrants were attracted by the prospect of this higher income per head to set up new additional co-operatives would the price be brought down once more to its previous level.

The importance of ease of entry for new co-operatives becomes even more marked when one considers the sign of $\mathrm{d}R/R$ in equation (4.7). An upward shift in the demand curve will raise the average income in each co-operative. But the effect of a change in the cost of hiring capital equipment is uncertain. If $\epsilon > \sigma$, then a rise in R will reduce W. But if $\sigma > \epsilon$, it will have the less obvious opposite effect of raising W.

Thus suppose σ to be very large and ϵ to be very small. An increase in R causes R to exceed Pk. As a result in each co-operative K is reduced. But since σ is very large, the reduction in K causes a very small rise in k; on the other hand since ϵ is very small, the reduction in the industry's output causes a large rise in P. In the new equilibrium with $Pk = R$ once more, W will again be equal to the value of the marginal product of labour Pl. But l will have fallen little (because σ is large) and P will have risen much (because ϵ is small). Thus $W = Pl$ will have risen.

In perfect competition in capitalist production with $\sigma > \epsilon$ a rise in R would cause a fall in output, a fall in K, but an *increase* in L. The main effect would be a substitution of L for K (with σ large) rather than any reduction in output resulting from the net rise in cost (ϵ small). This case emphasizes the much greater importance of entry of new firms in the labour co-operative economy than in the capitalist economy. In the latter each existing firm would have had an incentive to take on more labour if the change raised the value of the marginal product of labour above its reward in other occupations. This is not the case with the labour co-operative, where the industry must rely on the entry of new co-operatives if conditions raise income per head within the co-operative above the level ruling in other occupations.

V

With all adjustment carried out by changes in L we have

$$\frac{\mathrm{d}K}{K} = 0 \tag{5.1}$$

$$\frac{\mathrm{d}L}{L} = -\left(\frac{\mathrm{d}m}{m} - \frac{\mathrm{d}R}{R}\right)\frac{\epsilon\sigma}{\lambda(\epsilon - \sigma)} \tag{5.2}$$

$$\frac{\mathrm{d}k}{k} = -\left(\frac{\mathrm{d}m}{m} - \frac{\mathrm{d}R}{R}\right)\frac{\epsilon}{\epsilon - \sigma} \tag{5.3}$$

$$\frac{\mathrm{d}l}{l} = \left(\frac{\mathrm{d}m}{m} - \frac{\mathrm{d}R}{R}\right)\frac{\epsilon(1 - \lambda)}{\lambda(\epsilon - \sigma)} \tag{5.4}$$

$$\frac{\mathrm{d}P}{P} = \frac{\mathrm{d}m}{m}\frac{\epsilon}{\epsilon - \sigma} - \frac{\mathrm{d}R}{R}\frac{\sigma}{\epsilon - \sigma} \tag{5.5}$$

$$\frac{\mathrm{d}X}{X} = -\left(\frac{\mathrm{d}m}{m} - \frac{\mathrm{d}R}{R}\right)\frac{\epsilon\sigma}{\epsilon - \sigma} \tag{5.6}$$

$$\frac{\mathrm{d}W}{W} = \frac{\mathrm{d}m}{m}\frac{\epsilon}{\lambda(\epsilon - \sigma)} - \frac{\mathrm{d}R}{R}\frac{\epsilon(1-\lambda) + \sigma\lambda}{\lambda(\epsilon - \sigma)}. \tag{5.7}$$

The outcome is in this case dependent in a much more fundamental way upon the sign of $\epsilon - \sigma$. In fact the industry's output would, in the absence of the entry of new co-operatives or the exit of existing co-operatives, be unstable if $\sigma > \epsilon$.

This can be seen by supposing the industry to be initially in equilibrium with $Pk = R$ but then to experience an upward shift in the demand curve $(\mathrm{d}m/m > 0)$. The immediate effect of this is to raise Pk above R. K is then being paid less than the value of its marginal product, so that L will be receiving a W which exceeds its marginal product. In this case it pays each co-operative to reduce its membership. As a result X is reduced. But with σ large and ϵ small, this causes a large rise in P but only a small fall in k, so that Pk, far from being reduced again towards R, rises still further above R. As a result W exceeds still more the value of L's marginal product. The position is an unstable one. Equality between Pk and R could in fact be restored only by an increase in L which would cause a large fall in P (with ϵ small) and only a small rise in k (with σ large). Equilibrium requires an increase in L; each co-operative has an incentive to reduce L.[1]

Once more in these conditions in a perfectly competitive capitalist industry, there would be an incentive to employ more labour so long as the upward shift of the demand curve caused the return to labour to be above its reward in other occupations; but with a Labour-Co-operative structure the expansion of the industry would, with $\sigma > \epsilon$, rely in a quite basic way upon the entry of new co-operatives. Indeed stability might well require that the entry and exit of co-operatives was easier and more prompt than the adjustment of the size of membership within each co-operative.

With $\epsilon > \sigma$, the system of equations (5.1) to (5.7) would be a stable one. But an upward shift of the demand curve $(\mathrm{d}m/m > 0)$ or a fall in the cost of capital $(\mathrm{d}R/R > 0)$ would have the perverse effect of causing

[1] If $\epsilon = \sigma$, there would be no equilibrium point in either direction. With a change in L in either direction, the change in the price of the product just offsets the change in the marginal product of capital, so that the excess of Pk over R, and W over Pl, remains unchanged.

a reduction in L and in X — the well-known perverse backward sloping supply curve of labour-managed economies. Only ease of new entry for new co-operatives would offset this effect.

There is one further important feature of the situation in which labour co-operatives rely upon adjustment of L rather than upon adjustment of K to maximize income per head, namely the greater sensitivity of the level of income per head to variations in demand or in the cost of capital. In the case of a capital-intensive industry this sensitivity can become very great indeed.

The situation is illustrated by the following numerical example. Assume a 1 per cent upward shift in the demand curve ($dm/m = 1$ per cent) in an industry in which $\epsilon = 2$ and $\sigma =$ either 1 or 1.5. We ask what will be the resulting percentage rise in W on the alternative assumptions that the industry is labour-intensive ($\lambda = 0.9$) or capital-intensive ($\lambda = 0.1$) and that the adjustment is made wholly by increasing K or wholly by decreasing L. The following table derived from equations (4.7) and (5.7) gives the resulting percentage increases in W.

	$\dfrac{dL}{L} = 0$		$\dfrac{dK}{K} = 0$	
	$\sigma = 1$	$\sigma = 1.5$	$\sigma = 1$	$\sigma = 1.5$
$\lambda = 0.9$	1.05	1.03	2.2	4.4
$\lambda = 0.1$	1.8	1.29	20.0	40.0

The variability of W is in each case greater with $dK/K = 0$ than with $dL/L = 0$. This is to be expected. With, for example, a rise in the demand curve and $dL/L = 0$, K will be increased which will increase X and tend to moderate the rise in P. On the other hand, with $dK/K = 0$ L will be reduced which will decrease X and accentuate the rise in P. It is also clear that the variations in W will be greater with $\lambda = 0.1$ than with $\lambda = 0.9$. The variation in W depends *inter alia* upon the difference between PX and RK; and with PX or RK varying by a given proportion the difference between them will show a larger proportionate change the smaller is $PX - RX$ relatively to PX or to RK.

What is most marked in the above numerical example is the extreme variability of W when we combine $dK/K = 0$ and $\lambda = 0.1$. It is quite probable that in the real world it would be difficult for new co-operatives to be set up in very capital-intensive industries in which a large amount of capital must be borrowed per member of the co-operative; and it may be more difficult also in such a case for members of an existing co-operative to make any substantial changes in their capital stock. If this is so, then we must expect the incomes of the members of capital-intensive co-operatives to be subject to extreme variability in the face of market changes.

From the above table it can be seen that a high σ will moderate the variability of incomes in a co-operative which adjusts to an increase in demand by expanding K. The resulting fall in k will be moderated so that the needed reduction in Pk back to the ruling R must be achieved by a greater increase in output and reduction in P. On the contrary a high σ relatively to ϵ will cause great variability if adjust-ment is through a reduction in L. If σ is high, then k will be little lowered by any given reduction in L and the membership of the co-operative will have to be very greatly reduced to restore equilibrium. There will be a substantial fall in X which will accentuate the rise in P so that income per head is greatly raised. Indeed, we have already seen that if $\sigma > \epsilon$ the position will be an unstable one. In the above numeri-cal table with $dK/K = 0$, $\lambda = 0.1$, $\epsilon = 2$, and $\sigma = 1.5$ a 1 per cent up-ward shift in the demand curve would suffice to cause a 40 per cent upward shift in the income per head for the co-operatives' remaining membership.

VI

The above analysis is much restricted by the two assumptions of per-fect competition and of constant returns to scale. Nevertheless it is suggested that it points to three very important basic differences between a free enterprise market economy of the familiar capitalist type and one based upon competing Labour Co-operatives, particularly for those real world situations in which there is a fair measure of com-petition and in which economies and diseconomies of mere scale are not of great importance over a fairly wide range of a firm's size.

First, ease of entry and exit of firms plays a much more vital role in maintaining a balance between supply and demand in the case of Labour Co-operatives than it does in the case of capitalist enterprises.

Second, within any one Labour Co-operative appropriate adjustment to market changes can often be made either by changing the amount of capital employed in one direction or alternatively by changing the number of members in the co-operative in the opposite direction.

Perverse effects can occur if the individual co-operatives choose to react by adjusting the number of workers in their membership rather than by changing the amount of capital employed. Since a co-operative may find it particularly difficult to attract new members just when market forces have reduced its earnings per head or to persuade members to leave just when market forces have raised its earnings per head, there may be some general tendency for each co-operative to react by adjusting the amount of capital employed by it. However, perverse reactions through adjustment of the size of membership are not to be ruled out if, in an activity in which fixed capital cannot be very readily and rapidly changed, old members happen to be retiring just at the time that market conditions improve or an exceptionally profitable co-operative still remains attractive even after some deterioration in its market conditions. In such cases perverse adjustments of the size of membership can be offset only by the entry of new or exit of old co-operatives.

Third, there are serious dangers of extreme fluctuations in income per head in Labour Co-operatives in industries which are capital-intensive, for which entry of new co-operatives is difficult, in which substitutability between labour and capital is high, and for the products of which the elasticity of demand is low.

8. Some Economic Issues of a Workers' Co-operative Economy

by Brian Chiplin and John Coyne

In *The Workers' Co-operative Eeconomy* (see pp. 9–45) Peter Jay presents a cogently argued case for a market economy in which the predominant enterprises are workers' co-operatives. His analysis is based on two essential premises:

(i) that there is a central contradiction in the present political economy of the Western nations which portends a catastrophic failure of the system within a finite number of years; and

(ii) that the resolution of the contradiction rests on the suggestion that labour should replace capital as the entrepreneur of the predominant productive unit.

Both of these premises are open to debate. The problems of stagflation in the 1970s, both in the UK and elsewhere, are well documented. Considerable research has emerged to reappraise the traditional arguments and solutions, and this has taken place against a background of introspection within the economics profession concerning the progress and contribution of current economic science.[1] The search for remedies within the conventional political economy has produced a preponderance of short-run measures based upon the assumption that the economies are passing through a temporary disturbance, and that economic recovery will take place from a relatively unscathed economic base. In this context the extensive use of subsidy programmes by governments, particularly with respect to unemployment, can be understood.[2] Peter Jay argues that this is not a temporary disequilibrium

[1] W. Leontief, 'Theoretical Assumptions and Non-observed Facts', *American Economic Review*, March 1971. E. H. Phelps-Brown, 'The Underdevelopment of Economics', *Economic Journal*, March 1972.

[2] For a penetrating analysis of the current problems of the world economy see the report by the group of independent experts appointed by the OECD under the chairmanship of Professor Paul McCracken: *Towards Full Employment and Price Stability*, OECD, June 1977. For a discussion of subsidy programmes see B. Chiplin and P. J. Sloane, 'An Analysis of the Effectiveness of Manpower Policies

that will right itself in the short to medium term. He presents the economic difficulties as a long run decline to cataclysm, and sees Britain, amongst the OECD countries, as the front runner. Other writers have used the term 'British Disease' to describe the UK's position, and analyses of its nature and consequences have been well documented.[3] The advent of North Sea Oil has been heralded by many people as a solution to the 'temporary' decline in Britain's economic performance. However, whilst the emergence of this resource will lead to an increasingly favourable balance of payments on the oil account, there remains the significant problem of a worsening balance in manufactured goods. Continuing the idiom these symptoms have been labelled the 'Dutch disease'. The deindustrialization of the UK economy brought to public attention predominantly through the work of Bacon and Eltis, is a cause for real concern.[4]

The problems are, therefore, extensive. However, many would argue that serious and difficult as they may be, they are amenable to solution without the cataclysmic effect predicted by Peter Jay.

On the second premiss, it may be doubted whether a workers' co-operative economy would spontaneously emerge on the other side of the holocaust. Many countries have gone through such traumatic experiences and yet a worker–co-operative solution remains the exception rather than the rule. However a central thesis in Jay's argument seems to be that a workers' co-operative economy is a first best outcome which requires active encouragement and institutional change to bring about its existence. This is a serious argument which requires detailed consideration. It is the main concern of this paper to examine some of the issues involved in this complex question and to point out some of the shortcomings of the existing literature. In particular we will concentrate on issues which seem to us to have been unduly neglected and yet are fundamental items.

We shall approach these under two broad heads (i) the transition towards a workers' co-operative economy and (ii) the operation of such an economy.

and Related Measures in Curbing Unemployment in Britain and Sweden', in *Staat und Wirtschaft*, Duncker and Humblot, Berlin, 1979.

[3] See, for instance, the diagnosis in G. C. Allen, *The British Disease*, Hobart Paper 67, IEA, 1976.
[4] R. Bacon and W. Eltis, *Britain's Economic Problem: Too Few Producers*, 2nd edn., Macmillan, 1978.

The transition

It is perhaps unfortunate that much recent experience of workers' co-operatives in an economy such as Britain has been connected with failure. They are discussed not as a positive contribution to economic prosperity and efficiency, but as a last-ditch reaction to the threat of redundancy and closure. In the popular eye the Scottish Daily News, Meriden, and KME are obvious illustrations. Experiments of this kind are beset, at the outset, with difficulties in relation to the viability of the existing product lines, the availability of markets, and the existing asset structure of the enterprise. The newly formed government body, the Co-operative Development Agency, specifically excludes employment — saving co-operatives from consideration unless it can be shown rigorously that the unit is fully commercially viable. Success matters! It is misleading to seek solace in co-operation against the rigours of technical and economic change. The attention devoted to such cases obscures the positive successes in co-operation to be found elsewhere in the economy, both within co-operative manufacturing movements, and through partnerships. It seems to be overlooked, for instance, that partnership — a well-developed form of co-operation — thrives in a number of activities particularly amongst the professional classes. Many of these are, of course, small-scale and it is frequently argued that as such operations become larger it is necessary to have recourse to the capitalist mode of joint-stock production. It is a moot point, however, whether this is necessitated by institutional/legal factors or is an inherent weakness of the co-operative system. A modern study of partnership in the light of recent theoretical developments would seem to us to offer substantial promise as an area of research activity.

These issues raise the question of whether it is possible for capitalist and co-operative enterprises to coexist in any meaningful sense. After all, the one-man business still exists to a large, though declining extent, but the proponents of the co-operative system would surely not wish to see it confined to very small-scale activity. In the economic literature the issue is rarely discussed and authors concentrate on the analysis of two distinct economic systems.

The question of the possibility of coexistence is vital for the further development of the worker co-operative. For as Suckling[5] notes we need an answer to such a question if labour-managed firms

[5] J. Suckling, review of J. Vanek, *The Labor Managed Economy* in *Economic Journal*, December 1977.

(LMF) are not to achieve the status of a theoretical curiosity as opposed to a workable alternative to the mixed market and planned economies available at present. It seems to be a fairly common view that LMFs would face difficulties in existing alongside capitalist firms. Indeed, the mere fact that they do not exist to any great extent suggests some impediments but to what extent are these inherent in the nature of the enterprises themselves?

We shall argue that there are attributes inherent in the pure LMF that hinder its general emergence within a capitalist economy.

The conventional approach to the labour-managed economy is discussed in a later section. Here a simple model is outlined which brings out the elements of our argument. The firm, whether labour-managed or capitalist is presumed in the short run to be able to alter the quantity of labour services through changes in hours of work but the total number of workers (or members) is fixed. For the labour-managed firm this echoes a point made by Joan Robinson.[6] For the capitalist firm the importance of fixed hiring and firing costs reducing the employer's flexibility in terms of temporary lay-offs is well known.[7] Labour is assumed to be homogeneous and initially the shares attributable to the members of the LMF are equal. Premium payments for skill can be accommodated in the model if the relationship between groups is exogenously determined but the conclusions are no different than for the simple case.

Output (Q) is assumed to be determined only by the number of hours input (H) and the capital stock (K) which is assumed fixed in the short run.[8]

$$Q = Q(K, H)$$

$$H = Lh_i$$

where L = the number of workers in the firm and h_i = the hourly input of the average worker, i.

[6] J. Robinson, 'The Soviet Collective Farm as a Producer Co-operative: Comment', *American Economic Review*, March 1967.

[7] W. Y. Oi, 'Labor as a Quasi Fixed Factor', *Journal of Political Economy* 70 (Dec. 1962). D. O. Parsons, 'Specific Human Capital: An Application to Quit Rates and Lay-off Rates', *Journal of Political Economy*, 1972.

[8] A model along similar lines is contained in: K. V. Berman and M. D. Berman, 'The Long Run Analysis of the Labor-Managed Firm: Comment', *American Economic Review*, September 1978.

Whilst any change in the hours input (H) may in reality be made up of different changes by individual workers it is assumed here that they change proportionately, i.e.

$$\alpha H = \alpha \sum_{i=1}^{n} h_i.$$

The worker (member) has a continuous, twice-differentiable utility function

$$u_i = u(Y_i, h_i) \tag{1}$$

where Y_i is the income of the ith individual and $\delta u / \delta Y_i > 0$; $\delta u / \delta h_i < 0$. For simplicity it is assumed that the individual has no income other than that from work and in the labour-managed firm it is given as

$$Y_i = \left(\frac{PQ - rK}{H}\right) h_i$$

or from the assumption of proportionality

$$Y_i = \frac{PQ - rK}{L} \tag{2}$$

where P is the price of the final product, Q the quantity sold, and r the price per unit of capital.

Each member is presumed to maximize (1) subject to (2). Rearranging and setting up the Lagrangeian

$$\max Z = u(Y_i, h_i) - \lambda \left(Y_i - \frac{PQ - rK}{L}\right).$$

If the product market is competitive the first order conditions are

$$\frac{\delta Z}{\delta h_i} = \frac{(\delta u / \delta h_i)}{L} + \lambda P \frac{(\delta Q / \delta H)}{L} = 0$$

$$\frac{\delta Z}{\delta \lambda} = Y_i - \frac{PQ - rK}{L}.$$

But

$$\lambda = \frac{\delta u}{\delta Y_i}$$

therefore

$$-\frac{(\delta u/\delta h_i)}{(\delta u/\delta Y_i)} = P\frac{\delta Q}{\delta H}. \tag{3}$$

Thus, in equilibrium the LMF sets the input of hours such that for each individual (i) the opportunity cost of the last hour worked equals the value of the marginal product produced during that hour. We may now demonstrate how that compares with a traditional capitalist firm in which labour is hired for a given wage rate (W). In this case the budget constraint becomes

$$Y_i = Wh_i. \tag{2a}$$

Maximization of (1) subject to 2(a) yields as a first-order condition that

$$\frac{\delta Z^1}{\delta h_i} = \frac{\delta u}{\delta h_i} + \lambda W = 0$$

or

$$-\frac{(\delta u/\delta h_i)}{(\delta u/\delta Y_i)} = W.$$

But for the profit maximizing firm the optimum choice of hours is where

$$W = P\frac{\delta Q}{\delta H}$$

which thus yields the same solution as the LMF, i.e. equation (3). We can now relax the assumption of perfect competition and allow for some market power in the final product market such that

$$P = p(\beta, Q)$$

where β is a shift parameter with

$$\frac{\delta P}{\delta \beta} > 0 \quad \text{and} \quad \frac{\delta P}{\delta Q} > 0$$

the first order condition for the LMF is:

$$\frac{\delta Z}{\delta h_i} = \frac{(\delta u/\delta h_i)}{L} + \frac{[\lambda\delta Q/\delta H]\,[P + Q(\delta P/\delta Q)]}{L} = 0$$

or

$$-\frac{(\delta u/\delta h_i)}{(\delta u/\delta Y_i)} = \frac{\delta Q}{\delta H}\left(P + Q\frac{\delta P}{\delta Q}\right).$$

Thus, in equilibrium, the opportunity cost equals the marginal revenue product of the last hour. In the traditional capitalist firm opportunity cost to the individual is again set equal to the wage, but the firm will be in equilibrium where:

$$W = \frac{\delta Q}{\delta H}\left(P + Q\frac{\delta P}{\delta Q}\right).$$

This is identical to the optimum condition for the LMF.

Thus, whether under competitive or monopolistic conditions, if short-run flexibility is achieved through varying hours of work the outcome in both the capitalist and LMF will be identical.

In the long run H, L, and K are all variable. For competitive markets (3) remains the first order condition with respect to hours and in addition:

$$\frac{\delta Z}{\delta L} = \lambda \frac{(LP\delta Q/\delta L - (PQ - rK))}{L^2} = 0$$

but since

$$PQ - rK = LY_i$$

$$P\frac{\delta Q}{\delta L} = Y_i \tag{4}$$

$$\frac{\delta Z}{\delta K} = \frac{P\delta Q/\delta K}{L} + \frac{r}{L} = 0$$

or

$$P\frac{\delta Q}{\delta K} = r \tag{5}$$

Equation (4) states that the LMF will set the marginal value product of the worker equal to the average value product and hence would maximize the average value product. The conventional approach to the LMF yields the same outcome. Equation (5) shows that the LMF would employ capital until its marginal value product equalled the price — the same condition as for a capitalist firm.

If, for both the short-run and the long-run, within the models as demonstrated, we note no difference between the equilibrating behaviour of traditional capitalist firms and labour-managed firms, we must clearly investigate in more detail the incentives to set up LMFs. In the capitalist firm income per period, Wh_i: where W is the wage rate per hour and h_i is the number of hours worked by the average ith worker, is given by

$$Wh_i = \frac{PQ - rK - \Pi}{L} \qquad (6)$$

In competitive conditions in equilibrium $\Pi = 0$ and therefore

$$Wh_i = \frac{PQ - rK}{L}.$$

Since, as demonstrated above, the equilibrium for the LMF will yield the same output

$$Wh_i = Y_i.$$

In this simple model there is no benefit in the long run to the members from establishing an LMF under competitive conditions. On the other hand, if $\Pi > 0$ as it could be under conditions of market power then

$$Y_i > Wh_i \quad \text{by} \quad \frac{\Pi}{L}.$$

In this case there is a clear gain from forming an LMF since it must follow that —

$$U_1(Y_i, h_i) > U_2(Wh_i, h_i).$$

In this simple model the gain is clear. It is the possible reallocation of profits to workers and as such is a redistribution which does not affect any of the marginal conditions analogous, for instance, to first-degree price discrimination by the workers. However, there is one point that does not seem to have been appreciated in the literature. There is no necessary reason why the members amongst whom the surplus is shared should be equal to the number of employees. In other words it is quite possible to establish a mixture of contractual arrangements, e.g. some of the workers agree to work for a fixed contractual wage and others become members and share in the residual. Since, as has been shown, sharing in the residual does not affect the marginal conditions for determining the optimum hours, the LMF could pay some workers the equivalent wage to the capitalist firm. This would call forth the same quantity of hours and yield the same output. Thus the total labour force L could be split into at least two components

$$\gamma L; \quad (1-\gamma)L$$

with $0 < \gamma < 1$ where γ is the proportion on fixed wage contracts. The residual income for the typical (average) member (Yr) is

$$Yr = \frac{PQ - rK - \gamma wh_i L}{(1-\gamma)L}.$$

A decision variable for the members is γ and it is trivial to show that

$$\frac{\delta Yr}{\delta \gamma} > 0 \quad \text{if } PQ > wh_i L + rK,$$

i.e. if in comparable circumstances a capitalist firm would make positive profits. Hence it always 'pays' a member to try and exclude other members. The ultimate degree of exclusion occurs when the single entrepreneur sets up the firm and negotiates fixed wage and rental contracts with labour and capital owners respectively. With no entry-barriers workers excluded from membership of the LMF can always establish their own firm and extract the appropriate surplus. But the existence of positive profits in the long-run implies the presence of some form of entry-barrier and hence this adjustment route is hampered. (We say more about the importance of barriers to entry later in this paper.) In the circumstances the incentive exists for a small number of individuals to appropriate the available surplus. The constraint which operates is, in fact, related to the degree of risk. As γ rises the extent of fixed commitments increases as does the variance of the residual share with any variability in PQ. There is also the possibility of substantial personal loss. This can be alleviated in a number of ways: (i) decrease γ; (ii) spread the risk by negotiating some fixed contractual element with e.g. capital owners whereby capital return itself becomes at least partly variable and the return to worker-members becomes partly fixed by a contractual wage plus a share in the residual.

Once it is realized that the residual may be taken out in ways other than income, e.g. the quiet life, excess staff, etc. conditions clearly exist for the emergence of some form of variant on managerial capitalism.

The above analysis would suggest that the incentives are such that it is unlikely that a pure LMF could exist alongside a pure capitalist firm. If a pure labour-managed economy is to emerge, therefore, it appears that all other forms of organization would need to be proscribed by Law and every worker would have no alternative but to be given a share in the residual rather than a fixed wage contract. It is further implied that even if an economy of the type envisaged by Peter Jay should emerge as the result of a major upheaval its organizational form would tend to be unstable, and would revert to the equilibrium distribution of risks as in a private enterprise economy.[9]

This view is reinforced by a reconsideration of the utility function specified above. One claim in favour of workers' participation is that labour would benefit from the involvement with the enterprise implied by participation. Thus participation (I) enters the utility function directly so that

$$U_i = U(Y_i, h_i, I) \tag{1a}$$

where
$$0 < I < 1$$

and
$$\frac{\delta U_i}{\delta I} > 0.$$

When $I = 0$ the firm is a traditional capitalist organization, and when $I = 1$ it is a pure LMF. Taking a similar starting point, but with two classes of labour input — managers and workers — and with I as an argument in the production function, Steinherr[10] has shown that under fairly mild assumptions some profit-sharing and participation in decision making is always optimal. Further, in the presence of alternative technologies and differences in taste, firms offering different employment contracts can coexist. If this argument is accepted, neither the pure LMF nor the pure capitalist firm are likely to emerge as long-run stable institutional arrangements; a point which sits well with FitzRoy's analysis elsewhere in this volume.

A further point can be drawn from the above analysis. One possible disadvantage of the LMF economy is its inability to adjust to change. The establishment of new LMFs is an essential mechanism through which the economy adapts. But it might be argued that the establish-

[9] For a similar conclusion reached via a different argument see P. A. Samuelson, 'Thoughts on Profit Sharing', *Zeitschrift für die Gesamte Staatswissenschaft*, published by Rudolf Richter and Heinz Sauermann.

[10] Alfred Steinherr, 'On the Efficiency of Profit Sharing and Labour Participation in Management', *Bell Journal of Economics*, Autumn 1977.

ment of such an enterprise is more difficult than in the capitalist case even where institutional impediments are removed. It is unlikely that one would observe the spontaneous coalition of workers, either from other LMFs or from the unemployment pool, into new enterprises. Some agency or agent may be necessary, in at least a catalytic manner. The essential role of the entrepreneur is to spot opportunities and exploit them,[11] but why should he share these gains with others? However there is potential scope for the entrepreneur in the LMF system. Thus the entrepreneur could spot the opportunities, recruit, and organize the members of a new LMF and arrange for the hiring of capital. For this a fee could be commanded which at the margin could be set equal to the profits in equation (6). Further, the entrepreneurial services could themselves be supplied by LMFs. In this role the entrepreneurial LMF would be providing a brokerage service analogous to that provided in many other markets. The crucial question in these circumstances would be whether there were any barriers to entry at the entrepreneurial stage. Again the outcome is not likely to be dissimilar to that in a private enterprise economy.

Thus, we would agree with Peter Jay, but for different reasons, that it would seldom pay any individual enterprise to become a workers' co-operative. What we doubt is whether, even if established on a wide scale through a major institutional upheaval, such ventures would be self-sustaining; or whether they would rather revert to a quasi-private enterprise format. The importance of the supportive structure of laws able to sustain such a system is clearly evident in this context.

Leaving aside the question of whether it is desirable, let it be supposed that the transition takes place along the lines envisaged by Jay. There is one important problem: unless the transition is accompanied by wholesale destruction, the distribution of existing capital assets has to be taken as given. In particular the size distribution of plants and intangible assets such as goodwill are inherited by the economy. It is impossible to start from scratch.

In an economy such as the UK's it is well documented that both aggregate and market concentration have been increasing over time.[12] The 100 largest enterprises now account for over 40 per cent of net output in manufacturing.

[11] See for example I. M. Kirzner, *Competition and Entrepreneurship*, Chicago: University of Chicago Press, 1973.

[12] See e.g. S. J. Prais, *The Evolution of Giant Firms in Britain*, Cambridge University Press, 1976, and *A Review of Monopolies and Mergers Policy*, Cmnd 7198, HMSO, May 1978.

The current distribution of assets does suggest that even if all enterprises were split up into their separate plants (no easy matter) a substantial sector of the economy would be converted to large-scale LMFs. As Peter Jay himself admits both experience and *a priori* reasoning suggest that workers' co-operatives are likely to be most effective at a small size. Although the assets may require a common location for efficiency it does not follow that they have to be under common ownership,[13] or be operated by a common LMF. Some form of federal arrangement or set of inter-linked contracts is a possibility, as for instance was discussed as a potential scheme for *The Times*. Such negotiations would be complex and it may well be that common ownership is the optimum outcome which would explain the failure of federal-type solutions to emerge in a private enterprise economy. Over the longer haul a redistribution of assets could occur particularly if economies of large-scale production are insignificant. This seems to be the sort of development envisaged by Jay. But in looking at Jay's real world proposals it is important to bear in mind that the existing system has to be compared with the radical alternative of workers' co-operatives *given the existing distribution of assets.*

The Labour-Managed Economy

Our analysis has addressed itself to the problem of coexistence and the transition period but naturally it overlaps to a considerable degree with the analysis of the performance of a labour-managed economy, which is central to Jay's argument. It is necessary, therefore, to review the contribution of the major literature in this area and point out the similarities and differences between the traditional analysis and our own.

The theoretical work on the labour-managed economy has grown out of, and built upon, the contribution of economists such as A. P. Lerner, O. Lange, E. F. M. Durbin, and H. D. Dickinson who formalized socialist ideas to produce an economic analysis of a socialist system.[14] More recent work by B. Ward, E. Domar, J. Vanek, and J. Meade has analysed, in a partial equilibrium framework the implications of

[13] See O. E. Williamson, 'The Vertical Integration of Production: Market Failure Considerations', *American Economic Review*, May 1971.

[14] O. Lange, 'On the Economic Theory of Socialism', in B. Lippincott (ed.), *On the Economic Theory of Socialism*, University of Minnesota Press, 1938; H. D. Dickinson, *Economics of Socialism*, Oxford University Press, 1939; A. P. Lerner, 'Economic Theory and Socialist Economy', *Review of Economic Studies*, 1934; E. F. M. Durbin, 'Economic Calculus in a Planned Economy', *Economic Journal*, December 1936.

worker-owned and controlled firms buying and selling within conventional markets.[15] J. Drèze has extended their work in a Walrasian general equilibrium setting.[16] These authors have concentrated on the efficiency of the system and the way in which the LMF reacts to market signals as compared to, or contrasted with the capitalist firm. In both instances the objective of the firm is taken to be the maximization of a residual from production. In a capitalist firm it is the profit after all costs, including payments to labour in wages, have been met. In the LMF it is the sum left over to be divided amongst labour after the interest, hire, and depreciation charges have been made against capital together with the cost of other non-labour inputs.

In the standard model the firm is presumed to produce a single product subject to a production function $Q = Q(K, L)$ where K is the quantity of capital and L the number of workers. It is simple to show that the capitalist firm would set the marginal value product (or marginal revenue product) equal to the wage-rate whereas the LMF would set MVP (or MRP) equal to the average value product of labour. Thus a capitalist firm would continue to hire employees as long as their marginal contribution to the firm's revenue exceeds the wage paid to them but members would only be allowed to enter the co-operative as long as their contribution raises the surplus per head. If capitalist profits are zero, the same output and allocation of labour would occur in the two cases. Drèze has proved that maximizing total profits or maximizing the value added per worker lead to the same general equilibrium solutions with identical Pareto-optimal properties.

It is in the short run that responses to, for instance, price changes differ in the capitalist and LMF firm. In contrast with the capitalist firm, the LMF would tend to reduce its membership when the price of the product rises so that the residual shared out represents even more to each remaining member. If workers so dismissed can form new enterprises and enter the same industry, the long-run implications for employment and output are the same as in the capitalist economy. The analysis establishes as a critical facet the ease with which workers

[15] B. Ward, 'The Firm in Illyria: Market Syndicalism', *American Economic Review*, 1958; E. Domar, 'The Soviet Collective Farm as a Producer Co-operative', *American Economic Review*, 1966; J. Vanek, *The General Theory of Labour Managed Market Economies*, Cornell University Press, 1970; J. E. Meade, 'The Theory of Labour Managed Firms and Profit Sharing', *Economic Journal*, March 1972.
[16] J. Drèze, 'Some Theory of Labour Management and Participation', *Econometrica*, November 1976.

so displaced can form new enterprises to enter those markets in which firms are extracting high returns.

The results for equilibrium whether derived from partial or general analysis are not unexpected, but they do depend on the particular assumptions employed, namely that there are identical production possibilities, no change in production incentives, and perfect mobility of labour. Likewise the perverse short-run adjustments also depend on the precise specification of the model. In particular, allowing for multi-product production reduces the possibility of a perverse supply response to changes in the price of a final product.[17] But in our opinion even more crucial is the assumption that membership is variable in the short-run. It is both theoretically debatable and in practice counter-intuitive given the observed variability in overtime and firms' cycles of economic activity. This, therefore, seems a totally untenable assumption particularly when contractions are involved. James Meade has set out his ideas on the rules for the running of Labour Co-operatives.[18] As regards expansion, he suggests that there are two necessary conditions: (i) the new partner wishes to come in and (ii) the old partners wish to accept him. There are likewise two necessary conditions for the withdrawal of a partner: (i) that the partner concerned wishes to leave and (ii) that he should obtain permission to withdraw from the remaining partners.

These rules seem entirely fair and reasonable, and clearly demonstrate the interdependence of workers' and the co-operative's desires. Adjustment requires the coincidence of desires in the LMF, unlike the capitalist counterpart which requires only that management wishes to reduce the labour force, and implies that short-run adjustment via the number of members is probably not feasible. That is why we have emphasized the fixity of numbers but the flexibility of *hours* in the previous analysis. This seems to us more likely to characterize what would take place in a labour-managed economy and it is observed in the capitalist economy. We have already analysed the short-run equilibrium of the LMF and capitalist firm under this assumption and shown that in both competitive and monopolistic markets the output would be the same whether the firm was labour-managed or capitalist. It remains to consider the response of the firm to changes in the exogenous variables in the short-run. A rise in the price of the product, for instance, would increase the marginal return to hours of work and as long as the utility

---

[17] See Vanek, op. cit., pp. 53–6.   [18] J. E. Meade, op. cit., Section 5.

function is conventional and the substitution effect is larger than the income effect, would encourage the workers to expand the labour input. Output would therefore expand as a result of the increase in hours input of the typical member. This is an adjustment in the direction of efficiency and implies stable reactions in the LMF. Thus the potential problems emphasized by Meade, Vanek, and others are dependent upon the particular (and, we would argue, rather peculiar) assumption adopted concerning the mode of adjustment in the LMF.

Our earlier analysis was conducted very much in the spirit of the conventional approach to the LMF but with the one crucial difference outlined above. However, we are well aware that constraining the models in this way potentially restricts areas of interest, and could 'assume away' items of fundamental importance to LMFs. Many of the advocates stress that the act of participation itself will alter the production function and the hours/intensity of effort nexus. In our analysis it would be of the form:

$$Q = Q(K, H, I) \quad \text{where } \frac{\partial Q}{\partial I} \gtrless 0$$

accepting that the over-all effect on output is initially indeterminate given that there may be a time cost associated with the exercise of participation-decision making. For a case to be made on efficiency grounds then $\partial Q/\partial I$ should be positive. One of the major gaps in the literature is any rigorous analysis of the structure of incentives under the LMF *vis-à-vis* the capitalist firm. The relationship between incentive structures and economic efficiency, and the legal and property rights that establish them is only recently receiving attention in the 'traditional' neoclassical capitalist literature. In addition, the whole subject becomes more complex when we remove the assumption of labour homogeneity. Labour differs in terms of skill, age, experience, productivity, etc., so that we cannot talk about a unique relationship of effort/output per period of labour input. The nature of wage contracts, the penalty/reward structure, promotion ladders, etc., become paramount.

The question of internal organization has serious ramifications for the efficiency of the enterprise and attention to this aspect is a relatively recent phenomenon.[19] Discussion of exactly how an LMF would operate at anything other than on a very small scale is almost

---

[19] See, for instance, the Symposium on the Economics of Internal Organization in *The Bell Journal of Economics*, Spring 1975.

non-existent and there is no consideration of the precise way in which its organizational structure and incentive systems would produce a superior outcome to its capitalist counterpart. We may take one issue in this complex field and examine it a little more closely — the rewards to be given to workers possessing different skills, the acquisition of skills by workers, and the provision of training opportunities by firms. It is possible to generalize the model to allow for jobs or skills and if the income distribution schedule is known this is a simple tractable problem.[20] But how is the income distribution schedule derived? Is it truly exogenous? If we are considering a transformation from a capitalist to a labour-managed economy it is clearly endogenous to the system. Workers of each skill category must earn at least their transfer earnings either in another already existing LMF or in their own newly established enterprise. Are there any grounds for presuming that the pattern of rewards for skill would be any different to that arising under capitalism? In the Jay model, at least initially, it might be presumed that the LMFs would in fact inherit the skill and relative earnings distribution from the preceding capitalist mode. If so, we may ask whether forces would operate to change this pattern in ways which would not have occurred under capitalism and what such changes might imply for the economy?

At the same time consideration has to be given to the acquisition of skills. It has been found useful to distinguish between two types of training; specific, which raises the productivity of the worker only in the firm that provides the training, and general, which raises the productivity of the worker to all firms. Whilst there is a relationship between productivity and wages it is easy to see that workers would have an interest in paying for general training, whilst the firm may be prepared to pay for specific training.[21] Vanek argues strongly that the LMF would provide an environment more conducive to the provision of training than its 'capitalist twin'. Using the distinction above we may expect that this would be specific training, because the worker is more tied to the enterprise in an LMF economy. In terms of adjustments to skill requirements we may predict that the LMF would have the incentive to do this internally through retraining which may be slower than for a firm making a readjustment through a change in hiring. However, the firm's decisions being taken by workers may lead to a greater

[20] See the excellent discussion in Vanek, op. cit., Chapter 11.
[21] G. S. Becker, *Human Capital*, National Bureau of Economic Research, 1964.

provision of general training sponsored by the firm, which may be one way in which the workers could attempt to spread their risks.

Finance

In the standard comparison of the LMF with the capitalist firm, not only is the production function assumed to be the same, but also the capital market is presumed identical. In some cases the comparison is conducted in terms of a pure rental economy, but a careful discussion of the nature of the capital market under the two regimes and the implications for performance and control is essential if the viability of the LMF is to be established (see p. 00). There are a number of issues here.

Furubotn has argued that when dealing with leased capital goods workers can be expected to show little interest in protecting and preserving the equipment.[22] Rather they will tend to use rented assets unsparingly, maximizing returns in the short run, whilst minimizing or avoiding completely necessary maintenance services. Similarly, when borrowing takes place, efforts will be made to shift the repayment burden into the future, which may well be on to future groups of workers. These problems arise because workers do not have perpetual claims on the firm's net cash flows. However, this conclusion seems to depend on the rules for membership which would not appear to meet the Meade criteria outlined above. Further, the analysis seems to show no cognizance of the fact that shareholders can transfer their rights. If a particular set of property rights emerged in the LMF then the Furubotn analysis would have some substance but there is no *a priori* reason why this particular structure should occur. The obvious extreme implications on capital owners would surely lead them to attempt to respecify the contractual arrangements.

As Steinherr has argued[23] the investment behaviour of the LMF depends on the precise property rights structure. As he points out, if workers only acquire *usufructus* of the assets of the firm, these assets must promise a higher rate of return than a savings account or any other owned asset if the two investment alternatives are to be considered equally attractive. This arises because the member of the LMF cannot recoup his investment: therefore £1 invested in the LMF yields

[22] E. G. Furubotn, 'The Long Run Analysis of the Labour Managed Firm', *American Economic Review*, 66, March 1976.
[23] A. Steinherr, 'The Labour Managed Economy: A Survey of the Economics Literature', *Annals of Public and Co-operative Economy*, April–June 1978.

a return of $(1 + r)^t - 1$ whereas £1 invested in a savings account yields $(1 + i)^t$. Therefore, for the total returns to be equal $r > i$. The problem only occurs under self-financing and non-ownership of the assets. It is for this reason that Vanek has convincingly argued that self-finance is inappropriate for the LMF[24] — for it would lead to under-investment *vis-à-vis* a capitalist firm. But he himself argues that full external financing would not be provided by the conventional banking system. Thus on Vanek's argument the capital market itself militates against any coexistence of capitalist and LMFs. This, of course, is a totally distinct point from our arguments in the preceding section. A state organization such as a Lange-type planning agency is required which, it is argued, would have the ability to set the price of capital at the 'correct' level.

James Meade in a frequently quoted passage has pertinently noted that 'while property owners can spread risks by putting small bits of their property into a large number of concerns, a worker cannot easily put small bits of his effort into a large number of different jobs.'[25] The inability of labour to spread risks, he suggests, is likely to confine the LMF to activities subject to little fluctuation in the demand for the product and labour-intensive activities. The degree of risk from product market fluctuation can be offset at least to some extent by product diversification. There has been little, if any, discussion of investment strategies of the LMF in terms of product range decisions. Would the LMF, for instance, tend to be more diversified than the capitalist firm? Given any necessary economies of scale, increased diversification would imply a larger size of firm but it is generally thought that the effectiveness of the LMF is a declining function of size. Herein may lie one of the essential paradoxes of the co-operative economy!

However, financial arrangements can be made which seek to spread the risks between labour and capital.[26] Drèze examines the case where the LMF is financed by a combination of financial instruments: bonds, negotiable shares of stocks issued on the market, and non-negotiable shares of stock issued to workers. Where the shares issued on the stock

[24] J. Vanek, 'The Basic Theory of Financing of Participatory Firms', in J. Vanek (ed.), *Self-Management: Economic Liberation of Man*, Penguin 1975.

[25] J. Meade, 'The Theory of Labour-Managed Firms and of Profit Sharing', op. cit., p. 426.

[26] For an interesting discussion of risk in agricultural production and the role of share-cropping see D. M. G. Newbery and J. E. Stiglitz, 'Share Cropping, Risk Sharing and the Importance of Imperfect Information', *Economic Theory Discussion Paper No. 8*, Department of Applied Economics, University of Cambridge, 1979.

market are similar to those issued to workers it can be shown that it is always desirable for the LMF to issue shares on the *market* representing all of future output. Therefore the labour-managed economy requires a stock market and efficiency considerations necessitate that control rights are vested in shareholders. The second case, where the shares are different, is more difficult but Drèze tentatively concludes that some form of participatory decision-making of both labour and capital is called for. Again another paradox emerges. The fundamental objective of worker-control in the LMF seems incompatible with the necessary financing arrangements given the existence of private property rights in risky assets.

LMFs and Trade Unions

The major literature on labour-managed firms contains no reference to the existence of organized labour on an inter-firm or intra-occupational basis in the labour-managed economy. The implication is clearly that workers' representative desires are all met within the firm, and that trade unions therefore have no role to play. However, the issue is not so simple as this. If we are to consider either a transition from a traditional capitalist to an LMF economy, or an economy in which both forms of organization exist side by side, trade unions cannot be ignored. From the trade union point of view the fact that one now observes that money wages are rigid downwards is regarded as a major achievement of the movement in protecting the interests of those who are members of that union. Others regard this as a major problem in the necessary readjustment of a complex economy. Divided loyalties, vested personal interest, and a requirement that workers accept income flexibility of some form associated with their share of the risks in a labour-managed enterprise all pose problems for the emergence and stability of LMFs. Strong unions have consistently been able to improve the position of their members *vis-à-vis* non-union members, and members of weak and poorly organized sectors through the use of restrictive labour practices. They have been able to extract benefits from employers who have then sought to maintain profitability, where possible, through the use of similar restrictive measures in the product market. Eventually it is argued the consumer always pays. Restrictive practices amongst private enterprise firms in western economies have been widespread and pervasive. Restrictive labour practices are seen by some to be the root cause of many of Britain's economic problems. Will this propensity to collude, in both spheres, simply disappear under an economy of labour-managed firms as many advocates seem to believe?

It may be argued that, rather than disappearing, the collusive power against consumers (and Government?) may well be strengthened. The synonymity of 'bosses' and 'workers' may well mean that the power of trade union activities could be combined with the returns to commercial collusion to produce a much more harmful restriction of competition.

As Meade has noted,[27] the competitive pressures of free entry play a much more important role in a co-operative economy than they do in a capitalist system. Trade union activity of a particular form could therefore offer significant benefits to certain groups if they could organize on an inter-firm basis to erect entry barriers. They could directly increase the earnings per worker in the affected firms.

Organization on occupational lines depends upon the attitudes to the income/skill distribution and the means by which relativities are established. If the distribution were truly exogenous then there would be no room for craft or occupational unions. However, if some means exist by which groups of workers could restrict access to training and entry to occupations they could gain through an ability to change their place in the schedule. One might, therefore, expect some incentive for the formation of organized groups of workers under the LMF system analogous to a craft trade union.

If one started from a pure labour-managed economy then it might be possible to argue that the emergence of unions, or their equivalent, may not occur given a particular legal environment.

If a labour-managed economy were to replace an existing arrangement within which trade unions and professional associations have become dominant in certain sectors, it seems highly unlikely that such potential power would just wither away. A systematic, rigorous analysis of the scope and potential effect of collusive arrangements between LMFs or particular groups of workers within an LMF, is urgently required. We have merely suggested some of the implications. In the absence of such an analysis we do not find Peter Jay's arguments convincing (paras 97–113) and would be more inclined towards Brittan's[28] view that 'there is no reason to suppose that industry-wide monopolistic behaviour by organized workers would stop.'

[27] J. E. Meade, op. cit.
[28] *The Economic Consequences of Democracy*, p. 203.

A Middle Way?

Despite the increased attention devoted to the subject in recent years and the masterly seminal works by Jaroslav Vanek,[29] many vital questions remain unanswered concerning the operation of labour-managed firms within a market environment. In particular we have no clear indication as to whether workers' co-operatives could coexist for any substantial period of time alongside capitalist enterprises. There is a tendency to resort to labour-management when capitalism has failed but this is hardly a fair test of the system.

Mondragon and the other examples discussed by Robert Oakeshott elsewhere in this volume are illuminating and interesting, but it is difficult to assess the long term future of such experiments. It will be particularly interesting to see to what extent they have to surrender their management prerogatives to the providers of capital. In Mondragon the role of the central savings bank (The Caja Laboral Popular) seems crucial to its success. We have used a simple model, the predictions from which suggest that coexistence of pure labour-managed firms of the Vanek type seems unlikely.

The other simple models of the co-operative economy we have argued are based on a rather peculiar view of the scope for short-run adjustment. Economics is not the whole and may not even be the most important aspect of the question, but nevertheless market forces do impose constraints on the freedom of action of individuals to achieve other objectives. Considerations of risk and finance most elegantly dealt with by Meade, Drèze, and others do imply that one of the constraints is the extent to which the workers in the LMF system can retain sole control· of their enterprises. Most of the economic analysis leads to the conclusion that some middle way may be the most efficient and only solution to meeting the legitimate aspirations of human producers sustainable into the long run. The time is long past when we believed that the human agent was a passive perfectly motivated component of a productive system.[30] Some form of joint participation between the surplus of labour and the surplus of capital has already occurred to a large extent; it is the degree of such participation which

---

[29] *The General Theory of Labour Managed Market Economies*, and *The Labour Managed Economy*, op. cit.

[30] The work on the concept of x-inefficiency is a case in point. See e.g. H. Leibenstein, 'Allocative Efficiency versus x-insufficiency', *American Economic Review*, June 1966. G. J. Stigler, 'The x-istence of x-efficiency', *American Economic Review*, June 1976.

is open to doubt. It seems clear to us that such participation should involve a direct link between effort, responsibility, and reward and both the pure capitalist and pure LMF models emphasize the motive force provided by the residual reward. This is one reason, as we have suggested elsewhere,[31] for believing that a compromise as suggested in the Bullock report, and indeed later refinements, is not the way forward.

The discussion by Felix FitzRoy elsewhere in this volume illuminates a similar path to that which our analysis would lead to and suggests the potential supremacy of such a mixed solution. Whatever the predictions of authors, and the outcomes of practical experiments it is clear that the issue is complex and analysis tends to raise more questions than it offers solutions. Despite the energy and resourcefulness of its advocates the pure LMF has barely been elevated above the status of a theoretical curiosity.

---

[31] B. Chiplin and J. Coyne, 'Property Rights and Industrial Democracy', in *Can Workers Manage?*, IEA Hobart Paper 77, 1977.

9. Co-operation and Productivity:
Some Evidence from West German Experience

by John Cable and Felix FitzRoy*

1. *Industrial Partnership Schemes in West Germany*

Somewhere between traditional entrepreneurial firms and workers' co-operatives — on the spectrum of alternative types of firm — lies a range of industrial partnership models, involving varying degrees of worker-participation in decision-making and/or profit-sharing. In West Germany there are known to be more than seven hundred firms in this category, most of them small. Many belong to the Labour Association for the Furthering of Partnership in the Economy — Arbeitsgemeinschaft zur Förderung der Partnerschaft in der Wirtschaft e.V. (AGP) headed by Michael Lezius. Guski and Schneider, in collaboration with Lezius, have recently published a register of these firms. (Guski and Schneider, 1977.) Their analysis reveals a variety of legal configurations, heavily influenced by tax and company law; the size of employee profit and stock shares also varies greatly, most shares being relatively small. About half the firms in the sample have instituted some form of employee participation in what is normally regarded as managerial decision-making. The schemes introduced by AGP members range from employee control in a few worker-managed co-operatives to minimal consultative and informative practice in the larger firms.

This variety of schemes and practices revealed by the Guski and Schneider survey underlines the fact that no single, simple definition of worker-participation or industrial partnership can readily be given. But essentially participation involves at least access for workers to

*We are extremely grateful to the many firms who responded to our questionnaire and to Michael Lezius of the AGP. We should also like to thank for their helpful comments and suggestions Keith Cowling, Paul Kleindorfer, Bridger Mitchell, Dennis Mueller, Hans Nutzinger, Aubrey Silberston, Christian von Weizsäcker, and Bernhard Wilpert, together with F. C. Heng and Hartmuth Lohmann for programming assistance.

This is a revised version of a paper with the same title in *Economic Analysis*, 1, 1980.

information which is normally confined to management and, in most cases, some involvement also in the decision-making which traditionally defines the managerial function. It in general falls short of full workers' control.

The AGP members' schemes are voluntary. They are formally quite distinct from the system set up by the German Codetermination Laws, under which German firms with over 2,000 employees are required to have worker-directors on their supervisory boards, although they may have been indirectly influenced and encouraged by the legislative developments and the discussions surrounding them.*

The promotion of industrial democracy in some form is now a public policy objective in many countries. (See Garson, 1977, for a survey.) However very few, if any, results exist quantifying the impact of industrial partnership on economic performance. As a result some important questions remain unanswered. In particular, we cannot with confidence say whether the improvements in the quality of working life that might result from a move along the continuum from traditional enterprises to worker-control are available without loss of economic efficiency or whether, as some fear, they must be bought at a heavy resource cost. Still less are we able to judge whether or not industrial partnership, by combining certain of the characteristics of both traditional firms and labour-managed enterprises, might lead to superior economic performance to that of either of the two more extreme types of firm.

The comparatively well-documented German sample provides an excellent opportunity to make headway on these matters. With the co-operation of Michael Lezius and members of the AGP, the authors carried out an analysis of the impact of worker-participation and various types of profit-sharing on a number of aspects of economic efficiency. In selecting this emphasis, it should be stressed, we in no way wish to detract from the importance of other kinds of effect and benefit. Rather, we focus on this aspect as being an area particularly lacking in information at the moment.

We begin with an analysis of certain defects in the structure of traditional firms which worker-participation and profit-sharing might ameliorate. Our main concern is with the employment relation.

---

*The indirect influence of Codetermination law is discussed further in Section 5.

2. Defects in the Structure of Traditional Firms

Unlike most contractual arrangements in market economies, employment is usually a continuing relationship. To a large extent this may be traced to the prevalence of job-specific labour skills, which render mobility of labour costly both to the workers themselves and to employers. For the worker, skills learned on-the-job are often less productive or inapplicable elsewhere. Consequently to leave a job is risky, as well as involving search and transport costs. But the employer too faces major costs in replacing the specific skills embodied in his existing labour force, while much installed capital is also task-specific and immobile. Over a wide range of outcomes, employers and workers are thus stuck with each other.

Added to this, as has been emphasized in the economics literature, the complexity of production processes and uncertainty over future developments make it infeasible to regulate employment by means of detailed and explicit contracts covering every future contingency. As a result tacit or informal agreements are generally concluded, under which workers accept employers' authority to direct productive activity within certain limits. But because each side can inflict heavy costs on the other without their terminating the relationship, the traditional firm then becomes a bargaining arena, prone to conflict and endemic mistrust.

On the one hand the individual worker, immobilized by his specific skills, becomes open to employers' opportunism. In this situation collusion amongst workers and formalized collective-bargaining agreements are the rational response. With the tables now turned on themselves, employers will in turn seek counter-measures of their own. One strategy recommended by traditional economists is to resort to individual incentives. According to the traditional argument, individual incentives are superior to group incentives because a worker receives only a small fraction of his marginal product under a group incentive like profit-sharing, but receives all the benefits from shirking or leisure on-the-job. (See for example Alchian and Demsetz, 1972.) However in practice individual incentive schemes are unlikely to succeed since, as we have seen, workers' truly 'rational' motivation in the usual social context of productive organization is for collusive and strategic behaviour; (Fox, 1974; Oakeshott, 1978) and there is abundant evidence of 'negative collusion' to restrict output under traditional piecework schemes, where informal social sanctions and even violence against 'rate-busters' have a lengthy history.

More subtle forms of destructive effect on productive co-operation and communication in a closely-knit organization, arising from the rivalry for individual rewards and promotion, are also likely, yet entirely neglected in the traditional economists' analysis. Thus, distorting information-flows to obtain personal benefit is widely observed in such situations, whether by exaggerating one's own performance or denigrating a rival's. Faced with this kind of behaviour employers then find that increased monitoring costs must be incurred to counteract dishonesty.

Alternatively, employers may resort to ever-finer division of labour and specialization of tasks, in order simultaneously to aid supervision and to reduce the costs to themselves of replacing existing labour and training new workers. When they do this, work is de-skilled and workers' autonomy and job-satisfaction reduced, thereby adding to conflict and endemic mistrust as labour and capital expend resources on the socially unproductive activity of attempting to extend or defend their share of jointly produced wealth. (See Edwards, 1979.)

3. *Industrial Partnership as a Means of Joint-Wealth Maximization?*

Participatory firms — with or without profit-sharing — will produce better outcomes than traditional firms if the *negative* collusion to maximize one party's share, described above, can be replaced by *positive* collusion to maximize joint wealth. The hypothesis that worker-participation might achieve this effect would run as follows.

The negative collusion in traditional firms, together with associated behaviour including strike threats, stems from the fact that this is perceived as the only available method of countering employers' opportunism. However, the hypothesis runs, when workers participate in decisions affecting their jobs — in managerial activities — they acquire an alternative and more direct means of achieving this end. Moreover, when decisions are in some sense jointly taken, they are more likely to be regarded as fair. It should follow that such decisions will receive a readier acceptance and be implemented more efficiently.

However, workers are unlikely to agree to co-operate in maximizing the joint wealth of owners and employees (including non-pecuniary components) while some parts of that wealth accrue wholly to others — especially the residual element, profits, whose size depends most critically on effort and on decisions taken. Hence, if they agree to co-operate they will also require a share of profit, or any surplus above contractual rents and wages. Looking at it from the other viewpoint, participation with profit-sharing is much more likely to yield positive results than participation alone. We thus arrive at the conclusion that profit-sharing should motivate efficient behaviour. As we have seen, this contradicts received and authoritative opinion (see for example Samuelson, 1977), at least insofar as this is thought still to be valid in participatory settings. The divergence between our expectation and the orthodox one arises because we take explicit account of the social interaction among individuals at work in an organizational setting which is entirely neglected in the orthodox approach. Thus, with regard to the shirking problem, if the numbers involved in a group incentive like profit-sharing are not too large, and shirking imposes perceptible losses on co-workers with whom there is some personal interaction, then 'positive collusion' and 'horizontal monitoring' to encourage effort is the rational response for the peer group. Thus under group incentives, we would predict a reversal of the widely observed 'negative collusion' to restrict output which occurs under traditional piece-pay schemes.

The interaction between participation and profit-sharing is important and merits further exploration. It certainly seems reasonable that profit-sharing will seem to have more point to workers when they have some say in managerial decisions which determine the level of profitability. To the extent that this is so, the motivating effect of profit-sharing should increase. Moreover, when participation is present, workers may both be able to see a reliable connection between their individual effort and received profit shares, and also have less reason to fear that entrepreneurial opportunism will deprive them of the fruits of their extra labour. Conversely, in the absence of participation, profit-shares are likely to be regarded as random and unrelated to workers' effort, while fear of expropriation will be high in the typical low-trust, conflict-prone organization. In these circumstances — without participation — both the orthodox view of profit-sharing, and the preference of workers for wage increases rather than profit-related bonuses under collective bargaining, become understandable.

From our earlier arguments it is clear that the form which profit-sharing takes is important. What is required is a reward structure related to the performance of the firm as a whole. Profit-sharing in a literal sense via profits-linked bonuses etc. and other group incentive schemes have the advantage of not creating an incentive for disruptive, individually competitive, rivalrous behaviour. Individual incentives, on the other hand, are more uncertain in their effects. Unless they are devised in such a way as to penalize rivalrous actions (such as distorted signals, obstructing fellow workers, and lack of initiative in situations which do not affect one's own standing), the disruptive effects of such rivalry may still outweigh the incentive effects, even under the positive influence of participation in raising trust and fostering co-operation.

A final question remains, which is whether we may expect a gradual continuous improvement in firm performance as we move from traditional firms to full participatory, profit-sharing ones, with the improvement beginning at quite low levels of both participation and profit-sharing, or whether it is necessary to exceed some perhaps quite high threshold level of both before any significant improvement occurs. Ultimately this question can be answered only by reference to the empirical evidence. But it can be argued that even limited elements of participation or partnership are likely to generate a loyalty and attachment to the workplace which is rationally founded in the knowledge that personal prospects including promotion and job security depend heavily on the firm's growth and the profitability necessary to finance new investment. Thus, as the contractual status of labour becomes closer to partnership, incentives for joint-wealth maximizing co-operative behaviour should become progressively more powerful. Nevertheless, the uncertainty about where significant changes in performance occur as participation increases remains sufficient to make it advisable in empirical work to test both for gradual changes across the board and for discontinuous differences between groups of firms located towards the extreme ends of the spectrum.

4. *Experience of Participation and Profit-Sharing amongst AGP Firms* *

Our evidence on how participation and profit-sharing works in practice was obtained via a questionnaire designed in co-operation with Lezius, and sent to AGP members. The final sample selected for our analysis contained 42 firms. These firms were distributed over a wide range of mainly manufacturing industries. Their size varied from as few as 20 employees to around 6,000. None of the few existing co-operatives supplied data, but several of the firms who did respond are well known for the efforts of their owners or managers to introduce democratic practices into their internal decision-making processes.

*For a more detailed account of the data sources and statistical method see Cable and FitzRoy (1979).

Most of the information which was supplied consisted of accounting or other 'objective' data: statistics on numbers employed, sales, wages and salaries, dividends, capital employed, and so forth. For the great majority of firms in our sample were unquoted, GmbH companies, and because of the minimal information disclosure requirements binding this type of German company,* this information is not publicly available. The responding firms also supplied subjective evaluations of the degree of worker-involvement in various areas of decision making. Four of the areas were concerned with essentially job-related issues: the wage system; production methods; job design; and determination of piece-work bonuses, etc. However, the remainder extended into the highest reaches of firm strategy, covering advertising, product design, price policy, and investment policy. Each firm described itself either as having 'no participation' or as having workers involved as 'observers', as 'advisers', or as 'active participants'.

The information on participation has obvious limitations, in particular its subjectivity and onesidedness (coming wholly from management). The most serious bias it is likely to contain is a systematic tendency to overstate the degree of worker-participation. However this causes comparatively few problems for our purpose, which is to assess the effect of different *relative* degrees of participation between firms or groups of firms, rather than to measure the extent of worker-participation in absolute terms. In future work we propose to extend and refine the participation data with the aid of interviewing and detailed case studies. Meanwhile, the qualitative data provided through the questionnaire produced some interesting results in our preliminary analysis.

In order to measure the effects of participation on productivity we required quantitative indices of the degree of worker-participation in the sample firms. These we derived from the qualitative, questionnaire data, taking account of both the purposes of workers' presence and the topics discussed. The practical problem was to determine an appropriate weighting structure for the different purpose categories and decision-making areas, in order to derive a points score for each firm. Unfortunately there is to our knowledge no economic or sociological theory from which to derive an operational weighting scheme. We therefore experimented with many different specifications and schemes,

*Private companies – Gesellschaften mit beschränkter Haftung – are on average much smaller than public companies – Aktiengesellschaften (AG) – but numerically predominant in West Germany.

but found our results generally insensitive to the choice of weights over a fairly wide range. Two measures finally emerged which yielded results as good as or better than others, while using very simple weighting schemes. The first (P_1) attributed weights of 0, 1, 2, and 3 to 'no participation', 'observer', 'adviser', and 'active participation' respectively, and equal, unit weights for each decision-making area except for advertising, which attracted a zero weight, as being of marginal importance. The maximum P_1 score was thus 21, which very few of the 42 firms achieve. The second participation variable (P_S) used the same weighting structure for the degree of participation in each area, but was confined to the three 'strategic' decision making areas (investment, price, and product policy).

The questionnaire responses also yielded three variables relating to financial incentives offered to workers. The first, and quantitatively most important, was total employee remuneration in the form of incentive pay (I). Our impression is that this consisted mainly of piecework earnings, so that this variable must be seen as relating to the type of incentive about which our theoretical arguments were ambiguous or sceptical. The two other incentives variables were total profits distributed to workers (Π_E) and workers' capital (M). Unlike (I), these are related more to over-all performance than to individual effort, and may be expected to operate via peer-group pressure. Inspection of the data did not, interestingly, indicate that Π_E and M are confined mainly to white- rather than blue-collar workers, but the total amounts reported were typically very small.

To isolate and quantify the effects of worker-participation and incentives on firm performance, all of the above variables were incorporated in mutliple regression equations explaining differences in value-added (Y) across the firms in the sample, alongside other variables suggested by economic theory. The other variables comprised (various) measures of capital employed (K); white- and blue-collar labour input (L_W, L_B), included separately to permit later analysis of the differential effects of participation and incentives on production workers and others; and a series of eighteen industry dummy-variables, included to normalize for such influences as inter-industry differences in technology and market structure amongst the firms in our sample. Cross-sectional observations of the 42 firms in the years 1974–6 were pooled to form a single sample of 126 observations, and time-dummies for the years 1975 and 1976 were added to allow for changes in relevant prices and in economic conditions from year to year (and found to be significant). Following orthodox economic theory and previous empirical work, the logarithms of the continuous variables were used in estimation. In effect, the regression model shows the effects of participation and incentives by the way in which these variables shift the 'normal' relationship between output and factor inputs within the firm.

Using the P_1 participation variable the following results were obtained:*

$$(\ln Y) = -0.558 + 0.001 \ln K + 0.335 \ln L_W + 0.671 \ln L_B$$
$$\quad\quad (-4.70) \quad (0.02) \quad\quad (8.17) \quad\quad\quad (16.38)$$

$$-0.008 \ln M - 0.013 \ln I + 0.010 \ln \Pi_E + 0.149 \ln P_1$$
$$\quad (-1.11) \quad\quad (-2.34) \quad\quad (1.51) \quad\quad\quad (4.16)$$

$$\bar{R}^2 = 0.988.$$

Overall, the model explains 99 per cent of the observed differences in value-added across the sample, but this very high figure is due to the type of model used and should not be given undue emphasis. Of most interest for our analysis is the statistically significant and positive coefficient attracted by the P_1 variable. The incentives variables, however, do not perform well in this equation. I is statistically significant and negative, which could indicate the overriding influence of the disruptive aspects of individual incentives, discussed earlier, but both Π_E and M are statistically insignificant and M also attracts a coefficient of 'wrong' sign. Of the other reported variables, the labour input coefficients are highly significant and of plausible magnitude, but the results for the capital input variable are, in this case, unsatisfactory.

The estimated effect on value-added of an increase in participation in this equation is quite large: a rise of 1.5 per cent for a 10 per cent increase in the P_1 index. Thus, for example, a firm scoring 15 on the P_1 scale would, other things being equal, produce 7.5 per cent more output than a firm scoring only 10. A very similar result was obtained when P_1 was replaced by the participation variable relating only to strategic questions of investment, price, and product policy: P_S. This appears to suggest that, from the viewpoint of raising productivity, the existence of worker-participation on employment-related issues is

*Time and industry dummy-coefficients are not reported. t values in parenthesis.

immaterial, and it is the sharing of the highest level managerial prerogatives concerning economic strategy which is crucial in distinguishing
participatory from non-participatory firms. However, there may be
other considerations that need to be taken into account. In their recent
study of the development of economic democracy under the Allende
government in Chile, Espinosa and Zimbalist found that worker-
involvement usually began over work-related issues, with which workers
had previous direct experience, and only later spread to technical
questions and economic policy matters. (Espinosa and Zimbalist,
1978.) This sequence seems intuitively plausible. If true of the firms
in our sample, it could imply that the P_S variable identifies not only
the firms with participatory practices in strategic decision-making, as
intended, but also those with the longest experience of participatory
practices of any kind. These firms would have had more opportunity
to solve the problems arising from the adoption of participation
schemes, and to have hit on the most effective procedures for joint
decision-making in their own special circumstances. Clearly, this would
tend to lead to improvements in the effectiveness of participation in
all areas. Moreover, more time would have elapsed for the effects of
jointly taken decisions to work through to observed firm performance.
Unfortunately our questionnaire could not elicit information on the
length of time since the introduction of participation schemes in individual firms. From other sources, however, we know that the spread of
worker-participation increased significantly just prior to and during the
period of our study in the first half of the 1970s.* Thus there would
seem to be a distinct possibility that the P_S variable is picking up time-
related effects as well as effects due to codetermination in particular
areas. A further, separate possibility is that in some cases firms responding to our questionnaire may have interpreted 'participation' over the
wage system and piecework rates to include what are in effect collective
bargaining procedures. Clearly these ought not to be reflected in our
participation index, being characteristic of traditional rather than

*There were significant developments at the legal level over the period: the
1972 amendment of the 1952 Works Constitution Law (Betriebsverfassungsgesetz)
and the new Codetermination Law of 1976. The direct impact of the legislation
on our firms would not have been very great (for example the 1976 legislation
affects only firms with over 2,000 employees, of which there are only four in our
sample). But the encouraging climate of political opinion no doubt both reflected
and reinforced a more positive attitude in industry, especially among the member
firms of the AGP. For a succinct outline of the West German law, see Nutzinger
(1977).

participatory firms. Given the way the variables are defined, P_1 may have been distorted in this way, but this is unlikely in the case of P_S. Resolving these uncertainties over the participation data and consequently over the interpretation of the regression results for alternative indices is one of the priorities for our further work.

The regression model considered so far allows only for a restricted effect of participation on   efficiency. By simply adding a separate participation variable to the model, we provide only for a 'disembodied effect'. In practice we should expect participation effects also to work through to efficiency by enhancing the productivities of labour and capital inputs to the production process, which are reflected in the coefficients of these variables. Moreover, as we stressed in our earlier theoretical discussion, there are strong grounds for expecting an interaction between participation and the various incentive payments. Again the need is to allow the estimated coefficients for these variables to vary with participation itself.

A method of achieving this which avoids the statistical problems likely to be encountered with other methods is to divide the sample into 'high-' and 'low-participation' subsamples and estimate separate equations for each group. Two coefficients for each variable then emerge, differing to the extent that participation affects or does not affect the variable concerned, while any remaining disembodied participation effects will be captured by the difference, if any, in the first, constant term in the equations. The penalty for proceeding in this way is that, having divided the sample in two, and focused on the differences *between* the groups, we obscure the effects, if any, of variations in the degree of participation *within* the groups. However, as we stressed earlier, there are in any case good grounds to test for discontinuous increases in the effects of participation between groups, rather than for a continuous, gradual increase across the whole spectrum of firms.

A critical value of P at which to divide the sample was not imposed arbitrarily, but found experimentally following a conventional statistical method. Thus we carried out the analysis repeatedly, dividing the sample at various values of P over an extensive range in which the critical value was expected to lie. The critical value was then identified as that at which the explanatory power of the equations was at a maximum. In the case of P_1 this proved to be where the high participation group included firms with a score of 13 or more. Interestingly, in view of our previous discussion, this value requires a firm to have some degree of participation in 'strategic' decision areas, even if participation elsewhere is at a maximum, for inclusion in the high group.

By pure coincidence, the high and low groups thus defined contained an equal number of firms. The high participation group firms on average employed 914 workers compared with only 584 in low participation firms, but capital per man in the latter was much higher at 90,400 DM per man compared with 66,900 DM per man. The firms in the two groups were on average identical or nearly so in terms of the proportion of white-collar workers, hourly manual wages, and average earnings and hours per man.

The separate results for the two groups proved to be statistically different from each other as a whole,* and were as follows:

High group

$$(\ln Y) = -0.141 + 0.171 \ln K + 0.251 \ln L_W + 0.487 \ln L_B$$
$$(-0.44) \quad (2.15) \qquad (2.38) \qquad\quad (6.18)$$

$$+ 0.026 \ln M + 0.006 \ln I + 0.059 \ln \Pi_E; \quad \bar{R}^2 = 0.995.$$
$$(2.11) \qquad\quad (0.96) \qquad (7.24)$$

Low group

$$(\ln Y) = -0.039 + 0.128 \ln K + 0.375 \ln L_W + 0.489 \ln L_B$$
$$(-0.40) \quad (2.35) \qquad (11.88) \qquad\quad (10.72)$$

$$- 0.166 \ln M - 0.003 \ln I - 0.012 \ln \Pi_E; \quad \bar{R}^2 = 0.996.$$
$$(-2.46) \qquad\quad (-0.45) \qquad (-1.40)$$

No suggestion of a disembodied effect of participation on productivity remains in these equations, since neither of the intercept terms is statistically different from zero. However, efficiency differences do now appear that are embodied in the productivity of the three factor inputs. The coefficients for the relevant variables in these equations show the proportional increase in output that would result from given increases in the input level of each factor. To obtain an estimate of the actual increase in output that would result from a unit increase in each factor (i.e. the marginal product) we multiply each coefficient by the

*The Chow test yielded an F-value of 6.98, around four times the required critical value at the 5 per cent level.

average value of output per unit of the factor in question for each group. The estimated marginal products on this basis are:

	High Participation Firms	Low Participation Firms
Marginal Product of:		
Manual Workers (per hour)	13.87 DM	15.93 DM
Non-Manual Workers (per annum)	26029.00 DM	33414.00 DM
Capital (per 100 DM)	12.00 DM	3.00 DM

Thus labour productivity is higher in low participation firms, by some 15 per cent for manual workers and 28 per cent for non-manual workers. However, capital is four times as productive at the margin in high participation firms. This reversal is as we would expect from orthodox economic theory, in view of the relative scarcity of labour in the former, and capital in the latter. It may, however, be doubted that in determining unit costs the relatively modest excess labour productivity in low participation firms would outweigh the huge difference the other way in the productivity of capital. Moreover, when the statistical analysis was repeated for high and low participation firms classified according to the P_S index rather than P_1, manual worker productivity in low participation firms was only 13 per cent higher; non-manual productivity was actually 8.8 per cent less than in high participation firms; and capital productivity remained $3\frac{1}{3}$ times lower. Overall, these results generate a strong suspicion of lower over-all performance in low participation firms, due either to the choice of over capital-intensive methods or the inefficient utilization of capital or both.

This suspicion is confirmed by the evidence on over-all performance in the two groups. Thus the high participation firms on average outperformed the low group by 5 per cent, 177 per cent, and 33 per cent respectively in terms of output per man, output per unit of capital, and profitability (rate of return on capital employed) over the period of our study.

The differences in the effectiveness of economic incentives as between participatory and non-participatory firms that were anticipated in our theoretical discussion come through strongly in the regression results reported above. Thus in the equation for high participation firms, all three of the relevant variables exert a positive influence on output, and the two coefficients related to group incentives, M and Π_E, are statistically significant at the normal confidence levels. By contrast, in the low participation group all three coefficients are negative and one significantly so.

However, these differences were much less clear-cut when the high and low participation groups were classified according to the P_S index. Then, the results for *both* groups were very similar to those for the low participation group in the equation reported above, with the exception that the Π_E coefficient was positive, though very small and insignificantly different from zero. Taken together the results seem to imply an asymmetry in the interaction between participation and incentives: that incentives are effective only when participation covers work-related issues, but that participation (over strategic issues) can produce productivity gains by other means than via incentives.

The questionnaire returns yielded information on a number of other dimensions of economic performance. Much of this information has yet to be analysed in depth, but an initial survey suggests four preliminary conclusions.

First, there appears to be no difference between the high and low participation firms in either of two performance variables often used as proxies for 'alienation' or job-discontent: absenteeism and quit rates. Thus, on this evidence, worker-participation of the type under observation does not radically transform the work situation in a way or to a degree which is reflected in these variables. The only evidence which might conceivably be consistent with reduced 'alienation' is that earnings were no higher in the larger, high participation firms. The absence of a significant increase in wages with firm size was confirmed by a regression of hourly wage rates on relevant variables, and contrasts with Scherer's finding of a significant positive relationship between wage-rates and establishment size (Scherer, 1976), which he associated with the need to pay more in large firms to offset the higher 'alienation' levels to be expected there according to survey results.

Secondly, over the years 1972–6 of our data, which go from boom through recession to (partial) recovery, output at constant prices grew twice as fast in the low participation sample, although the high group itself turned in an above-average performance, leading GDP growth by four percentage points. Thus in this one respect the low participation firms have the better record — unless, that is, we are witnessing worker-participation acting as a constraint on the pursuit of growth as a managerial objective. (See Baumol, 1962; and Marris, 1964.) For beyond some limit, such growth would be excessive from the point of view of social welfare.

Thirdly, from 1972 to the recession year 1975, total employment fell by 12.1 per cent in high participation firms, compared with only 9.8 per cent in low participation firms. Unless explained wholly by technological factors associated with the greater capital-intensity of production in low participation firms, this is clearly at odds with the suggestions often made that worker-participation will lead to what in management eyes appears as downward rigidity in manning levels, and appears to workers as greater job security.

Finally, over the five years to 1976 output per man rose by more than 17 per cent in high participation firms compared with only 4.2 per cent in the low group. So great was the difference that the productivity level ranking reversed over the five-year period, high participation firms starting at only 93 per cent of the level of output per man in low participation firms, and finishing 5 per cent above them. This is of interest for at least two reasons. First, as we have already observed, we know from other sources that the first half of the 1970s was a period in which there was a significant spread of worker-participation in Germany. The relative growth of high participation firms' productivity could, therefore, reflect growth in the development of participation itself. Secondly, the fact that the high participation firms began with lower output per man tends to discount the argument that might otherwise be put, that worker-participation is a luxury which only the successful can afford, and that the in general superior performance we have observed in participatory firms stems from other causes.

5. *Concluding Remarks*

On the evidence available to us the participation and profit-sharing schemes adopted by AGP members have led to significant gains in their economic performance. These gains may even have been understated in our results. Bearing in mind the spread of participation that occurred in Germany during the period we studied, it may be that within our sample the introduction of participation has been quite recent. If so, the effects we have observed are unlikely to capture the impact of participation in full. In particular, at least some of the high participation firms are likely to have been experiencing transactions costs from the transition to more worker-involvement: developing and learning to operate new decision-making routines and so forth. Then our estimates of the impact on efficiency would contain a systematic downward bias.

The firms in our sample all lie in the middle ground between classical hierarchical organization and worker-control. Although economic performance seems to increase most distinctly with participation and profit-sharing in this region, it would not be legitimate to extrapolate this trend to these more extreme types of firm. Thus our results strictly do not permit a ranking of 'classical', co-operative, and intermediate firms in terms of productive efficiency. They do, however, render untenable the argument that any degree of worker-participation, whatever its advantages in terms of human aspirations and quality of working life, comes at a high price in terms of resource costs and efficiency loss, and this is of direct relevance to the policy measures now being taken in many countries to promote and extend industrial democracy in some form.

In view of the private efficiency gains found, it may seem surprising that such public policy measures should be needed, and that worker-participation is not already more widespread. Indeed, critics (e.g. Pejovich, 1978) of industrial democracy argue, by analogy with the Darwinian principle of natural selection, that only efficient organizations will survive the rigours of competition. If participation has not become widespread in the course of industrialization, then – the argument goes – it must be generally inefficient. Hence legislation encouraging any form of industrial democracy represents merely another step in the continuing erosion of property rights by using the power of the state through the political process to transfer wealth from owners of capital to special interest groups such as workers.*

However this critique has two main weaknesses. First the critics have tended to concentrate on one particular variant, namely codetermination. This – originally West German – system of union representation on supervisory boards seems to alter property rights in favour of labour, and certainly gives union officials new access to managerial information, if not the necessary majority to sway crucial decisions. Codetermination should thus enhance the 'voice' channels of communication between unions and management which Freeman (1976) has emphasized. However it is far from obvious that the bargaining 'power' of a union is thereby increased. In the steel industry, for example, there is evidence that the United Steel Workers of America has secured significant improvements in relative wages (at least for

---

*Both the substance and the language of the critique in some ways recall classical arguments against 'combinations' of workmen and unionization in its earliest phases. It is therefore interesting to note that unionization has been found to enhance productivity in the US, even where capital, training, and various worker characteristics are controlled for (Brown and Medof, 1978).

those with steady employment), and done much better for its members than has its codetermining German counterpart. The latter recently called the first steel strike in fifty years, and union board-representatives have shown no tendency to act as radical redistributors.

Secondly, the critique fails to take into account the productivity-enhancing role of co-operation and participation. At the same time, there is a valid aspect to the critique of industrial democracy, concerned with its possible redistributive effects. Paradoxically, this has not been formulated clearly by the traditionalist critics, because of their failure to appreciate the full role of co-operation in production. (But see FitzRoy, 1974, for an early version.)

For instance, it is not implausible that participation will reduce the (marginal) productivity of white-collar or administrative personnel below the level it would otherwise reach, as their exclusive decision-making power and access to information is modified. Some evidence of this may perhaps be seen in the lower coefficient (and implied marginal product) of white-collar workers in participatory firms in our regression results above. As long as the earnings of particular groups of workers bear some relation to their productivity, we would expect to find lower white-collar earnings where participation is high. In fact, in our sample of German firms we do not find that earnings of white- (or blue-) collar workers are significantly affected by participation. But this could simply reflect the rather rigid wage structure imposed by collective bargaining in West Germany in the short run, together with the relative novelty of participation schemes.

In the long run it must be regarded as likely that organizational innovations which increase rank-and-file worker skills, whether directly connected with their newly acquired decision-making role or deriving from increased levels of industrial training made worthwhile in partici-patory environments, will lead to higher wages at the lower levels, commensurate with going market-rates for the skills in question. Thus, even when the productivity of the organization as a whole rises, some managerial and supervisory functions may decline in relative and even in absolute importance, and monetary rewards will decline with them. Managerial resistance to innovation of various kinds is therefore to be expected and is in fact both widespread and well documented.* And

---

*For examples of revealing statements by managers, see Rosenthal (1978). One manager who refused to allow distribution of a questionnaire observed (p. 38): 'This company is democratic . . . but when it comes to managerial decisions, every company is a dictatorship . . . these questions are too socialistically inclined.'

opposition from management would constitute a very significant barrier to the spread of participatory practices, given managements' key decision-making role in large, complex firms with widely dispersed shareholders.

The other group likely to suffer a dimunition of role and consequent redistribution of power, status, and ultimately, earnings, are union officials. Again, they have generally been opposed to decentralized participation and profit-sharing schemes in practice. Cogent reasons for their opposition are not far to seek. Workers who share in both the making and the results of decisions can begin to approach the status of partners rather than employees in the traditional master–servant relationship. At the very least, the negotiating role of unions *vis-à-vis* management in collective bargaining would be significantly modified if industrial partnership were practised widely.

In the face of opposition from influential groups likely to lose from the redistributive effects of participation, we may expect schemes to go forward only where little redistribution takes place.* The evidence on gains to workers from our study is fragmentary, and needs to be augmented in future work. But at present workers in the high participation firms do not appear to receive higher earnings, and the proportion of profits distributed to employees was generally quite tiny. Moreover, if quit rates and absenteeism are any guide, changes in the quality of working life, reducing alienation, may have been undramatic, to say the least, while the evidence from employment statistics tends to point away from any significant increase in job security. If the gains to workers have in fact been as meagre as this suggests, and perceived to be so, workers elsewhere may understandably conclude they have little to gain from participation save higher responsibilities. Thus, distorted signals of the potential effects of participation can result in the addition of worker uninterest to managerial and union opposition as impediments to the diffusion of participation.

More generally, all change generates costs, and the contractual relations which define organizations like firms or unions can hardly be fundamentally altered without some redistribution of the benefits. When the gains are diffuse and their nature is not widely appreciated,

---

*It is probably also no accident that the experiments which have taken place have often been pioneered by owner–entrepreneurs with democratic convictions. In addition, smaller firms are probably better suited for participation practices, especially insofar as they do not have complex managerial hierarchies or give rise to the same need for union representation of workers *en masse* as in large firms.

but the costs appear well defined and concentrated among those with most influence and most to lose in the existing hierarchy, then realization of net gains is inevitably a slow process. Thus some form of legislation may be both legitimate and essential to reap the efficiency gains from reducing monopolies in information processing and decision-making held by management and, to some extent, unions, and encouraging learning processes involved in productive co-operation and participation.

The design of policy measures to secure benefits from co-operation is clearly a complex matter, and requires much more research before legislation can be put on a scientific footing. But clearly the blanket enforcement of any rigid system, whether based on German co-determination practice or any other model, could inhibit the variety of organizational innovation conducive to individual initiative at grass roots level. As we observed earlier, codetermination laws could have positive indirect effects on attitudes towards participatory practice. Conversely, ill-designed or presented legal measures may be expected to generate contention and a climate of opinion ill-suited to informal co-operation and experiment.

BIBLIOGRAPHY

Alchian, A. A. and Demsetz, H. (1972), 'Production, Information Costs, and Economic Organization', *American Economic Review*, vol. 62, No. 5 (December).

Baumol, W. J. (1962), 'On the Theory of the Expansion of the Firm', *American Economic Review* (December).

Brown, C. and Medof, J. (1978), 'Trade Unions in the Production Process', *Journal of Political Economy*, 46, 3 (June).

Cable, J. R. and FitzRoy, F. R. (1980), 'Productive Efficiency, Incentives and Employee Participation: Some Preliminary Results for West Germany', *Kyklos*, 33, 1.

Edwards, R. C. (1979), *Contested Terrain*, Basic Books.

Espinosa, J. C. and Zimbalist, A. S. (1978), *Economic Democracy*, Academic Press.

FitzRoy, F. R. (1974), 'Alienation, Freedom and Economic Organization', Alfred Weber Institute, University of Heidelberg, Acton Society Trust, Occasional Paper 1978/79, London.

Fox, A. (1974), *Beyond Contract: Work, Power and Trust Relations*, Faber.

Freeman, R. B. (1976), 'Industrial Mobility and Union Voice in the Labour Market', *American Economic Review*, vol. 66, No. 2.

Garson, G. D. (ed.) (1977), *Worker Self-Management in Industry*, Praeger.

Guski, H. G. and Schneider, H. J. (1977), *Betriebliche Vemögensbildung in der Bundesrepublik Deutschland*, D. V. Köln.

Marris, R. (1964), *The Economic Theory of Managerial Capitalism*, Macmillan.

Masson, R. T. and Qualls, P. D. (eds.) (1976), *Essays in Honour of Joe Bain*, Ballinger.

Nutzinger, H. G. (1977), 'Co-determination in the Federal Republic of Germany: Present States and Perspectives', *Economic Analysis*, 11, 3–4.

Oakeshott, R. (1978), *The Case for Workers' Co-ops*, Routledge and Kegan Paul.

Pejovich, S. (ed.) (1978), *The Codetermination Movement in the West*, Heath Lexington.

Rosenthal, R. A. (1978), 'Obstacles to the Diffusion of Worker Participation in U.S. Workplaces', unpublished Ph.D. Thesis, Boston University.

Samuelson, P. A. (1977), 'Thoughts on Profit Sharing', *Zeitschrift für die Gesamte Staatswissenschaft*, Special Issue: Profit Sharing.

Scherer, F. M. (1976), 'Industrial Structure, Scale Economies, and Worker Alienation', Ch. 6 in Masson and Qualls.

V. NOTES ON THE PRACTICAL WORKINGS OF CO-OPERATION AND PARTNERSHIP

10. Peter Jay's Project in the Light of Yugoslav Experience

by Ljubo Sirc

Peter Jay is justifiably concerned about the present trends of behaviour in Western economies, especially Britain, since their continuation could lead to a failure of the system within a finite number of years. (See Jay above, paras. 4-5.) He is also right in claiming that contemporary opinion no longer allows legitimacy to capitalist entrepreneurs (para. 28) although it is not clear whether he believes that the majority of the electorate no longer approves of capitalist arrangements, which is doubtful, or that they are rejected by those who have the power 'to stop the country' (or countries), which is indubitably true.

Despite being right in this sense, Peter Jay is wrong in my view when he suggests that the situation could be remedied by turning large enterprises with more than say 100 workers (para. 2) by law into workers' co-operatives (para. 13). I feel confident in giving such a categoric assessment because I have spent many years studying the Yugoslav 'socialist market' which Mr Jay mentions as of possible relevance to the evaluation of his blueprint (paras. 136-9) while claiming that its working is not sufficiently well known.[1] In fact, the shortcomings of the Yugoslav system have not been clarified because so many foreigners insist on describing its alleged attractive sides that its failings are common knowledge only within Yugoslavia, although there they

[1] My own recent publications on the subject: 'Workers Management under Public and Private Ownership', with a section on 'Theory and Practice of Workers' Management', in Chiplin, Coyne, Sirc, *Can Workers Manage?*, Institute of Economic Affairs, London (1977); 'Socialisme de marché et conflits en Yougoslavie', *Revue d'Études Comparatives Est-Ouest*, March 1977; 'The Yugoslav Experience of Enterprise', *The International Essays for Business Decision Makers*, Vol. III, Dallas, Texas (1978); *The Yugoslav Economy under Self-management*, Macmillan, London (1979).

became obvious some ten years ago. The stress on the alleged advantages is such that even the British Conservative leader, Mrs Thatcher, thought it necessary to say words of praise about Yugoslav economic achievements after her visit to President Tito in the autumn of 1978.

The downfall of the Yugoslav 'socialist market' is not due to any Yugoslav peculiarities, which seems to be Peter Jay's impression (para. 138) but to problems with economic first principles. Indeed, these problems are so intense that the Yugoslav communist authorities have been moving away from market mechanisms since at least 1970[2] and towards planning by social contracts which functions no better and possibly worse. All the problems besetting the Yugoslav system would not be avoided in the system as now outlined by Mr Jay, but would appear also there. In my IEA paper[3] I have tried to describe how and why the Yugoslav difficulties would make themselves noticeable also in an economy with privately owned capital if it was labour-managed.

Capital assets owned collectively

Mr Jay foresees a system where savings would be owned partly privately and partly by the workers of an enterprise collectively. He says: 'By workers' co-operatives I mean business enterprises in which the freehold ownership of the assets of the business is vested in the members collectively, in which the sovereign body is the members each having one vote and in which all employees and only employees are members. The rest is negotiable' (para. 1).

One of the most important requirements of an economic system is to bring in line the interests of workers as consumers with the interests of workers as producers. In other words, the sectional interests of enterprises and their staff have to be aligned with the general interests. In the capitalist system, this adjustment is achieved through the enterprise, particularly through the private ownership of the enterprise's risk capital, which Peter Jay calls 'the freehold ownership of the assets of the business'.

The owners, or people chosen by them on their behalf, invest some amount and hire labour at the wage determined in the labour market and additional capital at the fixed interest rate determined in the capital market. The owners (the term in this paper also implies 'their

---

[2] See Deborah D. Milenkovitch, 'The Case of Yugoslavia', *American Economic Review*, February 1977.

[3] See note 1.

representatives' if it is not clear from the context that it does not) determine what is to be produced and sold in the commodity markets. If the production is well chosen and produced at the cost which applies also to the firm's competitors, the revenue of the enterprise covers the outlays and produces some profits. If this profit is 'normal' for the economy, the value of risk capital will remain the same; if it is higher, it will rise; if it is lower it will fall. Supernormal profits and the rise in risk capital value are the reward for good investment and production decisions, while losses and the fall in the value of risk capital are the punishment for bad decisions. These arrangements bring the functioning of the enterprise in line with the general interest, which is that enterprises should produce goods which people, mostly workers, want at the cheapest possible price.

If the sovereign body, i.e. the decision-taking group, of a business becomes 'all employees and only employees', each having one vote, it is impossible to maintain this system of rewards and punishments essential to a market economy, that is essential to the alignment of the interests of workers as consumers and workers as producers. The reasons for this impossibility are:

 (i) the employees are not assembled when the enterprise is founded, so that somebody else must establish it, a private person, a political authority, a trade union, or whatever. If the freehold ownership is then vested in the members collectively by law, it has no market price when it passes into their hands because it is no longer marketable. The only price that is known is the historical value possibly minus depreciation plus some kind of interest. If the original decision to invest was wrong, the historical price is too high; if it was right, too low. Therefore it is sheer luck whether the 'sovereign body' is endowed with a good enterprise or a bad enterprise, while the quality of the investment decision can be in no way reflected in the financial position of the founder;

 (ii) the composition of the 'sovereign body' keeps changing so that 'members' who take a decision may no longer be there when the decision produces its favourable or ill effects. They may have left, or have been pensioned off, or even dismissed, because in a developing economy some people have intermittently to change their jobs. New members may have entered the enterprise and the consequences of decisions taken by others fall on them. No clear-cut responsibility remains for individuals; and the responsibility of a collective, let alone of a changing collective, is no responsibility at all. It is not that the distribution of risk and benefits is different (para. 36); risk is entirely obscured;

(iii) more than that, the consequences of risk such as it is can be expressed only in higher or lower incomes of member–workers. Higher incomes will be very acceptable, while lower incomes will be resisted as unjust not only by themselves but by public opinion, because it will soon be realized that there is no straight connection between the success of an enterprise and its members at a particular time. And even if there were, it will be felt that it is unjust drastically to reduce a worker's standard of living or even to deprive him of his livelihood, because his enterprise has failed. At any rate, some kind of 'right to work' will remain, which means that members of a failed enterprise will be given new employment presumably at the same wage as others in their new enterprise, or at least unemployment benefits like those whose enterprise has not failed.

From the study of labour-managed enterprises, it transpires that it is almost impossible to place the burden of risk-responsibility on to those who have average incomes only. The bulk of risk can fall without the danger of resistance by public opinion and hence its socialization only on to those who have higher incomes or higher wealth, so that they do not lose all or become reduced to poverty wages but only have their advantages taken from them. Further, people must incur risk voluntarily if they are so inclined and not see it imposed on themselves by law.

Mr Jay believes that, under his projected system, the financing of industries and enterprises would be less different from present arrangements than may at first blush have been supposed. Outwardly that may be so, but in essence it will be very different, because the lenders of fixed interest capital and other creditors of businesses will have to fall back — in the case of failure — on the 'freehold assets' owned collectively (that is by nobody in particular in so far as by anybody). Would these be supplied anyway in the first instance by the State or the society or 'by law', which makes all the difference?[4]

---

[4] Peter Jay wants to turn all enterprises with more than say 100 people into workers' co-operatives 'by law'. What will happen to their capital? It cannot preserve the form of risk capital because this solution would require that owners continue to manage, otherwise this capital would simply be turned into loss capital or even lost capital. Would it become a loan? What if the owners wanted to withdraw it? Would they become unwilling lenders 'by law'? Would the State or the society compensate them? How would capital be evaluated?

Conventional capital entrepreunership

Mr Jay suggests that all enterprises employing more than say 100 people be turned into workers' co-operatives and explains: 'The assumption behind this is that the creation of new enterprises to fill market gaps and to exploit new technologies is by its nature more easily undertaken (and therefore more likely to be undertaken) by an individual than by a spontaneous workers' co-operative sprung ready-made from the dole queues' (para. 73). This statement is a realistic admission that entrepreneurship is an individual rather than a collective activity.

More than that, entrepreneurship and management requires knowledge and continuous information, which cannot be acquired and digested by anybody in his spare time while having another full-time job to do, as the workers in an enterprise certainly have to. Some Yugoslav sociologists, therefore, claim that workers' self-management bodies do not make decisions but only take them, i.e. rubber-stamp what the managers have thought of. As a consequence, it can be said that at best the workers only elect persons who act on their behalf and in their interest.

As has been explained, there is no mechanism in such a system which links the general interest (the interest of workers as consumers) with the sectional interests of workers in an enterprise (their interests as producers). Their individual interest is to distribute as much as possible of the enterprise's revenue in the form of wages or 'personal incomes'. In Yugoslavia, this clash of interests leads to a situation in which enterprises as a totality distribute to workers more than their revenue; hence, there is no internal accumulation and no ploughing back but a continuous erosion of capital which has to be replaced from monetary issue. The same source also provides the largest part of the finance for new investment, resulting in rampant inflation.

Of course, it is also in workers' long-term interests that there be new investment, but they do not feel this interest as individuals; just as citizens do not feel it to be in their individual interest to pay taxes, and have to be obliged to pay them by law, although they wish to have government services at their disposal.

On the other hand, Yugoslav workers are quite prepared to save not for their enterprise but for themselves, i.e. when the savings become their own private property. However, their propensity for private savings is insufficient to provide more than a fraction of finance for new investment, albeit they are helped by remittances from Yugoslav guest workers abroad. Needless to say these savings are also eroded by inflation.

From all this it follows that social or collective ownership of the means of production and management by labour would, as suggested by Peter Jay, do nothing to close 'the alarming discrepancy between private and social goals which collective bargaining has caused' (para. 63). If the Yugoslav experience is anything to go by, it would be made much worse.

Under the Yugoslav system, the workers do not feel at all – and so they would not under Mr Jay's very similar system – that they are entrepreneurs or that they should identify with the enterprise. To remain on tolerable terms with the workers, the managers have (and so has the government) to allow excessive distribution and make the other decisions themselves. But neither their tolerance nor their decision-making makes the managers in general popular with the workers, let alone do they cause workers to identify with them. On the contrary, the managers in Yugoslavia have become in the eyes of the workers some kind of substitute-capitalists who are of use as scapegoats not only for everything that goes wrong but even for the simple impossibility of giving everybody, immediately, pie in the sky.

Conversely, the managers are not formally responsible for the decisions they make because in law they have to be rubber-stamped by self-management bodies. In the end, nobody is responsible for any decision and nobody is prepared to accept any responsibility. Every time the government tries to reduce the wages of workers in enterprises with losses, there are threats of strikes and political protests. The consequence is that investment money obtained from banks, mainly from monetary issue, is lavished on equipment in buildings that are badly underutilized, and up to 10 per cent of output is added to stocks and never sold. Yugoslav commentators complain that risk has been 'socialized', because in the end all losses are covered out of ever larger bank credits.

Yugoslavia does not suffer from under-investment as Mr Jay believes (para. 137) but from a flood of inefficient investment: 30 per cent of gross social product is invested yearly in fixed capital and another 10 per cent in stocks of 'rejects'. The Yugoslav workers or the managers on their behalf do not try to maximize income per head of enterprise members by limiting the number of employees per unit of capital as usually suggested by Western theoreticians of labour-managed firms on the basis of a static model, but by investing as much money as they can

lay their hands on and more – except that this investment is not done
according to any even approximate calculations. Of course, this also
leaves out of account the interest of unemployed workers (para. 39)
of whom there are about 750,000 at home, while another 750,000 have
to find work abroad, which is about 17 per cent of the total labour
force. In spite of all this, it is true that the Yugoslav economy grows at
the rate of 6 per cent annually – but this growth figure does not
indicate as great an economic success as it seems because of all the
enumerated inefficiencies but also because it requires a yearly increase
in foreign indebtedness amounting to 5 per cent of the gross social
product, while another 5 per cent is contributed by the remittances
of workers abroad. Without this yearly 10 per cent of additional
resources from abroad the Yugoslav system would probably soon break
down.

Another reason for high unemployment is that the very efficient
private workshops are limited to five workers. In order to produce as
much as possible with a limited number of men and avoid being turned
into self-management enterprises, private entrepreneurs use capital-
intensive methods of production instead of creating new jobs. This
would certainly also happen in the smaller enterprises suggested by
Mr Jay if they would be converted into co-operatives when the size of
100 employees were reached.

Share in surplus earnings

Mr Jay does not specifically discuss how the personal incomes or wages
of members of a business will be determined under his scheme. He does,
however, mention 'the monetary rewards the co-operatives are awarding
themselves' (para. 40) which seems to mean that he envisages the staff
of enterprises, somehow constituted, having the right to distribute the
net revenue of enterprises. The danger that this arrangement may leave
nothing for investment has been mentioned.

There is another, possibly worse, danger. Profits, i.e. the excess of
net revenue over workers' market wages, have little to do with the
workers themselves. They depend on 'freehold assets' which would not
be contributed by workers but handed over to them, since enterprises
of more than 100 workers would be turned into co-operatives by law.
They depend on further investment decisions which could not be taken
by workers, as explained above. At any rate, if workers obtain incomes
varying according to the results of enterprises, workers will feel that
this is not fair to them. Peter Jay correctly perceives that workers give

consent to income distribution on the assumption of some principle of fairness (para. 148). He believes that this demand for fairness precludes perfect competition in the labour market, meaning free individual bargaining instead of collective bargaining. But this demand for fairness precludes even more categorically the existence of differentials between payments to workers with the same skill and the elimination of differentials between payments to workers with different skills, the consequence of distribution according to the market results of different firms. There is an insurmountable contradiction in the demand for fairness as it exists today.

There are demands for distribution of profits in enterprises with profits and demands for parity in enterprises with smaller profits or losses. This happens in Britain but also in Yugoslavia under a system similar to Mr Jay's. Yugoslav sociologists claim that workers fail to perceive and accept any connection between their remuneration and market results. They all demand to be paid as in the best enterprises, which is the straight road to inflation. If they are not allowed to distribute more than the total revenue of their enterprises, they go on strike. In all probability, strikes would be even worse if Yugoslavia was not under authoritarian communist rule (para. 138).

Peter Jay says that the perception of a social advantage in general abstention from collective bargaining is too remote from the circumstances of the individual worker (para. 59) for him to desist from making collective claims on the economy which are impossible to fulfil. These demands which exceed the physical capabilities of the economies do not occur only under collective bargaining in semicapitalist economies, but also under supposed workers' self-management. The only place where they do not happen are the centrally planned economies where the population is afraid of the communist police.

The irony is that, in a democratic country with workers' co-operatives à la Jay, it would not be only all the co-operatives in a particular industry banding together to confront the government with a demand for privileged treatment (Samuel Brittan, quoted in para. 100) but all co-operatives wanting more from the government as if the government could produce plenty.

Misconceptions of our times

We have all been loosely talking about exploitation (para. 56) and alienation (para. 102) for such a long time that a large part of the working population has come to believe that by being difficult they can obtain 'justice' or 'a living wage' from the mythical capitalist or the capitalist government run by social democrats or somebody, while in reality they are fighting each other or reducing investment — tactics which can serve nobody: on the contrary (paras. 56-8). People have been led to despise organizational and technical work and hate those who perform it, although it is the organizers and technicians who have brought about the present prosperity. If we do not succeed in explaining the importance of organization and technical innovation to the working man and make him accept their role in producing his welfare, no system can work, least of all the market system which is the only one — as experience has taught us — to deliver the consumer goods. All reform movements in communist countries have been trying to reintroduce markets. And, in Yugoslavia, where the markets have been reintroduced, at least one sociologist said that they would function best if managers were made owners of enterprise capital and trade unions were restored to their free market role.[5] In fact, entrepreneurship cannot be a collective activity, only an individual one (cf. para. 73).

It is not even true to say that trade unions are indulging in monopolistic practices (paras. 5-9). If they were, they would still remain in the framework of the market and abide by financial discipline. In practice, they are using their social, political, and physical power to break out of the market and create chaos to the detriment of their own members, while claiming that they are fighting capitalism for their members' just rewards. As long as the real relationships are not clarified, no change of the system by switching from individual to unworkable collective entrepreneurship will function, and when they are clarified, the change will be superfluous.

When praising the market economy with individual capital ownership, one is not talking about a capitalist economy working with 'textbook perfection' (para. 31) but about capitalist economy as it has worked in practice up till now, producing untold economic progress, especially in the 1950s and early 1960s; progress which was then stopped by ill-considered actions of popular leaders and, of late, often by militants against the advice of their leaders. Many economists did not help by searching for faults in the working of an abstract market system (para. 52) which have never showed up in practice. As Peter Jay points out, we should be more interested in policy

[5] Veljko Rus, *Odgvornost in moc v delovnih organizacijah* (Responsibility and power in working organizations), Kranj (1972), pp. 200 ff.

and practicalities (para. 4) than in abstract failures.

One thing is certain, if people are allowed to make or take decisions on capital that is not individually theirs, they will distribute it among themselves and consume it. After all, they are human.

11. Some Aspects of the Mondragon Co-operative Federation

by Alasdair Clayre

As is known from several recent descriptions in the literature (especially Campbell, Keen, Norman, and Oakeshott, 1977), Mondragon is a group of over 70 mainly industrial co-operative enterprises in the Basque provinces of Spain which, in the generation since it was founded by a Catholic priest, José Maria Arizmendi, has been expanded from a single firm with 23 workers to a federation of about 13,000, with a turnover of about £200 m. There appear to be three fundamental reasons why Mondragon has succeeded to the extent that it has: the fact that the individual workers (not the state or a collective) own the enterprise; the fact that it is a federation, not a single firm, and can respond to changing market conditions by asking workers to switch between trades and even between firms (a condition of the contract of employment); and the role of the co-operative bank, the Caja Laboral Popular, in providing financial discipline and expert management advice. There are also questions to be pursued more closely about the role in its success so far of the Spanish tax structure and the history of Spanish trade unions.

The bank, founded in 1959, is owned by its staff and by the member firms. As with the individual co-operatives, an assembly of members elects a control board, which appoints the management. It lends money only to the co-operatives, and shares their interests (as a minor example, its staff receive the average profit-share of the federation). It has a management division which guides new co-operatives and monitors existing ones. If something goes wrong, instead of calling the loan (as a normal bank in the west would do) it investigates and helps put the problem right. In the first 18 years there had been only one commercial failure (a small fishing co-operative).

Workers put up an initial fee (currently about £800) to enter, and receive a share in proportion to their pay of some 70 per cent of the firm's annual profits. This is usually invested and drawn out only on retirement, so that 90 per cent of all profit is ploughed back in a normal year. A worker's share can be transferred to other firms within the group, but 20 per cent is lost if he leaves early, except for compassionate reasons. The problems that may be met when a large number of workers retire together require examination. Legal provisions and the standard contract between each firm and the bank require that 30 per cent of profits go to a reserve fund and a social fund, with a higher proportion to reserves in years when profits are more than 50 per cent of wages.

The individual interests of Mondragon workers as sole owners thus generally coincide with those of the firm. They bear the losses as well as profits. So they have an interest in hiring the most efficient management they can get, and there appears to be less inherited conflict between management and labour in the Basque country than in certain other parts of Europe.

A general assembly of all members (one man, one vote) elects the control board which meets monthly and can hire and fire top managers, while leaving them alone to appoint middle management and get on with their job. The highest paid manager gets a 4½:1 differential from the lowest paid workers. The quality of the management attracted to Mondragon is said to be high.

The small size of each particular Mondragon enterprise is no doubt one of the reasons for the harmony and constructive enthusiasm that impress most of those who visit the place. The only strike has been in the one large firm, ULGOR, which makes refrigerators, cookers, and washing machines and now employs about 3,500 workers.

Mondragon is devoted to education, and has recently been abolishing assembly lines and experimenting with group technology on the Volvo model. It stops short of creating a total co-operative environment like that of an Israeli kibbutz. Though it provides social security and health services (not offered by the state because co-operative workers are considered self-employed), workers live in their own homes rather than in any kind of collective housing.

There are special features of Mondragon that may make its success difficult to export wholesale: a local tradition of saving, strong Basque regional loyalty, benign neglect from central government and a tax structure which, in return for the 10 per cent social fund and the absence of social security benefits, has since 1969 let co-operatives off lightly. But some essential features of Mondragon appear to be quite possibly exportable to other countries in the west. These are:

(a) the fact that those who work both control and own their enterprise through deferred individual shares;

(b) capital lent at low fixed interest rates by a co-operative bank sharing the interests of all the co-operative members and lending only to them;

(c) provisions to ensure that a sufficient proportion of profits is retained for investment;

(d) management expertise (in the case of Mondragon supplied initially also by the bank);

(e) a sufficient number of enterprises in a federation to provide varying employment for all members as demand inevitably fluctuates (such fluctuations being a function not of the particular economic system but of all large-scale economies, although central planning may exhibit them in different forms, e.g. as queues, gluts, and unsatisfied or poorly satisfied consumers).

12. Industrial Co-operatives in Britain:
a note on enterprises owned and controlled by the people working in them and on some possible developments for the 1980s

by Roger Sawtell

The early co-operative movement in Britain in the last century was concerned with manufacturing as well as with retailing. The first Industrial and Provident Societies Act in 1852, which gave statutory legitimacy to co-operative societies, was pioneered by F. D. Maurice and a few colleagues who called themselves Christian Socialists, and assisted several industrial co-operatives making basic products such as shoes and furniture. Despite difficulties and failures, the number of these industrial co-operatives grew steadily, and finally they split off from the retail co-operative movement in 1882 to form the Co-operative Productive Federation.

However, from the turn of the century the number of these 'productive societies' gradually dwindled away until in 1977 only 15 remained. The membership of most of them has been diluted by admitting relatives of working members and retail societies, so that they are not owned and controlled only by the people working in them. Nevertheless these productive societies form part of the co-operative sector, and an enterprise like Equity Shoes,[1] formed in 1886, and with 206 people and a turnover of over £2 m. in 1977, demonstrates that survival is possible for nearly a century in an alien market place, without absorption into any larger grouping.

During this century the broad co-operative movement has not shown much interest in industrial co-operatives, and since the end of the second world war the initiative has passed to the so-called 'common ownership' companies. These spring from the views of liberal employers who are concerned to share both the financial rewards and the control of the enterprise with the whole working team which contributes to

[1] Equity Shoes Ltd., Western Road, Leicester. Registered co-operative society No. 2572R.

them. The original company of this group is Scott Bader Ltd. It became a common ownership enterprise in 1951 and had grown to 400 people and a turnover of £20 m. in the chemical industry in 1978. The original owner gave his shares to form the Scott Bader Commonwealth[2] which is collectively owned, in the sense that the people working in the company have no individual shares or personal loans in it. They make no money contribution on joining, nor do they have any claim on the assets when they leave, or on the liquidation of the company. The emphasis here is deliberately on the continuity of the company, as a means of livelihood for the neighbourhood and as a form of working community with social aspirations as well as commercial ones; it is clearly not a means by which any individual can get as rich as possible as quickly as possible. Other family owners and entrepreneurs followed Scott Bader in the 1960s and 1970s, and in 1978, there were ten industrial enterprises of this kind, mostly small and mainly in competitive manufacturing or service industries in which their entrepreneurs had former experience.

The third constituent of this emerging industrial co-operative sector is the 'Benn co-operatives', formed in 1974 with considerable government financial aid to three ailing orthodox companies, when Tony Benn was Minister for Industry. One — the Scottish Daily News — collapsed after six months and the others — Kirby Manufacturing and Engineering and Meriden,[3] making Triumph motor bikes — both encountered serious financial difficulties over the subsequent years. The same could be said of many orthodox companies, and the Meriden struggle to survive is not a criticism of its co-operative structure, but a warning that 'lame ducks' are still lame ducks whatever structure they adopt. Because of their political implications, the Benn co-operatives are the only ones to have received much publicity in Britain, and most people assume that they are the only industrial co-operatives in the UK. However the Industrial Common Ownership Act[4] of 1976 and the Co-operative Development Agency Act[5] of 1978 have meanwhile extended the sphere of co-operations in more substantial if less public ways.

The fourth and last constituent of the industrial co-operative sector

[2] Scott Bader Commonwealth Ltd., Wollaston, Northants, NN9 7RL.
[3] Meriden Motorcycle Co-operative, Meriden, Near Coventry.
[4] Industrial Common Ownership Act 1976 is administered by the Department of Industry (Small Firms Division), Abell House, John Islip Street, London SW1P 4LN.
[5] Co-operative Development Agency, 20 Albert Embankment, London E17 7TJ.

is the rapidly growing number of small new co-operatives initiated by groups of young people with high ideals and not much commercial experience, who see co-operation as a blindingly obvious expression of social justice at work, and who are prepared to make sacrifices for a better quality of life at work. They are mostly in labour-intensive service industries such as food preparation and distribution, printing, bicycle-hire, or building. There have always been people wishing to work in 'alternative' groups of this kind, but they have often been held back by lack of a simple structure which will enable them to develop a democratic form of control. In 1977 Model Rules[6] were published which had been specially prepared for this type of industrial co-operative; together with information about the quick and inexpensive registration process which did not need the services of a solicitor. Over 200 industrial and service co-operatives of this kind had registered with these Model Rules by March 1980.

There is sufficient evidence now to forecast some of the expected developments of industrial co-operatives during the 1980s. First, as knowledge of the simplicity of registering a Model Rules co-operative becomes more widespread, the number of new enterprises initiated as co-operatives will probably continue to grow. Second, as procedures are prepared and tested for changing orthodox companies into co-operatives there will be more 'conversions'. Most of these will be small- or medium-sized well-established companies controlled by one family or one person, for whom conversion to a co-operative structure will be more acceptable than selling to a larger company or going into voluntary liquidation when the family succession comes to an end. As more people with experience of conventional industry begin to work in the co-operative field, either in the enterprises themselves or in agencies concerned with co-operative development there will be a more professional approach to the operational problems of industrial co-operatives. There will be more precedents and more professional management competence, particularly in finding the knife-edge point of balance between the manager's need to take some decisions quickly to ensure commercial survival, and the need for working members to be genuinely involved in decision-making.

---

[6] All co-operative societies are registered with the Registrar of Friendly Societies, 17 North Audley Street, London W1Y 2AP, who publishes a list of sponsoring bodies with Model Rules.

13. Forms of Value–added sharing

by Alasdair Clayre and the staff of The Economist

Profit-sharing can be aimed at any desired balance between the interests of the company as such, those of its shareholders and the pockets of its employees. Up to a point, the three can coincide, but only up to a point.

The theory of profit-sharing and employee share ownership was first developed in 1848 by the German economist and landowner J. H. von Thünen. But little happened until nearly 70 years later, in America. Sears Roebuck, the retailing company, which later operated one of the largest schemes in the world, started its plan in 1916 with three declared aims: to allow employees to share in the profits they help to build; to encourage 'the worthwhile habit of saving'; and to provide for a more secure retirement.

It was partly the absence of other forms of company pension scheme that led to the wide spread of profit-sharing plans in America. They have been helped also by tax concessions. Today, the 1974 Employment Retirement Income Security Act (ERISA) is causing changes in the details of many American schemes. But profit is still mainly distributed in company stock, usually held in trust until the employee retires or leaves. In the late 1970s about 80 per cent of schemes gave shares only, 17½ per cent shares and cash, and only 2½ per cent pure cash.

This American practice of deferred share ownership gives employees a stake in the company's success; but meanwhile the company keeps most of the cash (tax-free) for new investment.

This form of payment is open to at least one major criticism: it leaves all the employee's eggs — his savings as well as his job — in one basket. American firms have met this risk by diversifying funds into other companies' shares, particularly as the employee nears retirement. Sears Roebuck started doing this in 1941. Since 1974 ERISA has made some diversifying mandatory, and has imposed a legal requirement on investment managers to act 'with prudence, diligence, care and skill', thus opening the way to two lawsuits when disgruntled employees (of

Marriott Corporation and Tappan Co.) saw their profit-sharing accounts slump in the recession.

Since 1974 the guaranteed income that pension plans offer — reinforced by a government pension-insurance programme — has made them increasingly competitive in America with traditional profit-sharing schemes. Some firms, such as G. D. Searle and Co., have dropped out of profit-sharing altogether.

The French example shows the dangers of placing too much trust in legislation. Profit-sharing has been given political prominence — but less popular acceptance. A 1967 law required all French firms employing more than 100 people to give workers a share in the company's devlewopment. Companies had to reserve money for this purpose either from profits or from a special investment fund based on capital. While the leading union movements, CGT and CFDT, condemned it as collaboration with the class enemy, French workers were indifferent to the scheme, mainly because it provided no great financial advantages. In 1978 only 7 per cent of Renault shares were held by workers (out of a 25 per cent maximum allowed); most workers had sold their annual ration as soon as they were allowed to (five years after issue), not unresonably, because a Renault share worth 100 Francs in 1970 was worth only 89 Francs eight years later. However some smaller private companies in France have done much better with their profit-sharing and employee share schemes. About 20 per cent of existing schemes are optional since they were in small firms exempted from the 1967 law.

Britain is well behind other industrial countries in both employee profit-sharing and employee share-ownership. About 2 per cent of employees benefitted from profit-sharing plans in Britain in the late 1970s; and according to the Wider Share Ownership Council there were only about 100 schemes open to all employees, though ten times as many for directors. In contrast, America had nearly 200,000 schemes in 1978.

Until the 1950s, profit-sharing in Britain was limited mainly to a few closed co-partnerships. Trustees rather than individual workers owned the shares, and the employees built up no stake to take away when they left or retired. The best known today is the John Lewis Partnership, whose profit-sharing scheme began in 1929. Until 1970 the firm paid an annual 'benefit' in non-voting fixed-interest shares, tradeable on the stock exchange. Now it pays cash: employees preferred it, and share performance was disappointing. All the employees (more than 25,000) are partners; they earn benefit (15 per cent of pay) from the day of joining.

In the 1950s, partly under the threat of nationalization of chemicals, cement, and sugar, ICI, Rugby Portland Cement, and Tate and Lyle began profit-sharing. ICI's scheme, the best known, began in 1954. Immediately marketable shares in the company are distributed as an annual bonus (5 per cent on pay in 1977, 7 per cent in 1976) at the middle-market price. They are taxed as income. Most employees sell them at once, and there is a temporary dip in the share price each year. A survey in 1971 showed that about 37 per cent of shares thus distributed were still in the hands of the employees who received them. ICI and its employees have since considered a ratio of payroll to value-added as a more objective criterion for profit-sharing than pre-tax profits.

Three schemes which may serve as practical examples are those run by Conder International, H.P. Bulmer, and Habitat.

Conder International is an engineering group based at Winchester which went public in 1979. Its 1976 turnover was £50.3 m, its wage bill £7.3 m, to which profit-sharing added £1.3 m. Shareholders' funds were £4.8 m. Conder's is a simple cash pay-out scheme. But the firm also assisted voluntary share-purchase by employees, with the result that more than half owned shares. This amounted to 22 per cent of Conder's capital in 1978.

Each quarter, every company in the group (there are about a dozen) separately calculates its own trading profit, defined as the profit earned after paying wages and all other costs, depreciation included.

From the trading profit is deducted interest on shareholders' money at a commercial rate, normally 15 per cent. The resultant figure (after a further small deduction to finance profit-sharing for the central services staff) is split 50:50 between the company and the employees. The company's share (half the divisible profit plus the 15 per cent on shareholders' money) is its pre-tax profit, available after tax, for distribution or retention.

The employees' share is paid individually in cash at the end of the second month after the trading quarter. The division is in proportion to basic salary, subject to a factor that increases the share of those for whom some extra effort is not directly reflected in wages: the factor is 1 for employees paid overtime, 1½ for those not paid overtime even if they work it, and 2 for directors.

The direct benefit of the scheme to the company is that the relatively high proportion, 50 per cent, of the divisible profit that goes to employees gives them a powerful reason to increase efficiency and avoid waste – the company has a slogan 'you pay half'.

Even so, the scheme falls short of the ideal of those who claim that profit should be split in proportion to the relative inputs of capital and labour. These can reasonably be measured by the respective costs of hiring the two factors of production: and at Conder labour's wage bill is over £7 m, capital's 'wage bill' – i.e. 15 per cent on shareholders' funds – a little over £700,000. So, given that depreciation is deducted before the divisible profit is arrived at, employees could argue for a split 90:10 in their favour. But the 50:50 split seems to be generally accepted as fair in the company. The 18 per cent that it adds to wages is certainly more than is common in profit-sharing schemes.

H.P. Bulmer, the cider company, runs a deferred profit-sharing scheme, based on value-added. Bonus is paid in shares, which are vested in employees five years after they are allotted. This is one of the schemes on which the Wider Share Ownership Council advised.

It was set up after study of the firm's historic ratio between value-added and the total payroll, and of five-year projections of prospects. Each employee is allocated shares worth a percentage of his total earnings, the percentage rising as the ratio actually achieved rises, e.g.:

Value-added ÷ payroll	Employee's percentage
1.50	1.15%
1.55	1.40
1.60	1.65
1.65	1.90
1.70	2.15
1.75	2.40

The plan is administered by trustees (including the finance director) appointed by the company and the employees.

Only people employed for more than an average of 16 hours a week during the company's financial year are eligible. The company allocates not more than 5 per cent of its audited annual profits to buy existing shares for employees, who are individually informed of their profit-share not later than three weeks before the annual general meeting. Shares are bought for them within three months after the AGM.

Trustees hold the shares for five years. They are then vested in the employee provided he is still with the company. Dividends on unvested shares go to buying more shares for the employee concerned.

The employee who leaves early may be severely penalized. According to the Wider Share Ownership Council, the main way in which share fortunes have been built up in America is by long-serving employees picking up additional shares forfeited by those who leave early. And at Bulmer too, people who leave voluntarily (or are fired for misconduct) within three years of receiving notice of a profit allocation forfeit the (still unvested) shares concerned. The trustees may, at their discretion, allow 3/5ths (or 4/5ths) of their unvested shares to those who leave within 3-4 (or 4-5) years. People who have served for at least seven years since they received notice of their first profit-allocation may receive all those shares owing to them that are still unvested. Forfeited shares are distributed among remaining members at the next annual allocation.

However, if the employee dies in service, retires, or has his employment terminated for any other reason than misconduct, all his shares vest in him at once.

For example, maternity leave counts as employment service. If the employee, six months after the date of confinement, has not notified the company in writing that she is returning, she is considered to have terminated her service; but all her unvested shares then vest in her forthwith.

The furniture company Habitat introduced its scheme in July 1976. It too is a deferred shareholding plan.

The company is divided into two profit centres for the purposes of the scheme, Britain and France/Belgium. The board allocates − at its discretion − a percentage of profits to the employee share plan, which is administered by a trust company (run by one Habitat director, one outsider, and one employee elected by all employees who have been allocated shares). If the total group profit is low, even though one profit centre has done reasonably well its allocation may be low too.

The trust company, with finance from the group, will buy shares from existing shareholders (i.e. Mr Terence Conran's family interests), up to about 15 per cent of the Habitat equity. It allocates them to individual employees who have worked for the full financial year, in proportion to their total earnings (a) provided these have exceeded a minimum figure (£750 for 1975-6), and (b) up to a ceiling which is three times the average earnings of all qualifying employees within the profit centre concerned. The 1975-6 allocation was £80,000-worth (plus another initial £60,000 for previous service); the 1976-7 figure was £117,000. Both figures were roughly equivalent to 10 per cent of the year's wage bill.

Shares become vested after three years. The unvested shares of 'early leavers' are treated much as at Bulmer.

Habitat being privately owned, share values are fixed annually by the board. The trust company will, if desired, buy back enough shares at current valuation to pay the income tax liability that arises on vesting; and it will 'endeavour' to buy back further shares offered, if the cash is available.

A scheme that aims solely to give employees a fair share in the profits they create will probably be a straight cash share-out; one that aims solely at the appearance of generosity at minimum cash cost will probably consist of the issue of new shares, perhaps unmarketable for several years. The commonest aim, employee motivation, is often supposed to be achieved by 'a stake in the company', i.e. shares: but hard cash may in fact do the job better − at a harder price which the finance director will be quick to lament.

Other questions to be asked by a company planning a profit–sharing scheme include, for example:

 (i) is the profit unit to be the whole company or individual profit centres? (Should employees in a lossmaking subsidiary share in group profits which they have helped depress?);

 (ii) what 'profit' (see below) is to be taken into account? Should the share-out relate to profit or to gain in profit above a threshold? Should it bear an obvious relationship to shareholders' dividends?;

(iii) who is to be eligible, and in what proportions? e.g., are new employees, casual employees, or pensioners even, to share? Or directors? Should long-service employees get special treatment? Is the share-out related to salary/wage levels, and, if so, to basic wages or actual earnings? On a straight percentage basis or in some other way?;

(iv) if the distribution is of shares, not cash (and why not offer employees the choice?), what kind of shares? Issued or bought in the market? Instantly marketable or not? How (especially if they are unquoted) are they to be valued? Will there be a bonus to encourage long-term holding of the shares?

Though there is a mass of technical questions (notably those of tax and of cash flow) these are the major ones whose answers are matters of 'political' choice. Answer them, and the planners can move to the next stage, the choice between the five main types of profit-sharing scheme − four of them, in reality, related to something other than profit:

(i) simple profit-sharing, based on either pre-tax profit, post-tax profit (not recommended), or the dividends paid on share capital;

(ii) value-added sharing (Rucker plan). The bonus fund is the difference between the actual wage bill and what the wage bill would have been if the company's 'historic' relationship between wages and value added had held good in the particular financial year concerned. The argument for the plan (developed in America in the 1930s) is that in any firm or industry the wage bill normally has a constant long-term relationship to value added: any short-term fall in the bill below its historic productivity should be made up as a bonus;

(iii) value-added bonus (a variant on Rucker). The bonus is related to increased added value above a given norm;

(iv) Scanlon plan. The bonus is based on a ratio between the wage bill and total sales. Again it is argued that this is normally a constant historic proportion, and the bonus fund should be any difference between this and the actual wage bill. Texas Instruments, in America, which started a new profit-sharing scheme in 1973, operates a plan based on total sales;

(v) productivity bonus. The bonus is related to increased output above a given norm.

VI. COMMENTS

14. Discussion of Practical Arrangements

19. *The working of the Caja Laboral Popular at Mondragon*

THOMAS: At Mondragon there is an intimate linkage between the bank
— which is not a normal bank — and the enterprises. Management
functions are performed partly by the managers in the 60-odd
enterprises and partly by the managerial division of the bank. Planning
and budgetary control are monitored by a division of the bank. Flows
of information from the whole group of co-operatives are being
channelled into that one enterprise; and the information of that one
enterprise immediately reaches the heart of the matter, where decisions
are to be taken. This is extremely important because it connects with
how they deal with losses and more serious problems. Information
reaches the nerve-centre very quickly.

With respect to management you see considerable internal mobility
by way of what could be called the workers' council. It is the way
many younger workers got an opportunity of training, an education
through which new managers emerged.

20. *Management at the enterprise level in Mondragon*

OAKESHOTT: There is a distinction made between policy and management. Policy-making is in the hands of the elected representatives in
an elected control committee, and day-to-day management is in the
hands of a management team appointed by them.

But they are worried that these two groups will pull in different
directions, and in the larger enterprises they attempt to protect themselves against this danger by yet another body which is called a co-
ordinating council, which consists of the senior members of the
management team on the one hand, and the senior elected representatives on the other. The whole object of the endeavour is to maximize
the legitimacy with which management is seen by the shop floor and
management's freedom to work in its own way once policy has been
decided.

MCGREGOR: I think that is very fairly put. It was only the phrase
'day-to-day management' that made me wince. It is used by most
people south of Watford who haven't actually worked in industry —
though this doesn't apply to Robert Oakeshott — and it is beloved of
civil servants. I don't know what the phrase means for anyone of any
seniority at all. I think the first senior job I had was at the age of 28.
My time-scale was never less than a year and a half from that time

onwards. So the idea that managers merely perform some day-to-day functions while other people take long-term decisions is ridiculous, and this applies to co-operatives as well as other structures.

21. *Management and council: the balance of responsibilities between them*

DENNIS LAWRENCE: Is it a function of management to advise the policy making council at Mondragon? And is policy made on this basis?

OAKESHOTT: Yes, I see the function of management at Mondragon and in co-operatives elsewhere as including the putting up of plans, the making of recommendations for the future.

LAWRENCE: But what decisions about what? If it is a decision about a new market to be explored or a new product to be made, that is a normal managerial decision. If it is about whether they should close down a factory or open up another factory or whether there has got to be a reduction in dividend to the worker-owners this year, that's a decision which the co-operative council could well take.

There is a great deal of ambiguity here in our discussion of industrial democracy. The Bullock White Paper is clear however. It has drawn on the German experience and other European experience of the separation between representation of interested parties and the functioning of a responsible but none the less independent professional management. This question is not any different whether you are talking about co-operatives or normal commercial enterprises: it is a problem of the twentieth century, in which we have accepted that the representatives of labour and the employees themselves have rights which in the nineteenth century we did not recognize; and there has been a diminution in the rights of the capital–providers – we are not quite sure how far it should be diminished – but it is different from the balance in the nineteenth century when most of our company law was originally drafted; and in the meanwhile there has also been the growth of the big companies with a professional management which has been detached from both. There is a need for creativity in institutions, both co-operatives and others.

22. *Size*

MEADE: There is all the difference in the world in the answer to these questions between working in a firm where you need capital of

£1,000 m. per worker and in one where you need £100 per worker. Is the Mondragon or other experience suggestive of what first principles would lead one to expect, that these co-operative arrangements work only in firms that are reasonably labour-intensive? For example buying your way into a steel mill with £800 would be inadequate.

OAKESHOTT: Mondragon co-operatives are more capital-intensive than most European co-operatives. They are what you might call good second division manufacturing industry. The latest batch of new enterprises have a capital cost of about £20,000 per job. The people at the bank are clear that certain kinds of enterprise — an integrated steelworks or a nuclear power station consortium — don't at the moment at any rate lend themselves to this kind of treatment. Nevertheless, you need not get down to the very minuscule enterprises like local bakeries. At Mondragon, they make consumer durables, earthmoving equipment, and so on.

23. *In practical terms, what is the nature of the 'stake' at Mondragon?*

THOMAS: The nature of the 'stake' at Mondragon is first of all a stake in a job; and in more than a job — in a feasible future of different jobs if necessary. It was clear from the 80 interviews we did at Mondragon that a lot of importance is attached not only to the security of a job but to the sense of security that if something happens to my enterprise somehow the movement takes care of me because they try to re-educate me so that I will be employed in one or two years in another line of activity.

The opportunity to accumulate 'human capital' — to be educated — is a second 'stake', and one sees agencies in many of the co-operatives; education is spread much more widely than would have been the case otherwise. Thirdly there is an earning pattern which has a sound base because it is part of the whole system, not just of one enterprise.

The provision of social security and pensions is a fourth and important point. In a co-operative, one is defined as self-employed. Now that the average age is creeping up to the mid-thirties and beyond there are big actuarial problems. Promised pensions are being readjusted, from 100 per cent of the past 11 years to 90 per cent.

Next there is the whole issue of the capital stake. There is a complex formula whereby only 10 per cent goes to a social fund, but as much as possible of the rest goes into cash flow for future employment, although there is the system of crediting into individual accounts. The worker not only earns above-average earnings compared with competition in the locality – they won the battle four years ago; actually there is a mini-inflation spiral because of the need to attract workers.

This is a major problem by the time people reach the age of 50 because these accounts are individualized and by law within a period of five years after retiring the whole capital account has to be paid out. This will be a major drain on the cash flow with considerable consequence for the whole movement.

A further point is the entry fee. A worker pays on entering somewhere about 15 per cent of the total cost of the job as an entry fee, of which a small part is a down payment and the rest is compulsory savings, with 24 equal monthly instalments.

MCALLISTER: Are 'capital stakes' intended to fulfil two functions; entry fees and guarantees of good behaviour? Should entry fees be related to the cost of jobs or to the desirability of jobs?

FITZROY: It is impossible to lay down an exact formula. Each enterprise, each group of workers has different tasks, different risk preferences and earning opportunities, different human capital; there is a great danger in legislating structures such as workers' co-operatives for all firms of more than a hundred employees. It is a thoroughly arbitrary imposition on what could be a continuum of arrangements that was anarchic and free in the sense that it included in the human capital market facilities which the present market economies essentially do not. Such a free market would throw up the variety of satisfy each group.

24. *Practical experience of entry contributions*

SAWTELL: Views on entry contributions will vary. Some will say 'no entry contributions', as Peter Jay says and as Scott Bader have always said; some would say there should be comparatively large individual contributions to obtain sufficient commitment. There is not enough experience in this country to see which way it is going to go; but in the last few years rather over 100 industrial co-operatives have started up – mostly small – and each has had to decide on this. The majority have decided in favour of individual contributions, and prospective members are often prepared to contribute about £500. Sometimes that is redundancy pay which is put into a new co-operative; more likely it is a deduction from wages or salaries of say £5 a week for 2 years.

OAKESHOTT: If we are talking about a piecemeal development in Britain now, then, as Roger has told us, it is almost bound to involve capital stakes.

Now it may be that if you ever got to a world where all enterprises were of this form it might be more desirable or more elegant to swtich to Peter Jay's arrangements. But it seems to me if we want actually to get there all the evidence points to the need for capital stakes.

In Yugoslavia surely you get just the kind of dangers that Dr Sirc has described from a complete absence of capital stakes in the enterprise on the part of individual workers.

MEADE: On a point of information, are there fall-back wages at Mondragon and in British co-operatives?

OAKESHOTT: At Mondragon you have what you could call a 'fall-back wage' or an amount stated as the normal distribution. But it is really only an advance on your residual share. In fact it is called that: an 'anticipo'. Theoretically it could be set too high and you would get a negative residual.

MEADE: And is that the same in Britain?

SAWTELL: It varies enormously. Some people will accept a below-average wage in order to get the co-operative off the ground.

MEADE: Do they call it a wage?

SAWTELL: The sophistication of calling it an 'anticipo' has not yet reached Britain. People tend to think of it as a wage.

MEADE: Does that mean that at the beginning of the year you say, 'The weekly wage will be such and such'? But that may be topped up or reduced according to results.

SAWTELL: Yes.

OAKESHOTT: You don't say the weekly 'sub'; you say the wage. And as you become more sophisticated you might say 'sub'. And there is a question whether the Inland Revenue would tax those subs as wages.

25. *Trade Unions*

MEADE: And do the trade unions come in and say, 'We won't have undercuttings of this kind'?

SAWTELL: Yes.

MEADE: I think it is very important. Does this kill some co-operatives?

SAWTELL: Yes, it can stop some getting off the ground: for instance in printing. But in small labour-intensive companies, broadly speaking, unions are not particularly strong.

OAKESHOTT: You have had examples the other way, where the unions come into a small labour-intensive co-operative, both here and in France, saying, 'You've got to hoist your wages because they've gone up at the firm down the road and we've got a linkage agreement', and the enterprise saying, 'I'm sorry: we actually control this enterprise, not you. It is our livelihood that depends on its continuing in existence, and we know that we would price ourselves out of business if we hoisted our wages.' And the trade unions have had to accept that. In certain cases the enterprise hasn't survived after that kind of set-to, but in other cases it has.

26. *The working of the Caja Laboral Popular at Mondragon – payroll policy*

THOMAS: A large conglomerate, which is about 45 per cent of the movement, sets its payroll according to the comparable payroll in the surrounding area; so there is very careful tuning of the central core of the movement to competitive average wage-rates. From this the Caja Laboral (the co-operative bank) sets a wage-rate, and all the firms associated through the contract of association are permitted to set the standard 10 per cent higher or 10 per cent lower. In general the rest of the movement follows the pattern. Although it is called an 'anticipo' – an advance – it is really a wage policy, and in fact Mondragon wages are just slightly ahead of their competitors nearby. But if an enterprise is anticipating losses, it will immediately drop to 95 per cent or even to 90 per cent. And the Caja Laboral gets the information straight away that something is wrong in that enterprise, and it moves in with budgetary controls, with advice, and tries to get things back into shape again immediately, perhaps within a year.

27. The importance of the individual stake at Mondragon

OAKESHOTT: If you look at the choice between entering a taxi co-operative where there is an owner–driver relationship and the person owns most of his own taxi and therefore looks after it, on the one hand; and on the other hand entering one where the taxis are presented to the driver by some set of arrangements such as Peter Jay's, and if you think which taxi co-op is going to work better, it seems to me manifest that the taxi co-op where there is an owner–driver element is going to have taxis that are better looked after, greased better, be better maintained, and have a longer life than the corresponding system which Peter Jay has suggested.

CHRISTOPHER ZEALLEY: I am involved in setting up co-operatives, doing it through the conventional mechanisms: limited liability companies with conventional shareholding by workers. I am against generalizing from Mondragon and from what they consider important. They have a very complex structure, and they have no way of knowing the importance of any one element in it, such as the individual stake. I am very doubtful about the importance of the individual stake. I am not at all convinced that commitment to the enterprise is conveyed that way and I can think of many enterprises — particularly small enterprises — where there is at least the same level of commitment, where the capital structure is absolutely conventional and what matters is a sense of achievement and an awareness that they are indeed buying a lifetime's income and a pension in working for that business.

28. The findings of the survey of participation and profit-sharing in a sample of German firms

FITZROY: We took a sample of firms all of which have some degree of worker-participation which goes beyond what is required by German law on co-determination, and some firms which had some degree of profit-sharing. There are no workers' co-operatives; but there is a fair range.

(a) Participation and profit-sharing in conjunction
There are theoretical reasons why participation and profit-sharing should work best together. If you have only profit-sharing and no participation in decision-making you may get dilution of incentives, in the sense that the individual worker feels that his contribution to profit is negligible and it doesn't motivate him. On the other hand there are two

factors working against this, particularly if participation and profit-sharing go together.

One is through social interaction within the work-force. In a conventional firm where the worker who is shirking is shirking at the cost of distant shareholders, all the other workers are likely to be doing the same thing. On the other hand if he is doing so at the cost of his co-workers under profit-sharing, they are likely to put pressure on him, particularly if there is a cohesive group. These pressures may run all the way from social sanctions to physical violence. Previous experience of these pressures come mainly from the opposite direction − from the classical individualistically motivated system of piece-rates where workers form a coalition to reduce production so that management will not lower the piece-rates, a situation which arises where there is a low degree of trust. Even under the conventional system, if workers have complete faith in management and believe that their individual efforts will be recognized, then piece-work incentives can work; and one way to promote a high degree of trust is to give workers an added say in management decisions. This does not mean workers' control: it can stop well short of that.

Further arguments for profit-sharing, given that you have participation, and vice versa, are that if workers are going to take part in decision-making they are going to want a reward from this decision-making; while if they receive a profit from managerial decisions made by others they are going to regard this as a random variable and that will have no effect on motivation.

These arguments add up to the point that if you combine participation with some kind of residual sharing you are more likely to get high trust, which is in turn a pre-condition for individual incentives to work, and also a pre-condition for better communication, for the absence of disruptive conflict, absence of deliberate falsification, and so on.

(b) Test of the hypothesis

To test the hypotheses, we divided our firms into two groups. One had a high degree of participation, the other low. In the group with high participation we found that profit-sharing had a positive and statistically significant effect on productivity, whereas in the group with the low degree of participation profit-sharing had no statistically significant effects.

(c) The pecuniary benefits that follow

There is evidence that participation in combination with profit-sharing is workable in various degrees and also yields significant benefits in a basically capitalist competitive market environment. That of course immediately raises the question, 'Why is there so little of it?' Perhaps we should not raise that here.

(d) The non-pecuniary benefits

There are pecuniary benefits then in measured productivity. But we have a hint about non-pecuniary benefits too — psychic income, the reduction of 'alienation', and so on: effects whose importance one certainly would not want to put lower than the material benefits; but which are simply much more difficult to measure.

Now, in general, workers in large organizations express more dissatisfaction with their work than in small firms, and perhaps to compensate for this workers in large firms tend to get paid more than workers in small firms.

We found that although our high participation firms were larger than our low participation firms there was no corresponding increase in quit-rates or absenteeism, and no evidence of a compensation differential: wage rates were very similar in the two groups.

29. *Participation in Yugoslavia*

SIRC: I believe that 'participation' in Yugoslavia is very complex: it may be that it is because of the changes of line of certain ideologists. However if you ask workers in Yugoslavia what features of the firm they are most interested in you usually find they say 'high wages', 'pleasant work-mates', and 'management' — and 'self-management' fourth and last.

The workers seem in general completely uninterested in the entrepreneurial decisions. Where they use their powers is when it comes to distributing wages or advances. But the advances are usually so high that they go over the top of what is available in real terms. The latest results are that for all Yugoslav enterprises, what was paid out in personal income was 6 per cent higher than the total value-added.

30. *Who owns social capital in Yugoslavia?*

SIRC: There is a feature of Peter Jay's idea as I have understood it so far which reminds me of Yugoslavia, which is this vagueness about to whom the ploughed-back capital belongs. In Yugoslavia the main problem is that capital belongs to nobody: capital is social, nobody looks after capital, and if you leave you don't get anything to take away with you. This is discussed in Yugoslavia under the term 'past labour': the term simply means 'capital'. And they have not been able to find a solution. They cannot introduce workers' ownership. That would be against the ideology. The Yugoslav economy is a very good example of what happens if you organize a system where people make decisions about capital which does not belong to them. They first distribute it and then expect that somebody else is going to provide more capital — which in Yugoslavia somebody else does.

Because in spite of the fact that there is practically no ploughing back in Yugoslavia — that is to say accumulation has been more or less wiped out — banks lend so much money that the percentage of fixed investment in the GSP as it is called — the 'gross social product' — is 30 per cent. If you take it together with stocks — because the production is to a large extent not usable and in fact 10 per cent goes straight into stocks — it becomes 40 per cent of the national income.

31. Decision-making in Yugoslavia

SIRC: Another point is the difference between decision-making and decision-taking. According to legal definition, the whole jurisdiction in Yugoslavia is vested in the workers' councils from which the administrative committee and also management derive their authority. But it has been suggested by sociological research that in fact the whole power remains in the hands of management; that all important decisions are merely taken by managers and then rubber-stamped by workers' councils.

Now a curious situation develops because of that: in a way managers are not responsible for what they do, because formal accountability falls on workers' councils; in fact it is sometimes said that the workers' councils are in a position of powerful impotence and the managers have all the rights and no responsibilities.

Sociologists are trying to find a solution to this problem and it is widely suggested that the power of managers should be embodied in the legally defined positions. One sociologist (Veljko Rus) came to the conclusion that the best way of dealing with the present problems of management in Yugoslavia could be to transfer the ownership of capital to the managers and allow the workers again to create their free trade unions. It is a rather curious solution, especially if one looks at Yugoslavia from the west, but there you are.

32. *What would the capital market be like in a workers' co-operative economy?*

MEADE: It seems to me that there are three ways in which a producer co-operative of the kind we have been discussing might finance its capital: the first is by fixed interest debt from outside; the second is from Peter Jay's equity type capital, with a 'distribution' that is first decided by the co-operative; the third is by ploughing back some of the value-added.

There is a fourth way which I'm not going to say anything about in the context of capital raising. That is by buying entry into the firm by some combination of equity capital and fixed interest capital.

Now I'd like to consider the problem by asking what would happen with these various forms of capital if, starting in some broad sense in equilibrium, the demand for the firm's products goes up.

If you first take the case of fixed interest, there is no reason why that form of saving and investment should not take place as easily with a co-operative of this kind as with any other kind of enterprise. And Peter Jay I thinks says this in his paper. Theoretically, both the labour-owned enterprise and the capitalist-owned enterprise would go on hiring capital — in the economist's jargon— until the rate paid for it was equal to its marginal product. Thus there is no difference in the incentives between the two kinds of firm although there may be a difference in what the lender thinks is the security behind his asset, which is very important: Peter Jay there suggests you might have a mortgage-type arrangement for the co-operative enterprise. I leave that on one side.

The other two forms raise very considerable difficulties and problems. That doesn't mean to say they should be ruled out.

I am not convinced by Peter Jay's argument that you could have this system of equity capital with a distribution that was just decided by the workers in the concern. This is for the reason I gave in my shorter remarks earlier. If the demand for the firm's products goes up I can see an incentive for the co-operative then to increase its capital investment and expand in so far as it is borrowing capital on interest; but I can see no incentive for it to take on more labour. Earnings or income per head will go up in the workers' co-operative economy and there won't be any incentive to take on more labour — unless they can take on new labour at a lower share than the existing labour; in which case you are, as it were, reintroducing a labour market.

Broadly speaking if the new labour must have the same share as the existing labour then I can't see any great incentive for expansion of labour in existing concerns when their demand goes up; and therefore the argument that you can rely on the distribution being made because they will want to raise more capital is a weak one.

The only incentive to expand the labour force will then be to set up new concerns; but if there is no incentive to savers to put their money as share-holdings into old firms, then there is also no incentive for savings to be put in to buy shares in a new concern; because as soon as it is set up it will pay the workers who happen to be there to take the whole of the residual and not make a reasonable distribution.

I think there is a very real problem there.

Ploughing back expansion by not distributing the whole to the workers is a possibility; but I think you can rely on that only if you give the individual worker some ownership in this capital; if he can take out some of it with him; and this has been brought out by the Yugoslav experience, as has been pointed out.

I conclude that fixed interest debt and ploughing back profits are both possible, provided you make some arrangement to have the latter owned by individuals rather than owned by nobody.

I have considerable scepticism I'm afraid about Peter Jay's equity interest from outsiders unless one can think of some way of ensuring that they will get a distribution.

33. *A practical example of an 'equity-type' investment*

ZEALLEY: May I say that I have devised a scheme for a co-operative to do exactly that: it involves a sleeping partner collaborating with the worker-shareholders and gaining a variable equity return.

MEADE: How do you decide which share goes to whom? That is an economic problem: unless of course you choose the other possibility and have the full, not 'profit sharing', but 'value-added sharing' arrangement, where you just have workers and capitalists, and you all have a contractually determined share in the value added.

ZEALLEY: Here is how this particular scheme works in a printing co-operative. Outside shareholders put up a special form of debenture alongside the money that is being put up by the 12 co-operators or co-operative directors. The whole scheme is arranged on a contractual working basis for 8 years with a self-destruct clause at the end of the 8 years. You can't arrange such a scheme in perpetuity. There is a formula for increasing the interest on the debenture, which is geared in our case to the increases which the co-operators award themselves in their wages and salaries. (In our case when we started 5 years ago the interest rate we were getting was 12½ per cent; it's now 23½ per cent on the same loan, so we are doing quite well; in fact the worker–share-holders are looking forward enthusiastically to three years' time when we are all going to have to sit down together and they will either have to return our money, which they won't want to do, or come to some new arrangement with us for a further period.) We recognize that we have got to be not excessively greedy as shareholders; the total cost of wages and salaries will rise far more sharply than the benefits that we have obtained from our interest. Unlike the wage in conventional company structures, we accept that this distribution of wealth created will be equitable overall, and that the workers' share should rise more sharply than our share.

That is one case. But you can devise other kinds of contracts between an outsider putting in equity and relating his equity interest to the interests of the workers, so they don't feel they are competing with each other over the company's surplus.

Incidentally in this case it was the only way that these people could have got off the ground. There was no other way of raising the capital required.

34. *An Eastern European parallel experience of variable return on capital (to overseas investors)*

SIRC: That sounds like the arrangement they usually make in Eastern Europe with investments from abroad: that's very much like what Fiat has done. The payment may be either in money terms or in material terms — in component parts, for example. These East Europen investment agreements usually give the investor the right to interfere in management. He is not the owner, but he has the right to participate in management.

ZEALLEY: We would not have that right. But we certainly have fall-back powers; as with any conventional investment. They have to be very remote so that the co-operators do not feel we are inhibiting what they are doing.

35. *How helpful – or how essential – is the special 're-employment'
    agency of a federation such as exists at Mondragon, to guarantee
    re-employment and retraining in a new line of trade when the tech-
    nology or demand for particular products changes and causes the
    demand for labour in any one trade to fall?*

FITZROY: Employment guarantees are possible without a federal
structure, by work-sharing. For example, there is a firm in the US
called Lincoln Electric which makes welding equipment where there
is an employment guarantee. It has 5,000 employees. They have
weathered the recession and they have practised a certain amount of
work-sharing. They guarantee more than 30 hours work a week so they
have had to have some shortening of the week, but no lay-offs. Though
like Mondragon it is a very exceptional firm, it is only one firm; it is not
part of a federation, it is not diversified, it is very specialized.

Workers' income consists half of profit-share; the other half is either
wage- or piece-rate earnings, and the earnings level is very much higher
than the average.

In connection with this interchange of workers between firms in
the federation at Mondragon; one wonders why the market couldn't
channel workers between firms. What advantage does the federation
have over the market?

CLAYRE: Presumably retraining workers and guaranteeing them
employment. Is there not insufficient incentive to individual firms
to do this in our system?

FITZROY: If that is so, it shows the imperfection of the human capital
market in the present system.

OAKESHOTT: In fact the Mondragon federation, quite apart from
its re-employment guarantees and its training facilities – which are
much more extensive than is usual here – is committed to a policy of
continuous job-creation and to the creation of new enterprises. This is
in fact a matter of ideology: they are not behaving as economic man.

VII.   SUMMING UP

15. Summing up. Peter Jay's reply

36. *The distinction between the arguments for systematic change and for piecemeal change; and their non-contradictory relationship*

JAY: There are two different views flowing into each other here: and there is a certain amount of turbulence where they are meeting. I want to make the distinction clear.

It is one thing to argue that there is a specific and defined systemic defect in current political economy which would be responsive to the establishment of worker co-operatives, supposing that one could take that as a general change, and to argue that the benefits that would accrue from curing that systemic fault would accrue only from curing it as a fault of the system.

That is not to say that no benefits of any other kind might accrue from establishing co-operatives on a piecemeal basis. In addition to my macro-economic concern I have a personal — if you like emotional — sympathy with the idea of establishing worker co-operatives, and if people can make them work and do it on a piecemeal basis there's nothing in my argument that says that that's a bad thing to do.

All I want to do is protect myself very carefully and explicitly in advance from people saying: 'Because in some cases where people have done that it hasn't achieved the results that they expected, therefore that is evidence that it wouldn't achieve the benefits to the system that I look for if you introduced it as a change in the system as a whole.'

Therefore when I talk about the analogy of the rule of the road, it is not to be construed as saying I'm against what other people are doing on a piecemeal basis.

One is also judging by different criteria. Some of the evidence we were discussing about the contribution to productivity that comes from higher degrees of participation and higher degrees of profit-sharing or worker-stake in enterprises, is, I think, very interesting information and has a bearing on whether it may be in the interest of existing firms and possibly new firms to go in that direction.

But it does not go directly to what was my concern, and my case does not stand or fall on whether or not evidence of that kind accrues. Whether the statistics produce positive or negative correlations would have no bearing on the question whether or not there is a benefit to be gained for the system as a whole as a result of changing to a co-operative system as a whole, because the key benefits that I am concerned with derive from the withering away, which I allege would occur, of collective bargaining and certain other things once the whole system changed.

I think it's important to distinguish those two streams.

37. *How is the world of the workers' co-operative economy to be reached?*

Now I was asked by Alasdair the question: how do you get to my 'world'?

The short answer is that in free and democratic societies the only way you can make systemic changes is by a national political legislative act. In order to get to the point where you can do that, certain very important things have to have happened, including the development of a set of ideas that a body of qualified critics finds coherent, the dissemination of those ideas to wider and wider circles of people who are concerned with these things, and then the further dissemination of them to the general public until such point as there is a general public support expressed once or twice or three times in the electoral process for such changes, and then the changes are made through the parliamentary process.

38. *The unilluminating nature of parallels drawn with Yugoslavia*

Much has been made of Yugoslavia. I want to say something by way of diminishing the relevance of Yugoslavia as an analogy. It is supposed to be the home of market socialism and in some very broad senses it is. I don't myself however think it is a good or relevant testing ground for what we're talking about. Quite apart from the dramatic economic and cultural and historic differences between Yugoslavia and our own country or other countries that we might be considering, it is a country in which the central government plays an enormous and central role in political life and in economic life including investment decisions, and that is fundamentally different from what we would have under the political settlement that I am talking about.

39. *The relationship of management to the entrepreneur in the workers' co-operative economy*

I picked out a number of references to the idea of management as a third force or an independent force in the industrial process, which according to some people needs legitimizing; and this seemed to lead to some ideas of writing into company law certain specific definitions of what was the role of management, what was the role of the suppliers of the capital, what was the role of the suppliers of labour.

I would like to say again briefly that that is a very dangerous blind alley. I think we're much safer in a world in which managers are a form of skilled worker: where they are hired by the entrepreneur, be he capital or be he labour, to the extent that the entrepreneur needs his skills or wants his skills; and his reward depends on the bargain that is struck between them and his rights and functions depend on his abilities to satisfy the person who hires him. My personal belief as I've already said is that under a system of workers' co-operatives in a market environment where one has established the credibility of the government's non-availability as a wielder of a safety-net, both the rewards to management and the recognition of the importance of management will be greatly enhanced. Though I don't underestimate the fact that in the transitional phase there will be a number of rather nervous managers, I would expect these to be more the bad managers than the good managers.

40. *The capital market*

The most important points for me that have been raised are the ones that James Meade with his usual unique lucidity and insight has raised about the essential financial mechanics of the firm: how it raises capital and how it deals with the capital market. I would say briefly in reply to the question how I think the capital market will function in general: if you want a description of how I think the capital market will operate you will find it in paragraphs 16–29 of the paper.

But on this central question whether there is enough incentive to distribute to establish the credibility of the co-operative as a borrower in the capital market, I do think James Meade has made a very effective point and I think it would be totally effective if it really were true to say that people only borrow or in the overwhelming majority of cases borrow in order to expand. I haven't got statistics to hand, and there are practical businessmen here who can correct me, but my impression has always been that a very substantial part of the capital requirement of concerns has to do not with increasing your total productive capacity but with keeping adapting to changes in technology, adapting to changes in consumer preference, while (at least in terms of volume of activity) standing still; and that these requirements will continue to be financed on a very significant scale in a workers' co-operative economy — quite enough to give any normal co-operative a strong need for investment finance.

The point would still be a weak one if it were supposed that all or the great majority of these needs would be met from the company's internal resources. I find some difficulty, as I say, in reconciling the two arguments that are sometimes made: one, that the companies will finance all of their needs from internal resources and therefore there will be no sufficient dependence on the capital market; and the other that they will distribute or pay to themselves or use inefficiently all of their monies to the extent that they won't have even enough resources to cover their existing commitments.

I don't see why it is not reasonable to assume that they could have a considerable dependence on the capital market for these purposes even if they had some internal resources.

From a purely theoretical point of view, I must say I myself wouldn't be opposed to a change in the existing companies law which prohibited people from retaining anything for purposes of investment. I'm not at all sure whether it isn't much better that all savings should be arbitrated through the capital market where proper market forces apply to their use, rather than as it were hijacked by the firm in which they happen to have arisen, and applied; and that might be one way of dealing with this problem if it turned out to be a really substantial problem.

41. *The distribution on equity capital in a workers' co-operative economy*

On the question of an equity formula for determining the variable distribution, I am not opposed in principle to that, though I would rather it came about as the result of free bargaining in the capital market between the co-operatives and the savers than that it were imposed by part of the general companies law as a requirement on all companies. However if the co-op found it could not borrow the money on the basis which I have described, and if it could borrow it on the other basis and was willing to do so, and there were willing lenders or the rates were more attractive that way, then I would certainly have no objection to its being done.

42. *New entry and the cut-off point for conversion from capital-owned to worker-owned firms*

I think we have not sufficiently discussed the problem of new entry and new formation which I think is an enormously important one: I would only like to say in passing that I personally place great importance on the ability of the old-fashioned individual entrepreneur, namely the man who provides risk capital and starts up in his back garage, being able to continue doing that; because it seems to me that is in practical terms always likely to be a very important source of new enterprises and should be so. No systemic problems arise about people doing it in very small units.

But if you want to do what I want, you have to have an arbitrary cut-off point; it is of course arbitrary, and whether or not you say the right number is when you employ the 100th man or the 150th man or the 50th man is something one could argue about.

What is extremely important is of course to be able to provide a clear account of why it would be in the interest of the man who employed ninety-nine people to go ahead and hire the hundredth and come under the law and therefore be required to give up what until then would be his conventional capital entrepreneurial role in the firm.

The answer to that I think gets back to what we've been discussing all along about the ability of the firm to borrow on the capital market. If it is able to borrow on the capital market on those kind of terms then the entrepreneur who hires the hundredth man will become the inheritor of those kinds of rights. He will at that point own 100 per cent of the equity-like capital in the firm and therefore he will have had an incentive to build it up to that point. He will then have some choices to make — which can't be entirely made by him — as to whether he continues in an employed management capacity with the firm or whether he prefers to go out and start another one or indeed to retire and live in the South of France or a number of things of that kind. But his position will change and one has got to be able to show that it will not change in ways which will provide him with a disincentive for going ahead and hiring the hundredth man. I think that can be shown but I think that is an important point to have in mind.

43. *The workers' stake in the firm*

There is one further point that I wanted to mention about the workers' stake in the firm. It does seem to me that one of the problems with Mondragon — sympathetic as I am to the general enterprise — is that if the workers have stakes in the firm they have the right to take something away with them; and that a good part of the favourable investment financing of Mondragon has been due to the fact that the total Mondragon population was rising, and rising quite briskly. It is no not entirely clear to me that if and when the demography changed as you got a mature population of mature age — with an equal number of people dying and retiring and so on to the number being recruited — that that would not make a rather radical difference to things which ought not to be made just because you have reached demographic stability. I mean if the thing becomes unstable just because you reach demographic stability there is something inherently wrong with the arrangement. You need to be sure that it is not one of those things that you have to pedal faster and faster in order to stay upright. And it did seem to me when I looked at it to have that characteristic.

44. *Would labour be in a position to form monopoly groupings in restraint of trade in a workers' co-operative economy?*

Again there is the important point which is always raised and rightly raised about whether or not in this new form of economy the trade unions — or labour — will not continue to have great monopoly power. I did respond to this once before, though I can see I did not persuade Mr Chiplin and Mr Coyne. I would draw your attention to paragraphs 97–113 of the paper.

I don't deny the theoretical propriety of the question they ask (see p. 72) and the validity of the answer depends on whether or not the institutional change would make it possible to do something which it is not possible to do by just Anti-Combination Acts at this moment.

But it is extremely important that one should be able to give a good answer to that question.

45. *Quality of working life, and size*

Finally I would like to say that there are quite a number of other things that we have not talked about and could not talk about: a number of other reasons why people might want to be interested in workers' co-operatives as a way of doing things, which have to do with the quality of working life. They have a considerable connection I suspect with that whole large and very important topic — one that is hard to discuss in a methodical way — of 'small is beautiful': the whole business of the relations of people to their work and to one another and their ability to behave in reasonable ways and make sensible decisions in smaller groups rather than in larger groups and the idea that the difficulties arise when the groups and organizations become too remote.

If I may hazard some general rather wild shorthand in the history of political thought: in my judgement, towards the end of the nineteenth century both capitalism — or economic liberalism if it prefers to call itself that — and socialism took serious wrong turns; and they took serious wrong turns in both, in their different ways, turning away from the notion of the producer co-operative in a market environment.

In the case of socialism the Webbs were very much to blame for this, and in my opinion they are very much to be criticized for this. It took socialism in the direction of what — again using shorthand — I might call 'big labour' and 'big government', which is now seen to be not easily reconcilable with the basic objectives and tenets of socialism as it was developed in the eighteenth and nineteenth centuries and earlier.

And likewise capitalism got itself involved with a contest of big corporations which, while undoubtedly they have their role — there is some discussion in my paper about whether there are some firms which for technical reasons have to be very large indeed in terms of employment — nevertheless led to a war between the dinosaurs, or a three-way war between big labour, big government, and big corporations, which people sometimes seek to resolve by what, in my judgement is the worst of all possible ways — merging them all together in some great national committee. And I think that it is therefore extremely fruitful to go back and try to unravel some of those false knittings in both those two heritages; and one of the enjoyable things about it is that in doing so one finds very surprising areas of agreement between people who are supposedly not ranged in the same places or similar places on the political spectrum. I regard that as an encouragement to believe that one is probably on the right track.

16. Conclusions

When the discussion started it seemed that there were supporters of three different and clearly defined positions – of an employee-owned economy; of a co-operative sector within a mixed economy; and of an alternative to both, in a combination of profit-sharing and participation – besides a number of interested participants who were unconvinced by any of the three. By the end of the conference, the differences between the first two had apparently been reduced but the other major division remained.

Both Peter Jay and Robert Oakeshott believed in a co-operative solution to the problems of the economy. Peter Jay advocated whole-sale change to economic co-operation through the ballot-box and legis-lation, but he was not, as some critics had expected, opposed to the piecemeal approach, and indeed he welcomed it in the discussion. He simply thought it less likely than a once-for-all legislative act to achieve the ends he looked for and he did not want to be saddled with the argu-ment that existing co-operatives in a mixed economy gave valid evidence of what co-operatives would be like in the wholly worker-owned economy he advocated.

There was still at least one important difference between the two positions. Oakeshott saw workers' individual stakes in the capital of their enterprises as valuable sources of commitment as well as of funds. Jay was opposed to the whole idea of capital stakes held compulsorily by workers in their own firms, on the grounds that capital should be allocated in a free market undistorted by any such requirements, while it would be unwise for workers, in principle, to have their jobs and their main savings concentrated in the same firm. Here too, however, the differences proved not to be diametric in practice: the Mondragon Co-operative Federation, favoured as a model by Robert Oakeshott, invests pension funds elsewhere than in its own enterprises, while Peter Jay would not object resolutely to some very small capital stakes for workers in their own firms if these were wanted, though he would never argue that they should be compulsory or would make much difference

to commitment. If a sufficiently small capital stake is in question —
such as the £500 to £1,000 accepted by most new co-operatives in
Britain as a reasonable entry stake — possible compromises seemed
negotiable between the two positions. What neither side advocated for
co-operatives was State money or any funds contributed by anyone
otherwise than voluntarily.

But from elsewhere in the conference a different set of ideas
emerged, ultimately in conflict with those of both Jay and Oakeshott,
although perhaps starting from similar sympathies. Felix FitzRoy
argued strongly against the need for any fundamental change in
property rights such as Peter Jay's proposals would require, and also
against the necessity for a sector of fully employee-owned and
controlled co-operatives as advocated by Oakeshott. Two already existing devices, employee participation in decision making, and profit-
sharing or value added sharing, if combined — but only if combined —
could achieve the main ends desired by both groups who favoured co-
operatives. If applied separately, he stressed, they could not be
expected reliably to have any such effect. Cable and FitzRoy produced
theoretical arguments and also evidence from West German data to support their conclusions.

The tension between these two sets of ideas — co-operation on the
one hand and participation combined with profit sharing on the other
other — is reflected in the theoretical work which forms the centre of
the volume, and in particular in the ideas contributed by Professor
James Meade: in a co-operative sector or economy, ease of entry for
new firms to the market or a policy of active expansion in the membership of individual co-operatives, or both, could become of exceptional
importance; and 'partnership' — value-added sharing and participation
— is worth examining as an alternative solution to some of the difficulties identified by Peter Jay and others in the present system of political
economy, and also to some of the difficulties of the fully co-operative
solution itself.

Notes on contributors

JOHN CABLE,
Dept. of Economics,
University of Warwick.

BRIAN CHIPLIN,
Dept. of Industrial Economics,
Nottingham.

ALASDAIR CLAYRE,
All Souls College,
Oxford.
and
Antelope Films Ltd
London

JAMES CORNFORD,
Outer Circle Policy Unit.

JOHN COYNE,
Dept. of Industrial Economics,
Nottingham University.

FELIX FITZROY
Internationales Institut für
    Management und Verwaltung,
Berlin.

PETER JAY,
The Brookings Institution,
Washington D.C.

SIR DENNIS LAWRENCE,
Dept. of Industry.

RICHARD MCALLISTER,
Dept. of Politics,
University of Edinburgh.

PETER MCGREGOR,
Anglo-German Foundation for the
    Study of Industrial Society.

JAMES MEADE,
Emeritus Professor of Political
    Economy,
University of Cambridge.

ROBERT OAKESHOTT,
Job Ownership Ltd.

ROGER SAWTELL,
Daily Bread Co-operative

LJUBO SIRC,
Dept. of Political Economy,
University of Glasgow.

MARTIN SMITH,
Banker.

HENK THOMAS,
Institute of Social Studies,
The Hague.

CHRISTOPHER ZEALLEY,
The Dartington Hall Trust.

INDEX